A

HISTORY

OF

THE WHIG PARTY,

OR

SOME OF ITS MAIN FEATURES;

WITH

A HURRIED GLANCE AT THE FORMATION OF PARTIES IN THE UNITED STATES, AND THE OUTLINES OF THE HISTORY OF THE PRINCIPAL PARTIES OF THE COUNTRY TO THE PRESENT TIME, ETC. ETC.

BY

R. McKINLEY ORMSBY.

"It should be the peculiar care of Great Britain to foster divisions between the North and South." JOHN HENRY, *the British Emissary.*

BOSTON:
CROSBY, NICHOLS & COMPANY.
1859.

PRINTED BY
GEO. C. RAND & AVERY.

Stereotyped by
HOBART & ROBBINS,
NEW ENGLAND TYPE AND STEREOTYPE FOUNDERY,
BOSTON.

PREFACE.

THE object of the writer of these hasty sketches has been to give the outlines of the principal parties that have existed in the United States to the present day, and notice the more important and leading measures of the various administrations of the general government. Of the administrations prior to that of President Jackson he speaks according to the impressions he has received from reading and tradition; but of the politics since Jackson's day, with which he has been contemporary, he speaks from personal observation, and gives his own views as to public men and measures. He is aware that his outlines are very imperfect, and in many things may be erroneous. He has had no access to libraries, nor public documents; and his statistics are sometimes given from general recollection, and are but approximations to accuracy. But feeling that some history of the parties of this country is needed, he has the temerity to offer this till its place shall be supplied by one more reliable and satisfactory.

THE AUTHOR.

BRADFORD, Vermont, Aug., 1859.

CONTENTS.

INTRODUCTION.

THE origin of political parties which have existed in this country cannot well be understood without a recurrence to the events and circumstances in the mother country from which many of our political principles took their rise. Many of the principles considered when our forefathers established the institutions they bequeathed to us were, at different times, the subjects of agitation in England before the American Revolution commenced. If the Anglo-Americans are truly the descendants of the ancient Saxons, the American Revolution only had the effect of restoring to the race the primitive but greatly modified independence it enjoyed upon the shores of the Baltic. The subjugation of the Saxons in England by the Normans (a conquest of fillibusters by fillibusters), and the establishment in that island of the Feudal System, was a reduction of our ancient ancestors to a pretty severe state of bondage. As in the process of ages the Saxon blood so flourished as to check the power of that haughty line of iron rulers, a greater degree of liberty and freedom was gradually acquired. All such acquisitions, or rights and immunities, by the commonalty of Old England extorted from their lordly masters, were usually secured by solemn writings, called charters, constitutions, etc. The freedom of speech; the liberty of conscience in matters of religion; the principles of taxation and representation; the right of jury trial; the right of relief from arbitrary imprisonment by writ of *habeas corpus;* and very many other principles considered and guarded by our constitutions, had their birth in the British isle, and were brought to this continent by the early settlers. To see the Saxons thus gradually make their feudal lords relax their tyranny, and by degrees break up that uncouth system of military tenures, and to see them secure those great principles of civil liberty so rarely enjoyed by mankind, was to witness the triumphs of more than an ordinary race. The ancient Britons, who were subdued by the Roman arms, and held in subjection for some four hundred years, were by that subjugation and dominion rendered spiritless and helpless. Scarcely a family of the old Sclavonic race has ever made much progress, but take the servile as a normal condition. The pure Celtic race has ever been slow in the development of the principles of popular sovereignty. But the Saxon is an aspiring blood. The tutelage it has received and is receiving from the Norman,—a kindred, but for a long time in military discipline a superior people,—though rough and severe, may, under Providence, prove an instrumentality of good. Without it the Saxon would but slowly have thrown off his primitive barbarous filli-buster state, so as to have emerged from England in a different condition from that in which his ancestors, under Hengist, entered it. The nomads that for centuries wandered over the vast plains of Scythia, and in process of time were crowded upon the coasts of north-western Europe, entered Britain as metal enters a mould, to receive the form and impress suitable for the purposes they were designed to subserve. To subdue the nomadic habits of a race, and imbue it with feelings, capacities, aptitudes, sympathies, and the principles of nationality, and fit it for civil liberty, is no small undertaking, and requires not only severe discipline, but also time. From the conquest of England by William the Norman, about the twelfth century, to the discovery of America, near the dawn of the sixteenth, we see that the reformatory rule of tyranny had been applied in England with so strong a hand as to very much modify the native disposition of the Saxon, and he began to experience those national feelings which caused him to exult in the idea that he had a country. The constant wars for centuries with France had contributed to inspire the islander with patriotic feelings. And the occasional quarrels between the king and the turbulent nobility of early ages, enabled the people, by siding with one or the other of the parties, to extort from the crown those charters which have changed the British government from almost an absolute despotism, to a limited, constitutional monarchy. But for several centuries the British monarchy submitted to changes but gradually, and very reluctantly, and concessions had to be many times extorted from the crown before they were sacredly regarded as the inviolable rights of the people. The earlier ages of that monarchy were devoted more to warlike enterprises than to the arts of peace. The susceptibility of the Saxon for civilization, as disclosed by his history while upon the coast of the Baltic, as well as by the administration of Alfred, was quite apparent; but the Feudal System, with such masters as the Norman brought into England, though well calculated to nationalize those migratory tribes, was not well adapted to develop the pursuits and arts of civilization. The Saxon upon the Baltic repressed all civilizing arts by the dire necessity of his situation, and not as a matter of choice; he was never insensible to the ameliorating influences of peace and social commerce; but without a government which is the gift of mental and moral discipline, such influences can never be enjoyed.

The Saxons were early addicted to the sea, and were, in their rude vessels, spirited navigators; under Alfred and his successors they took much pride in their fleets; but England, until after the discovery of America, had accomplished but little in the way of commerce, or the arts and sciences. The early British monarchs were warriors, and are prominent in English annals as soldiers; but the trades, and those pursuits which now render England the first of nations, were but little encouraged. The earlier kings, for their support, and to defray the expenses of their armies, were obliged to resort to robbery, and, as a fruitful resource, frequently plundered the Jews. They had no commerce. Edward the Third (about A. D. 1350) began to encourage the manufacture of woollen fabrics; but he prohibited the exportation of all articles manufactured of wool and iron. This shows how crude must have been the ideas of the British rulers of those days in regard to commerce. The exports and imports of England about a century before the discovery of America (merely nothing) will show how little the English had advanced in the arts of peace and civilization. It was about this time that her vessels began to reach the Baltic for the purposes of trade, and they did not trade to the Mediterranean until about the middle of the next century, or about fifty years previous to the discovery of America. But the discovery of America, and of the passage to India round the Cape of Good Hope, late in the fifteenth century, gave an impetus to commerce; and at about this period modern civilization began to take its rise. Since the discovery of America, England herself, in her political as well as in her social institutions, has passed through an entire revolution. For many hundred years Great Britain was but a sort of military despotism, without a king or statesman capable of comprehending the principles of political economy as practised by civilized nations. But commerce is the magic power before the touch of which the harshest features of feudalism have long since given away, and its last relics are fast disappearing. The spirit of feudal aristocracy is anything but compatible with what by modern politicians is called progress; and the regulation of the arts, trades, and commerce, under her earlier kings, shows England, until comparatively a late period, acting in defiance of the principles which have in modern times, in despite of her rulers, elevated her to the first rank in greatness. Her trade has been of slow but sure growth. It is interesting to trace its progress, as with it came her civilization and power. Her first rude statutes, adopted to aid her merchants; her efforts to compete with her Dutch rivals, and then her naval warfare with those audacious Dutchmen, in which the English navy, triumphing over the gallant Van Tromp, laid the foundation of her future greatness; the relaxation of the doctrine of entails about the middle of the fifteenth century, by which feudalism received a check and commerce an impetus; the discovery of America; the invention of the art of printing; the introduction of the use of gunpowder in warfare, by which national difficulties could the more speedily be brought to a close; and the revival of letters; all are events which, falling out nearly in the same century, were the precursors of the changes which have been witnessed in modern times. The Saxon is certainly a promising race. Its origin is involved in mystery, being but an offshoot of the still more mysterious German race, from which the principal civilization of the present age took its rise.

The revival of letters came with the discovery, by the German mind, of the press, which at once reproduced the ancient civilizations, and enabled the nations to leap from infancy to maturity at a bound; and hence the ideas of progress which have so startled the thinkers of the present age. But although great revolutions have swept over Europe, and over England in particular, they were but such revolutions as we witness in the vegetable kingdom when some coarse shrub puts forth a bud, the old and the new — the rough stock and its blossom — remaining inseparably connected and mutually dependent on each other. In consequence of the causes alluded to, England, for many hundred years, has been undergoing a change in the spirit of her institutions, and the change will continue its progress hereafter; and nature has in the human as well as in the vegetable kingdom her subjects so effectually under her control, that we may expect the future development of the fruits of civilization will proceed with that gradual and regular course which shall indicate them healthy growths. Hot-bed plants are pleasing and luscious, but can only be preserved by an artificial atmosphere. In the moral world it is not singular that some minds, impatient at what they conceive to be the slow advancement, as by a natural growth, of ameliorating principles, should seek, by stimulating expedients, to hasten their progress. But as yet no revolution produced in advance of its proper time, by the application of such excitants, has been productive of useful fruits.

Prior to the commencement of the English colonies in America political parties had an active existence in the mother country, of which the parties in America, especially during and preceding the Revolution, were the offspring. The earliest parties in England were the gift of religious controversies, and were, subsequent to the Reformation, very violent. One has but to read the history of the times of the Cavaliers and Roundheads, or of England down to and during the time of the Commonwealth, to see with what rigor party spirit reigned in that country. The persecution of those who embraced reformatory views in matters of religion, under James the First, drove the Puritans to Plymouth Rock. The titles of Whig and Tory, which have designated the two principal parties in England for the last two hundred years, originated in the time of Charles the Second. It is not a little interesting to trace the history of parties in Great Britain; and in the perusal the reader is struck with what he must regard as their providential direction. As a general thing the two parties in question have been both national and conservative. For much of the time during their existence it would be puzzling for one to discern the principles that divided them, their contests having been more for place, or office, than anything else. This is by no means true of the whole period during which those parties have existed. During the ministries of Grenville, the Pitts, and Fox, we find that they were divided on important political measures. But what is worthy of remark is that throughout the whole existence of those parties, they have, with scarcely more than one exception, been founded on a conservative and national basis, and, though at times degenerating into mere factions, rarely ever have taken an attitude dangerous to the integrity of the British dominions. With the exception of the Tory measures in regard to the American colonies, neither of those parties have been sectional, nor composed of one class of society as antagonistic to another. In each have ever been individuals of all classes. The Whigs have in later times been regarded as the most liberal; but the Duke of Monmouth was the first Whig, and ever since his day the Whigs have embraced a fair share of the aristocracy. At the revolution of 1688, when the bigoted James was divested of his crown, and William of Orange placed upon the English throne, the masses of Whigs and Tories seemed to coöperate. In short, throughout the history of these parties, embracing England's history for two hundred years, the evidences of their beneficial effects are apparent. They have been the schools in which the greatest statesmen have been educated, and the unparalleled prosperity of England in modern times has been much owing to their instrumentality. Within proper channels, restrained within legitimate, reasonable, and natural limits, political parties may be instrumental of good; but, beyond these limits, devastating floods.

A HISTORY

OF

THE WHIG PARTY.

CHAPTER I.

POLITICAL PARTIES PRIOR TO AND DURING THE REVOLUTION. — THE SECTIONALISM WHICH CAUSED THE SEPARATION. — THE CONSERVATISM AND POLICY OF WILLIAM PITT, THE ELDER. — THE EFFECT OF THE REVOLUTION ON PARTIES. — THE INCONGRUITY OF THE DIFFERENT COLONIES.

Two large political parties have existed in this country nearly from the period of the adoption of the Constitution. Since the times of Jefferson, the measures of these parties have undergone many changes, and many of their respective members have changed sides; but still we can trace in the present Democratic many lineaments of the old Republican party; and the late Whig was in many respects the representative of the old Federal party. The policy, tactics, and measures, have not continued the same, and perhaps the modern parties contain but few traits to identify them with their predecessors. When the relationship of the modern to the ancient parties is spoken of, we have more particular reference to their perpetuation as political organizations, than to the transmission of party principles. These two original parties were organized and brought into action soon after the adoption of the Constitution, but were formed, in part, from elements previously existing. In sketching their origin, we will glance at only some of the more prominent events that gave them birth. During the Revolutionary struggle the old English party titles of Whig and Tory were in vogue; and, at the outset of the difficulties that led to that struggle, the parties represented by those titles in England and America were nearly identical; but at a later period the American Whig and Tory lost all identity with their transatlantic namesakes. In this country the title Whig came to represent one who was in favor of popular rights as opposed to all regal government, while that of Tory was applied to those who, although opposed to the usurpations of George the Third, were still in favor of monarchy, and opposed to the stand for independence taken by the colonies. The Tories of that period were, in America, divided into two classes, it is true; viz., those who sided with the ministry of George the Third, and those who dissented from that monarch's project of taxing the colonies, but still adhered to the royal cause during the Revolution. The change in the spirit of parties progressed with the Revolution, and kept pace with the body which that event produced. The American Revolution was not, compared with the French, and other revolutions, a very bloody struggle; it was indeed attended with some agony, but was in reality but the throe of a great nation in giving birth to a child. As we look back upon the conduct of the mother country prior to the separation of her colonies from her, we see how entirely, in the whole course of her proceedings towards them, she was guided by the hand of Nature, or of Providence, who had apparently foredoomed that separation. As the party politics of the United States at the present day are liable to lead to as unexpected and undesired results as did those of Great Britain which produced the dismemberment of her empire, we should often look upon the example of the latter as a warning, and endeavor to profit by it. It seemed to the British government as reasonable and entirely right that her colonies should contribute, by way of taxes in some form, to defray the expenses of their protection, as it was called. One method, and a fruitful one, of raising money in the mother country, by way of tax, was by making a law that all paper used for commercial, legal, and business purposes, should be stamped, and that all contracts, writings, and all sorts of obligations used without such stamp, should be void. The officers of the crown sold the stamps at fixed prices. They were small pieces of paper, on which were printed the words, under the picture of the royal crown, "*Honi soit qui mal y pense;*" and the person executing a contract, note of hand, bill of sale, deed, will, or other instrument in writing, was obliged to paste on one of them, or his writing would be void. It was one of the many ways adopted by England to raise the necessary funds to defray the enormous expenses of her government; and about the year A. D. 1764, immediately after what in America was called the French and Indian war, it was thought advisable to extend the stamp system of taxation to this country. The colonists remonstrated and protested; but the American Stamp Act passed Parliament with great unanimity,—by a majority, in the House of Commons, of about two hundred, and in the House of Lords unanimously. The conduct of the colonies, in refusing to submit to that tax, was regarded by our forefathers across the deep as most unnatural, unreasonable, and undutiful. George the Third, who incurred so hearty a detestation of our ancestors, was not what his more worthy countrymen called an immoral man ; he was in all the private walks of life regarded as virtuous and upright ; but he had a monarch's notions of royal authority, and of the subject's duty of obedience. That his people in distant colonies should presume to question his power, or the rightfulness of its exercise, excited him strongly against them. The ideas of the king were a part of his being ; and, although they were his misfortune, perhaps they were not his fault. But few men are responsible for their opinions. The question of taxing the colonies was one that affected all England ; and England generally, at first, participated in feelings of indignation at the idea that they thus should refuse to submit to taxation. Her statesmen, her orators, her jurists, and her writers, with few exceptions, united in putting their rights at absolute defiance. The contest soon became sectional, and the bitterness between the two portions of the British empire became so extreme, that thousands in America, who at first were disposed to espouse the side of the mother country, were forced to turn against her.

There were a few intelligent, clear-sighted, and conservative men in England, at that time, who foresaw the tendency of the measures, policy, and course, pursued by the ministry ; but the warnings of these brave patriots were unheeded, or only met with derision. They foresaw and predicted that the bitterness likely to be engendered between the two portions of the common country would lead to a separation, and a final loss of the colonies; and whenever such disunion was thus, in spite of the seeming omnipotence of the British throne, predicted, the speaker was uniformly made an object of ridicule. At that very epoch in English history there was in England a statesman whose wisdom had really laid the foundations of the unparalleled greatness which, notwithstanding the loss of her best colonies, that kingdom has since attained. To none more than to William Pitt was our ancient mother indebted for the inception of a course of policy which has made Britain one of the greatest of modern powers. Had his views been regarded by his countrymen, the British empire would long since have been the greatest, and altogether the most powerful and magnificent, the world has ever seen. Pitt was the first of English statesmen; he was more than a century in advance of his age; his penetrating mind saw clearly the advantages, in a commercial point of view, of the position of Great Britain and he understood better than any of his cotemporaries the real resources of his country, and in what her true wealth and power were to consist. He gave the impetus and direction to her commercial system, which all the blunders of later statesmen, and all the impediments thrown in its way by ignorance and folly, have not been able to arrest. The colonial system of England Mr. Pitt regarded as the right arm of her power, without which her commerce, for which she seemed designed by nature, could never be developed. Under his administration the Canadas were added to the crown; and, had his prudent counsels been heeded, it is very clear that the loss of the American colonies would not have taken place. But what signifies the voice of wisdom when opposed to the prevailing sentiment, or passion, or ideas of a nation? His sense of right, justice, prudence, and expediency for his country, prompted him to stand up almost alone in the British Parliament, and resist the first steps of that power in a course that was to cost England the most valuable portion of her empire; and, by taking such a stand against the settled feeling of his day, he placed himself in a small minority, and his great wisdom and unparalleled faculties were lost to the administrative service of his country.

It should always, in reading the history of American politics, be borne in mind that, at the time when the troubles between England and her colonies commenced, those colonies were far from being composed of such homogeneous materials as to facilitate their ready union into one people. The New England colonists were generally religionists; people of severe morals, and disciplined in the school of adversity. They were mostly, especially the first settlers, persons bred in poverty, with but little education, saving in scriptural matters. The Puritans, in England, were looked upon as fanatics. To escape from oppression they sought refuge in New England. On the other hand, Virginia was settled by a portion of those same Englishmen whose religious and political sentiments had driven the Puritans from England. Virginia was the most favored of the American colonies; her charter was liberal and her grant of territory magnificent. Many of her planters were from high families, and, as a general thing, the settlers of that colony were of the Anglican church, and attached to the English institutions. Maryland, also, settled under the auspices of Lord Baltimore, received many wealthy planters, who sought asylum from religious persecution; but, as they were Catholics, they would not be likely to find much sympathy amongst their Protestant neighbors. The Pennsylvania colony, commenced under Penn and his followers, who were driven from the mother country by harsh usage, was, like that of Maryland, exceedingly tolerant of other sects, and, like that colony, also received into her midst with fraternal affection people of all lands and religions. The Carolinas were settlements of English planters, commenced under the auspices of the British nobility, and were generally attached to the English church, saving a moderate mixture of the Huguenots, who in early times found their way into the South. New York was a mongrel colony. She was in early times settled by the Dutch, and was afterwards overrun by Englishmen of all degrees and qualities. These settlements, prior to the Revolution, had no political connection, and but little intercourse with each other. Their only bond of union was through the mother country, to which they all hung like clusters of grapes to the parent vine. So gracefully and naturally were the colonies attached to the mother country, and, left to themselves, so little were they adapted to a union amongst themselves, that, had it not been for extreme violence from that mother country, they would not have been shaken from her attachment. But King George had no conception of the policy which should govern his administration. Pitt saw in England's colonies but the pillars of her commerce and manufactures, which should make that country the richest and most powerful of nations; but George's minister, Grenville, though accomplished and fully equal to the age in which he lived, looked upon them with a narrower view. He only saw them beneficial in proportion as they could be made tributary to the treasury by means of taxation. The death of George the Second in 1760, after the conquest of the Canadas under the ministry of Pitt, was followed by the coronation of George the Third, and the peace of Paris, in 1763, brought about through the counsels of Bute, and in spite of the wishes of Pitt. In the French war, which resulted in the fall of Louisburg, Quebec, and the surrender by the French of the Canadas, the Americans had truly shown themselves of great service to England, and had taught France and Europe fearful expectations from the fast growing power of Britain. What would have been the career of England, had she continued to hold her colonies, can only be imagined; it was perhaps well for the world that the dismemberment took place; and France was far from censurable for seeking her own safety by the only measure that could prevent her rival's becoming at once the mistress of the world. The French minister (Choiseul) saw, better than either North or Grenville, the importance to England of the American possessions. In considering the early politics of this country, the motives of France for intriguing for American freedom should be carefully examined into; for, on account of the interposition of that country in our behalf during the Revolution, American party politics were sensibly affected, especially during the progress of the French Revolution.

CHAPTER II.

THE PERSISTENCE OF ENGLAND IN HER REVENUE ACTS UNITES THE COLONIES. — ACTION OF VIRGINIA AND SOUTH CAROLINA. — THE FORMATION OF THE UNION BY THE ADOPTION OF THE CONSTITUTION. — THE DIFFICULTIES IN THE WAY OF A UNION. — PROBABLE RESULTS IN CASE THERE HAD BEEN NO UNION. — THE SACRIFICE OF THE LARGE AND GAIN OF THE SMALLER STATES BY THE UNION. — CONSTITUTIONAL CONVENTION. — THE PART TAKEN BY VIRGINIA IN ESTABLISHING THE UNION.

The passage of the Stamp Act taught the ministry of George the Third two things, by neither of which did they seem to have the ability to profit. It taught them the great importance of the colonies as consumers of English goods, and the spirit with which they were evidently disposed to meet encroachments on their rights. The resistance of the colonists was not regarded at first in a serious light; but the loss of trade with America, consequent on that resistance, disclosed the fact that, even at that time, the mercantile and manufacturing interests had begun to acquire some importance, although they had no decisive influence in the administration. They, perhaps, contributed greatly to the repeal of the odious Stamp Act; but the infatuated ministry were so wedded to their project of taxing America, that the Stamp Act was only repealed to give place to other systems of taxation. Unlimited submission of refractory subjects was the only thing to satisfy a haughty feudal monarch, and hence the enforcement of attempted taxation became a matter of pride with the king and his ministry.

The infatuation of the British ministry and king cost England the best of her American colonies. But these colonies, thus indebted to England's injustice and folly, and to the jealousy of France, for their independence, were a long time at the mercy of chance, and, unless actually under the control of Divine Providence, indebted likewise to the hand of fortune for the true greatness they have since attained. As early as 1776 the Americans declared themselves independent of the mother country; and the struggles of the Revolutionary War taught them that mutual dependence on each other which well prepared them for the formation of the Union, and the adoption of the Constitution under which we now live. The colonies, by the war of the Revolution, were not attempting to work out schemes of ambition, and but few of those persons who saw the revolutionary drama successfully closed, had anything like a correct idea of the future greatness destined to attend their new-born country. The contest between the colonies and the mother country was a struggle on the part of the former for their legal rights, — a battle against oppression. In this resistance they were all a unit. Massachusetts had already made wonderful progress in every species of prosperity. Upon the ocean and the land her commerce had begun to expand, and all the trades flourished in her bosom. For virtue, intelligence, and industry, she was in advance of her sisters; and when that first project of taxation, the Stamp Act, was put forth, the voice of her intelligent and manly sons went forth through the land in loud remonstrance. But Virginia! all have heard of the electric shock which that colony sent through the continent! Patrick Henry drew the resolves which her House of Burgesses passed, declaring, in effect, that the Stamp Act was not binding on the colonies, and that, without representation in the British Parliament, that legislature had no authority to tax America. These resolves found a cordial response in every colony, and on none did they fall with more animating effect than on Massachusetts. In the threatened conflict Massachusetts had much to encounter, and her brave sons felt no common joy when they heard from Virginia in thunder-tones such a bold defiance hurled at the tyrants over the deep. It was truly said that "Virginia gave the signal for the continent." Massachusetts was not insensible to the nobleness of Virginia patriotism. In those days, no matter in what section of this land he was born or bred, every true American's heart thrilled with one sentiment, and all united in the conflict with the oppressor with a kindred spirit. Massachusetts was the first to suggest the idea of an American Congress to unite on means of redress, but South Carolina was the first to appoint delegates. The spirit of resistance was everywhere, and the concert of action necessary to render that resistance effectual was attained; and, after the most glorious struggle the world has ever seen, the colonies in 1783 became what they had declared themselves to be — Independent States.

The Constitution of the United States was perfected and adopted in 1788. The Federalists of that day were not precisely the party that afterwards went by that name. Of the questions before the American people, on the adoption of the Constitution, it is impossible here to give any adequate account. The greater portion of the most prominent American statesmen manifested the deepest solicitude for the formation of the Union of the American States, by the adoption of the Constitution. France had evidently aided the colonies to achieve their independence with a view to the formation of a close and profitable connection with them, as well as for the purpose of abridging the increasing power of England. Should the states, after becoming independent and sovereign, remain separate, and each under its own control, they would, it was feared, become a prey to European powers, until civil war, superinduced by foreign intrigues, and the clashing of internal interests, should overwhelm them in ruin. There was but one hope; that was felt by every statesman and patriot to be in union. Washington's great and patriotic heart was deeply enlisted in the measure. It was hard to form a constitution that would give perfect satisfaction to all sections of the country, and much was yielded, by way of mutual concession, out of a patriotic desire to secure to posterity the liberty which had cost so much treasure and blood. Although the Constitution had the support of Washington, and the greater part of the most prominent patriots whose labors and counsels had guided the colonies through the Revolution, it had, nevertheless, many powerful opponents. The most eloquent advocates in its favor, whose writings have come down to us, were, perhaps, the authors of the *Federalist* — Jay, Hamilton, and Madison. As the opinions of those who took part in the discussions upon the formation and adoption of the Constitution were regarded in the political party organizations which subsequently came into existence, it is clear that any one who would thoroughly comprehend the origin of political parties in the United States should look attentively into the history of that interesting period. The period was truly an interesting one, and it is feared that we are too little accustomed to revert to it for lessons of political wisdom and patriotism. Do we not show too great a disposition to be governed by considerations of the present, with too little regard to the past and future? It may be safely asserted that the statesman who, in shaping his political theories, shall disregard the landmarks afforded by the past, will never prove a safe counsellor for the state.

At the commencement of the Revolution there were none but colonial governments. The colonies, in 1776, declared themselves states, after which there was nothing, excepting the Confederation, but state governments until the adoption of the United States Constitution in 1788. The Congress, which was formed by delegates from the different states, having no power, saving what those states voluntarily accorded to it, continued its patriotic labors from 1774 till the adoption of the Articles of Confederation in 1781. By the Articles of Confederation no general government was formed, with power to raise armies, levy taxes and imposts, regulate commerce, or otherwise provide for the general safety and well-being of the whole country. The Congress, as constituted under the Articles of Confederation, could recommend measures necessary for such purposes; but each state was independent, and there was no compulsory power to insure compliance with the congressional recommendations. The revolutionary struggle ended in 1783, and for a few years the states attempted to proceed under the Confederation, but were soon discouraged, and fearful apprehensions were entertained by the patriots of those days for the future welfare of the country. Considering the original diversity as to manners, habits, customs, religion and caste, of the people of the different colonies, it could not have been expected that they would all readily merge into a general government which should absorb all their nationality; nor could such a consummation have been possible, but for the fraternal feelings inspired by their long and united resistance to the mother country. It is true that there were multitudes in those days who were opposed to the Union as finally formed; and there were many who were not in favor of any union at all, but would leave each state a sovereign power. And had there been no union, this must of course have been the case. No one capable of a slight degree of reflection can fail to see that the result, in such an event, must have been disastrous in the extreme. Here would have been a cluster of republics; but the kind feelings engendered by their common efforts for liberty might not have endured forever, and probably would not; as, under the relationship of a closer tie, the states are not always in the best of harmony with each other. Each state would, as a sovereign power, have required navies, armies, and foreign ministers; and, in the regulation of its trade and commerce, would have had its peculiar scheme of duties. Had there been no union effected, and had no foreign intrigues ensued to subvert the independence of one or all of the states, the result must in time have been an absorption of all the smaller by a few large ones, which, being situated favorably for commerce, would have received a monstrous growth.

In the formation of the Union, the surrender of ambition, and of transcendent prospects, was wholly on the part of the larger and commercial states. The small states had nothing to lose, and everything to gain, by the union; but, for the larger ones, such as Massachusetts, New York, and Virginia, with their Atlantic positions and large territories, to enter such union, placing themselves on a par with the least, was a step that might require some estimate of the gains to accrue therefrom. The gains were duly estimated, and those states, with the others, met, by their delegates, at Philadelphia, on the second Tuesday of May, 1787, and continued their session until the 17th of September, before they could agree upon a Constitution, under which they were willing to become merged in a national government. In that Convention, fortunately, were some of the first statesmen and patriots of the revolutionary period. The Convention was presided over by GEORGE WASHINGTON, who threw his whole soul into its objects. Virginia had other distinguished men in that body, such as James Madison, Edmund Randolph, and George Wythe. From Pennsylvania were Benjamin Franklin, Robert Morris, George Clymer, and others of talent and note. From New York were Alexander Hamilton, John Lansing, and Robert Yates. John Rutledge, the Pinckneys, and Pierce Butler, were there from South Carolina; Roger Sherman and Oliver Ellsworth from Connecticut; and Elbridge Gerry, Rufus King, and Caleb Strong, from Massachusetts. In short, the members from all the colonies were prominent men. Minutes of the debates of that Convention were kept by Mr. Madison, and they form one of the most interesting works we have connected with the origin of our government. The labor upon the hands of that Convention was the most weighty and important probably that ever devolved upon mortal faculties. The selection of men for that labor was fortunate. It seems as though the Deity inspired Virginia to send Washington, as nothing could have been more fit than for that truly great and good man to preside at such a convention. Virginia was not only among the first to adopt the Constitution, but she did more than any other state for the formation of the Union. At the close of the Revolution she owned all the north-western territory, now comprising many flourishing and powerful states, and voluntarily surrendered it to the general government, as an act of justice to her sisters, and as a consideration for the formation of some closer union. But, notwithstanding the precarious situation of the states at that time, and the deep anxiety of the greatest and best men then living, and, notwithstanding the general good feeling pervading all the states, it was with the greatest difficulty that the delegates could agree on a Constitution. It is said that the Convention was several times on the point of breaking up and dispersing in despair. But, finally, after a session of months, the Constitution that was subsequently adopted, was agreed upon, and transmitted to the old Congress for submission to the states for approval. It is certainly an astonishing production; but while we read its provisions with grateful attention, we should not forget that many of its choicest principles were the gifts of our ancient English ancestors. Our Constitution was, fortunately, modelled on the English constitution, so modifying the latter as to suit our situation and condition.

CHAPTER III.

THE ELEMENTS OF POLITICAL PARTIES DEVELOPED DURING THE ADMINISTRATION OF WASHINGTON. — METHOD OF ELECTING THE PRESIDENT BY THE COLLEGE OF ELECTORS PROVIDED BY THE CONSTITUTION, AND THE FAILURE OF THE SYSTEM. — THE EFFECT OF THE FRENCH REVOLUTION IN CREATING PARTIES IN THE UNITED STATES. — SOME OF THE CAUSES OF THE FAILURE OF THE FRENCH REVOLUTION.

THE Constitution of the United States was adopted in 1788, and Washington's administration commenced in March, 1789. Washington was unanimously chosen president by the college of electors. Political parties were not fully developed during his administration, although, as we shall see, their elements, during that period, began to manifest themselves. The college of electors, as constituted under the Constitution, answered the purpose for which it was designed at the first presidential elections ; but soon it became a useless piece of machinery. It was judged by the wise framers of the Constitution that if the election of the chief executive of the nation were left to the voice of the mass of the people, demagogues might triumph over modest and meritorious statesmen. They had the experience of the past ages of the world to warrant them in this belief. In Greece and Rome, and every other land, where there been liberty enough to call for elections at all, the prejudices and passio s of the masses had invariably prevailed over the wisdom and patriotism of the few. Ambition, in all ages of the world, has always clothed itself in a winning garb. Under pretensions of friendship for the people, the fiercest tyrants of old won their way to power. What though a few could always see through the ambitious designs of an aspiring demagogue? Has it not ever been the case that the less fortunate and less intelligent portions of the people have been influenced uniformly by the pretensions of those seeking their suffrages? And, as merit and worth are usually modest and unassuming, and as corrupt ambition is brazen and pretending, it is not so strange that demagogues are generally the surest to succeed, in the race of popularity, with the people. The premises and conclusions here are undoubtedly correct, as they are borne out by all history; but woe to the politician who should dare to assert them! Republican governments have uniformly been destroyed by demagogism; and it was not singular that our fathers, in establishing a government for this country, should endeavor to provide some safeguard against the shoals on which all other free governments have foundered. The college of electors was the result of their precaution in this respect. The Constitution provides that the people of each state shall vote for presidential electors, instead of voting for a president. It was contemplated, by the framers of that instrument, that the electors should be selected, by the people of each state, on account of their being the most intelligent, weighty, and patriotic, of their fellow-citizens; that the election of the president should be left solely to them; and that, in such election, they should act their unbiassed judgment. But, as every one sees, the *patriotism* of parties has swept away the provisions of the Constitution, and, instead of being elected by the electors, the presidents are now elected by the people. That is, the electors are mere men of straw, committed to their course of conduct before their election.

But scarcely had our government been organized under the Constitution, before an event, or a train of events, commenced, which greatly hastened the formation of political parties in this country. The French Revolution is alluded to, which broke out in September, 1789. We say revolution; but perhaps it would be more proper to say, series of revolutions. Louis the Sixteenth, a virtuous and amiable monarch, was then the occupant of the French throne. He had placed himself in a singular attitude, with respect to the monarchs of Europe, by lending a helping hand to the British colonies in their struggle for independence; but Europe saw that it was with no censurable *motives* that this had been done. As Austria, Prussia, and, in fact, all the continent, looked with dread upon the fast growing power of Great Britain, under the policy of Pitt, Louis was not only pardoned for, but was encouraged in, his efforts to establish the liberties of the American colonies. But the results of this interference in our affairs are well known to the world. It is not safe for a monarchy to send its soldiers abroad to fight with patriots for the rights of man. French officers and soldiers fought under the immortal Washington, and while these battles were raging, the scarcely less immortal Franklin walked the streets of Paris, a minister at the French court. And it was with the spirit of liberty as with the lightning, of which Franklin had taught the world how to disarm the clouds; it was not, and never can be, safe for a body in a negative condition to be put in contact with one in the positive state. Franklin once, in connecting his electric jar to the clouds by a kite, came near bringing down the lightnings upon his head; and Louis, in attempting to experiment with the spirit of freedom on this side of the Atlantic, was not sufficiently cautious in making use of non-conducting instruments, and Europe was shaken to its foundations by the shock occasioned by the passage of a spark of that subtle spirit across the deep. Louis, that gentle monarch, whose name must ever be regarded with respect and gratitude by Americans, lost his life as the result. There were many things to predispose France to a revolution. The two prior monarchs, Louis the Fourteenth and Louis the Fifteenth, had been extravagant and improvident, and the crown came to Louis the Sixteenth, charged with burdens which proved insupportable. The state of bankruptcy into which the kingdom had been brought, by the extravagance of those monarchs, rendered the convocation of the States-General necessary; and this step was but the signal for the revolution. That grand national convocation had not been assembled before for about two hundred years, and had never been called together but upon very extraordinary occasions. It consisted of the representatives of the nobility, clergy, and the people, or the *tiers etat*, as they were called. The popular branch which had, at this convocation, been doubled at the instance of M. Necker, contained many daring spirits. But what not a little surprises the reader of the history of that period, is the fact that large masses of the clergy and nobility of the States-General were disposed to unite with the popular branch in wresting from the crown of France some of its oppressive prerogatives, and securing for the nation a more just, liberal, and equal constitution. The press in France had been for some time free, and the subject of popular rights had been agitated boldly by the ablest writers of that age. The result of the Revolution in America, and the majestic march of the Americans to independence, and the establishment of a national government, had produced a profound sensation in the minds of all intelligent men in Europe. The profligacy and debauchery of the French court, under Louis the Fifteenth, had disgusted the nation, and, in view of the deplorable condition into which the crimes of the monarchy had plunged France, it was not strange that her best people, whether noble, clergy, or lay, should feel inclined to take advantage of the crisis to lay the foundations of a safer, purer, and more just system of government. The period was right for the effort, and the spirit of the nation favorable. The reigning monarch himself, Louis the Sixteenth, seemed willing, and pleased, to yield to any reasonable demand; and nothing was wanting to secure France a safe, just, equal, and durable constitution, but political wisdom on the part of the French people. The popular power met with no obstacle to anything it demanded, until revolution after revolution swept away all rights. There were in France intelligent and somewhat conservative Republicans, whose counsels, if heeded, would have conferred blessings on that country; but when the foundations of all government are once up-turned, and everything made to hinge on the popular voice, of what importance, in a nation of millions of people, are a handful of intelligent and conservative individuals? It may be easy for a few innovators, by dint of constant agitation, to induce a nation to become dissatisfied with, and throw off, their government; but when all government is once at an end, and the popular will made supreme, it is not always so easy to make that popular will again submit to the control of constitutional restraints.

The first fruit of the French Revolution was the establishment of the National Assembly, which wielded the legislative power of the kingdom; but between 1789 and September, 1792, when the monarchy was wholly overthrown, and Louis the Sixteenth beheaded, the system of government adopted by the revolutionists was several times changed. In fact, scarcely any constitution that could be invented would endure a year, and many of them but a few months. The government was in the hands of the Jacobins, and every measure of importance was arranged at their club, and rarely anything transpired in the Assembly as an act of deliberation. The history of these French Jacobin clubs ought to teach every sensible mind the extreme danger of suffering any nation for a moment to surrender sacred constitutional rights. Perhaps the world has never seen anything bloodier or more cruel in the way of civil war. Power reigned without justice, reason, or mercy; and for a period the government in France was rightly called the Reign of Terror. Marat, Danton, and Robespierre — well may the world turn pale at the mention of their names! But, after all, probably they did no more than any leaders, under like circumstances, seeking at all hazards to carry out peculiar views, would be obliged to do. They are not all spoken of as men by nature innately cruel and bloody-minded; but it was the exigency of their mission that called for the assassination and murder of millions of the French clergy and gentry. To render France safe under the government that ignored their castes and rights, those privileged classes must be extirpated ; and, should a like predicament occur to a large popular faction in any other country, — should all government be swept away, and the prevailing faction, true to their mission of crushing out the rights of other classes regarded as privileged, unless disposed to compromise with sin and injustice, which leading political saints are rarely disposed to do, — the bloody acts of the French Revolution would necessarily be reënacted. Reformers are too little apt to reflect that without compromise no government nor society on earth can possibly exist. In France, how many trials were made during the revolutionary period ! The history of their National Assembly, their Convention, their Directory, their Consular government, and their Imperial government, will show. Had moderate, wise, and conservative measures been acquiesced in at the outset of these revolutions, the people, clergy, nobility, and monarchy, would all have concurred, and France would have taken a step forward in the career of freedom and prosperity; but rash, impracticable, and head-hot and head-strong men rushed into the storm as champions of the people, and of divine popular rights ; and the result was that the progress of the grand nation, in everything beneficial to the human race, was backwards.

CHAPTER IV.

THE AMERICAN GOVERNMENT FORMED ON THE PRINCIPLES OF THE ENGLISH CONSTITUTION, MODIFIED TO SUIT OUR REPUBLICAN CONDITION. — NARROW ESCAPE FROM THE CONTAGION OF FRENCH JACOBINISM. — THE FEDERALISTS IN FAVOR OF THE CONSTITUTION AS ADOPTED. — THE ANTI-FEDERALISTS. — THE FEDERALISTS AND REPUBLICANS.

On the breaking out of the French Revolution, it was very natural that Americans should feel deeply interested for the French people; and undoubtedly that event had a powerful influence in establishing the Republican party in this country. In France, the moderate Republicans were anxious to adopt a Constitution based upon the principles of the English or American Constitution; but the popular party were not to be satisfied with any institution that infringed in the slightest degree on liberty. America had been more fortunate. At the close of her Revolution, which placed the supreme power of the country in the people, it fortunately happened that the principal leading men throughout all the states were, with but few exceptions, unambitious, upright, conservative, and judicious statesmen. The Revolution had successfully terminated under the auspices of these men; and, when the adoption of a constitution was undertaken, their influence remained unimpaired with the masses of the people. They were partial to the laws and institutions which had been their birthright, and which were peculiarly adapted to the spirit and genius of the Anglo-Saxon race. As America was really the offspring, the child of England, it was natural enough that the free spirit of the British Constitution should animate her. The American Revolution itself, seen during all its stages, seems more like a birth than a civil war, and the colonies, from their first appearance, were really but the imperfectly defined lineaments of an embryo kingdom or state. After emancipation from the control of the parent government, although this enfranchisement had only been achieved by a bloody struggle with that domineering parent, the best wisdom of young America instructed her that her future safety, power, and glory, were to be attained by a preservation here of that Constitution which had grown up with the growth of the Anglo-Saxon race, and which was her legitimate inheritance. That, in cleaving to the British form of government, modified, of course, to suit their changed circumstances, our fathers not only obeyed the dictates of nature, but likewise acted wisely, subsequent events have fully demonstrated; still, at the time of the adoption of our Constitution, there were many who were opposed to it. The controversies in regard to it, during the years 1787 and 1788, were carried on with a great deal of spirit. Those who favored the Constitution as adopted, following, in the division of the legislative assembly into an upper and lower house, and in the construction of the judiciary and the creation of the executive departments, the English system, were called Federalists; and those who were opposed to that proposed federal system were styled anti-Federalists. The people at large were so incensed against the mother country that any system of government acknowledged to resemble hers, would naturally encounter great prejudices ; but men of clearer and deeper views saw, in the recent contest with England, not the test, but the abuse of her admirable Constitution. Under that Constitution, the wisdom of England, as a general thing, rules ; and hence her unexampled stability, power, and prosperity. But what would she probably have accomplished under the auspices of a Convention, a Directory, a National Assembly, or a Consulate? France, no doubt, with a form of government that had mingled the popular with the aristocratic element, and had secured, in the service of her legislature, the wisdom of the kingdom, would have attained all that the heart of patriotism could desire. Fortunately, America was called upon to establish her national governmental charter before the minds of her people had been poisoned and distracted by the terrible isms of demagogues. At that day her wisest and purest citizens stood high in the confidence of the people, as there had not been time for the envy and jealousy of conceited reformers and restless agitators to undermine and destroy their influence. If, at the present day, a Constitution for this country were to be framed, it is doubtful if it would be formed by its best intelligence. As it was, the Constitution met with much opposition from prejudice and ignorance.

On the breaking out of the French Revolution the sympathy for France and hatred of England were more apparent and decisive, in this country, than ever. France seemed to claim, as a matter of right, that America should espouse her quarrel with England, and many Americans were disposed to join their Gaulic friend, as in a crusade in behalf of the freedom of the world. That that was a trying period for the republic of the United States, is very evident. Fortunately for the destiny of this country, Washington was at the head of government, and there can be no doubt that the preservation of the newly-established Constitution was, in a great degree, owing to his great personal popularity. His administration was in many respects contrary to the feelings of large masses of the people, and it is doubtful if the Federalists, with a president less influential, could have succeeded in the measures they carried out under Washington's presidency. It was under his administration that the Democratic or Republican party, as then called, began to have an existence. Thomas Jefferson, one of the most enthusiastic and thorough-going patriots of the Revolution, one of the first to bid defiance to George the Third, and who was venerated as almost equal to Washington, on account of being the author of that production more cherished and thought of, by the masses of the people, than any other human composition, — the Declaration of Independence, — was, at the time of the formation of the Constitution, absent from the country. He was at the French court from 1784 till 1789, when he returned, and, at Washington's solicitation, took a seat in the cabinet, as Secretary of State. Born and bred to free principles, and instructed in the revolutionary doctrines at home by such men as Patrick Henry, and then for five years thrown into the association of those powerful French revolutionists, many of them philosophers and men of genius, it would be by no means singular if his ideas were fully up to his age for sound and unwavering democracy. No one has doubted the entire sincerity of Jefferson's democracy. He was a natural lover of freedom and free principles, and probably no man lived, in his age, who labored more ardently than he for popular rights; and but few exceeded him in the amount of services rendered in behalf of our independence. But Mr. Jefferson was not wholly satisfied with all the features of the Constitution, and was far from relishing the admiration expressed by the Federalists for the British form of government. He would not have such a body as the senate; would simply have representatives immediately from the people, that in all measures the pure popular will might more readily and certainly be realized. This would form a government much, if not precisely, like the National Assembly of France. The fact is, Jefferson was an intense hater of the haughty and overbearing lords and aristrocrats of England, and was not pleased to see the English theory of government embraced in the American institutions, and looked with impatience upon those Americans who, he thought, took too fondly to the British model.

Alexander Hamilton, also a member of Washington's cabinet, — the Secretary of the Treasury, — was one of the leading Federalists; one who had almost idolized the fundamental principles of the English Constitution: we mean, of course, that Constitution when divested of its aristocratic privileges. Mr. Hamilton, it was asserted, had been in favor of a Constitution more resembling the British model, than the one adopted. He favored, so his opponents said, a longer term for the office of senator; and the executive he would have hold his place during good behavior. These were alleged to be propositions advanced by him in the Convention, or otherwheres, although not insisted on against the opinions of others. Excepting Washington, perhaps there was scarcely any one whose labors accomplished more in establishing the Constitution than those of Hamilton.

He was truly an able and brilliant statesman. He had been much associated with Washington during the Revolution; had been his *aide-de-camp*, confidential secretary, friend and adviser, on many critical occasions. Washington evidently reposed great confidence in his intelligence, penetration, and judgment; and looked with the greatest partiality on his probity, honor, and patriotism. As the friend of the Father of his country, — one in whom that illustrious character reposed more than usual confidence in affairs of the highest moment, and of whose worth and friendship he never had a doubt, — Alexander Hamilton's name will go down to the latest ages. John Adams was Vice-President of the United States, and was ranked among the first of the Federalists, although he was absent from the coun try, as a minister to France, until after the formation of the Constitution. Adams was one of the first that raised his voice against the encroachments of England upon the rights of the colonists, and was one of the main spokes in the wheel of the Revolution. He was a man of superior judgment, extreme clearness of views, incorruptible integrity, unblemished honor, and unexcelled patriotism. When the question of the formation of a government for these states arose, Adams was, with other statesmen, in favor of a strong and durable one. His partiality for what was called the British Constitution — that is, for the principle of dividing the governing power into three departments: an executive, a judiciary, and a legislative body consisting of an upper and lower house — characterized him as a Federalist. The Secretary of War, under Washington's administration, was John Knox, a well-known revolutionary general. It is said that he ranked as a Federalist; but the

Attorney General, Edmund Randolph, of Virginia, was, like Jefferson, disposed to encourage, in the formation and administration of government, principles of a more democratic tendency. In short, without going into a minute history of the controversies and discussions attendant on the adoption of the Constitution, and the administration of the government under it, it is sufficient here to state that the Constitution itself was a compromise between those who sought for a strong government, and those who were for having one of a more democratic cast. But as that was an age of democratic ideas, and as anything savoring of popular rights was exceedingly palatable to the masses, the expressions made use of by Hamilton, Adams, and others, favoring the principles of the British Constitution, were caught up and repeated much to their disadvantage, by those who looked upon anything British as unfavorable to liberty. The Federalists were charged with meditating the establishment of a monarchy, and orders of nobility; and doubtless many of those days credited such charges. That the Federalists, especially of a somewhat later period, were too partial to England, and were even too much in favor of the aristocratic, to the exclusion of the democratic, element of society, many even to the present day believe; but that they were ever anything but pure republicans it would be ridiculous to assert.

If this were, instead of a hasty sketch of the origin of political parties in the United States, a history of the administration of Washington, it would afford us great pleasure to record the triumphs of Hamilton's genius in his administration of the Treasury department. All accord him transcendent abilities; and that the principles, at the outset of our republic, when all was in chaos, developed by him, remain the basis upon which our government, in the department presided over by him, has ever since been administered, is ample evidence of his abilities. But few men were ever more unlike in feelings, views, and principles, than Hamilton and Jefferson. They disagreed on many important questions, and it was but a short time after the formation of the government under the Constitution, before each had his friends and admirers, who were gradually arranged into opposite parties. There were many things to promote these party divisions. The French Revolution has been alluded to, and was the prominent one. In 1792, when France was declared a republic, enthusiasm in favor of that country ran high in the United States. Banquets were held in honor of the French Revolution, and sympathy in many ways expressed. At first, the course taken by European affairs seemed so auspicious for liberty, that Americans generally felt their hearts pulsate in unison with the strides of freedom in France; but the displays of unbridled license and cruelty, which soon ensued, filled the minds of the judicious with concern, and strengthened the federal administration in those feelings of neutrality as to European conflicts, which their judgment had taught them to be in accordance with correct principles. After revolutionary France had become enlisted in war with England, it was natural that those Americans who would suffer their feelings to act in defiance of correct policy, if not of correct principles, should think America ought to espouse the cause of her old ally against her recent enemy. But Washington and his cabinet were too faithful guardians at the head of government to suffer such a suicidal step. When, therefore, in 1793, Washington's proclamation of neutrality was issued, the friends and sympathizers of France, and bitter enemies of England, were greatly excited. Washington was generally spared denunciation; but the Federalists, in and out of his cabinet, and Hamilton especially, were violently denounced. In 1793, "Citizen" Genet came to the United States as a French minister. He landed at Charleston, S. C., and voyaged to Philadelphia. The warmest demonstrations of popular favor greeted him wherever he appeared, the people meeting him in vast numbers, rendering his progress that of a triumphal march. But, notwithstanding he everywhere was warmly greeted by the masses of the people, he found he could not prevail on the President nor his cabinet to depart from a course of strict neutrality. The mission of Genet seemed to be to enlist the United States with France in the war against Great Britain; or, failing in this, to himself carry on war against that country from the United States, by enlisting men, fitting out cruisers, etc., etc. But when he found that the President would in no case permit such transactions, it is said that he threatened *to appeal from the government to the people!* At the request of the President, "Citizen" Genet was recalled; but his mission showed the precarious situation of the country at that time, and enables us to see how much we are indebted to the moral power and influence of the great and good Washington, whose arm alone, unsupported by the mass of his countrymen, protected our infant republic from the wiles of foreign intrigues. As, perhaps, the fruits of Genet's visit, democratic societies were formed in this country, in imitation, it has been said, of the Jacobin clubs of France. They were secret organizations, holding correspondence with each other; and it has been supposed that it was to them that Washington alluded in his Farewell Address, where he warns his countrymen against secret political societies. They had but a short existence, but were probably serviceable in concentrating into a party organization those who were growing distrustful of the Federalists. There were, it is true, other matters agitated by Congress under Washington's administration, on which there was a difference of views between the Federalists and their opponents. The question of state rights was warmly debated. There was quite an excited controversy as to the debts against the government, and touching those against the states to be assumed by the general government. In 1791, the Bank of the United States was chartered, occasioning some controversy; the Federalists generally maintaining its constitutionality, — their opponents the reverse. Also the impressment of American seamen by British men-of-war was a subject of much perplexity, none apologizing for, but the opponents of the administration loudly condemning, such acts as illegal, and a cause of war. But perhaps the excitement at no time ran so high against Washington, as on the negotiation of the Jay Treaty with England, 1794 and 1795. But, notwithstanding the popular clamor of the day, time, it is believed, has fully confirmed the wisdom and entire propriety of that measure.

These different events and measures are alluded to, to show by what steps the opposition of those days came into being, and into power; by what means and causes those old Federalists, the heroes of the Revolution, and the Solons of the constitutional convention, were rendered unacceptable to the American people, and were made to yield their places in the national councils to persons of other views, feelings, and principles. That there should be a revolution occasionally in the parties of a country is no doubt beneficial and necessary. Within certain limits parties are useful; as without them we can hardly conceive that political economy, as a science, would receive much attention. To party is America, as well as England, indebted for the highest orders of statesmen. It gives life to political science, and is no doubt a safeguard as well as sometimes a destroyer of free institutions. That the Federalists in some things, especially at a somewhat later period, went too far in submitting to the domineering power of England, many will, at the present time, concede; and likewise, that the Republicans, as the opposition were called, on the other hand, were, in many things, too radical, and too little inclined to submit to constitutional restraints, will be conceded by just as many. That the Federalists should be at the helm in the outset, and lay the foundation of the government, and then yield to a party that had had the influence of their example and discipline for twelve years, was, doubtless, no unfortunate thing for the country, as then situated; nay, the event shows that it was for its substantial service. The overthrow of the Federalists was, like the overthrow of any political party, only a political defeat, with a free course before them for future triumphs. These parties have continued from their origin until a recent date, both occasionally changed as to names, adherents, leaders, and principles, and alternating in their ascendency in the government of the country. As the Federal was in reality the parent of the late Whig party, and as it is of the latter that we propose to give some account, it will be necessary to pursue a little further its destiny.

CHAPTER V.

JEFFERSON THE FOUNDER OF THE REPUBLICAN PARTY.—THE DECLINE OF THE FEDERAL PARTY.—WASHINGTON'S RETIREMENT AND FAREWELL ADDRESS.—JOHN ADAMS' ELECTION IN 1796.—TREATMENT OF THE UNITED STATES BY ENGLAND.—IMPRESSMENT OF SEAMEN.—THE NEUTRAL POLICY OF THE FEDERAL ADMINISTRATION, ETC. ETC.

WHATEVER may be said of the Republican party, as it existed in the times of Jefferson, as to the propriety of its issues, no one can deny that the Republicans themselves, so far as they espoused party measures, meant well for the country. They were patriots, warmly devoted to the cause of human liberty, and willing to perish in the defence of their country. The party was no sectional organization, but was, and ever has been, intensely national. Jefferson, the founder of American Democracy, was in heart and soul a lover of freedom. The party that formed around him was one whose watchword was Liberty. It was a party consisting of men who were fired with fierce indignation towards England for attempting to fasten the chains of slavery upon them; and although that party had not, at the outset, so many men of wealth, and of highly cultivated minds, as composed the Federal party, it nevertheless abounded in patriots—those who were willing to face the cannon's mouth in the defence of their liberties. It is but natural that freemen should be jealous of their liberties. The greatest fault that can be charged upon the old Republicans is, that they were perhaps a

5*

little too jealous of their rights, and carried their politics somwhat too far; that, in their excess of zeal for the world's freedom, they were in danger of wrecking the vessel freighted with their own. But, if this charge be just, it was fortunate that they encountered the old Federal party, whose prominence in the land thwarted and counteracted their less conservative principles. The history of Washington's administration shows the gradual decline of the Federal organization, and the corresponding growth of the Republican party. As early as 1793, on some party measures, the Federalists were in the minority in Congress, although it was not until 1800 that the Republicans had an ascendency amongst the people. At the close of Washington's administration John Adams was by a majority of three in the electoral college elected President, and held the office one term; after which, in 1800, Thomas Jefferson was elected by the House of Representatives, there having been no choice by the people. When Washington, at the clóse of his second term, took leave of the presidency, he presented to his countrymen his FAREWELL ADDRESS. In making that address, he consulted propriety less than duty. The propriety of the act was unquestionable, and recognized by the whole world. He had been the leader in the Revolution; his discretion, wisdom, and prudence, had saved the revolutionary army, and exhausted, and finally captured, the forces of the adversary; he had throughout encountered every obstacle that envy, jealousy, and the passions of man, could throw in his way; generals in the army, and knaves out of it, had conspired against him; and nothing but his firmness, patriotism, and heroism, enabled him to hold together naked and starving men, and finally lead his countrymen to victory and peace. Every candid reader of history will say that, without Washington, our independence could never have been achieved. And then, when peace was established, and the passions of disunited and jealous states were wrangling about state rights and confederations, it was only under the auspices of the beloved Father of his Country that the people of the United States could be led to unite their destinies under a general government, and consent to the adoption of the Constitution. And finally, when, with shrieks for freedom, anarchy reared its awful head, and the peace and stability of the new-born American republic were threatened by the yawning gulf of French Jacobinism, nothing but the composed, serene and majestic brow of Washington could speak safety to his countrymen, and allay the fiend of discord. He felt that the newly adopted government was an experiment, but an experiment freighted with the liberties of America. More nations have conquered freedom than have preserved it. Courage, which is not uncommon, may extort freedom from the oppressor; but only wisdom, which is very rare, can render the acquisition secure.

Washington had done so much towards establishing the liberties of his country, that, on ceasing longer to take a part in public affairs, he felt he could not with propriety withdraw from his elevated position, as chief magistrate of the nation, without giving his countrymen his parting advice. And the counsels of that affectionate Farewell Address now speak to us as a voice from his tomb. They were the counsels of one who wished the American republic to be perpetual. His eyes glanced down to future ages; he foresaw the difficulties which coming time had in store; and with marvellous wisdom he laid down the principles, and put forth the cautions, which, if regarded, will unfailingly secure the lasting union and prosperity of these states. Washington was acquainted with the ill-success which had, in past ages of the world, attended the establishment of republican and democratic governments; and he well knew, and most keenly felt, that there was but a single hope for the success of the government here, in the formation of which he had taken so great a part. Would or would not the Americans have the wisdom and stability to seize hold of, and stand by, the only possible means of rendering the republican institutions, for which there was so great an exultation, permanent? His Farewell Address shows with what intense anxiety the Father of his Country saw this republic launched upon the "tide of experiment," and how impressively he besought its helmsmen to never lose sight of that compass by the aid of which there can be no storm it cannot outride. If republics can ever become successful and permanent, it must be through the instrumentality of constitutions. So long as the constitution of a country is regarded as a sacred law, — so long as all parts and sections of the commonwealth are united in yielding full and entire obedience to it; feeling that it is an instrument on which their dearest rights are dependent, — a republic may be safe; for all republics have been destroyed by enemies from within, not from without. In his Farewell Address Washington dwells long and intently on this. In fact, to teach one to observe and cherish the Constitution, is to teach him union, and every other principle and duty embraced in that instrument. He warned his countrymen against all sectional animosities, and recommended that union, above all things, should be cherished as the palladium of their liberties, and pointed out the many methods by which, unless the American people should remain constantly on their guard, their government might be shipwrecked.

John Adams succeeded Washington as President in 1796, having been elected over Thomas Jefferson by a very slight majority. Jefferson was the candidate of the Republican party. Notwithstanding the excesses of the French Revolution had very much dampened the ardor of that portion of the American people who had been in favor of espousing the cause of France in her war with England, still much occurred to nourish the hatred of Americans generally towards the latter. England, in the peace of 1783, did not yield to her destiny with very good grace. As she had, in the war against her colonies, to encounter France and Spain, our venerable mother saw the necessity of giving up the struggle; but as soon as the weapons of her two European foes were withdrawn from her breast, she was far from honorable, or just, in the manner of executing the treaty of peace with the United States. The forts and stations, held by Britain upon our borders, were not given up with any degree of cordial alacrity, nor were her forces withdrawn as readily as they might and ought to have been. Our country had much to suffer from her unfriendly and haughty disposition. The states were not united, and had no government worthy of the name. Immediately on the announcement of the peace, our ill-clad and unpaid army was disbanded. Of course there was no navy; and what could be done but to submit to the superciliousness of a power which, under all the circumstances, could not have been in a very amiable humor towards us? American officers, throughout the Revolution, had been the objects of ridicule amongst the aristocrats of the British camp, as, indeed, had the American patriots, and everything American, amongst the parasites of the English court. This feeling of contempt for everything American,—this disposition to treat with ridicule the manners, habits, and customs, of Americans, and to sneer at American institutions,—is not even at the present day entirely subdued in the lordly heart of Mr. Bull. For years after the Revolution nothing could more nauseate that gentleman than to hear the name of Jonathan; and when it was in his power to be governed solely by his own sentiments of propriety, in his treatment of his pretending son, he was never known to err on the side of magnanimity, or courtesy. The fact is, Mr. Bull had no faith in his son Jonathan; did not believe he would ever amount to anything; was very sure that he was a graceless, unmannerly scamp; and was far from feeling disposed to recognize his rights in anything, further than absolutely *obliged*. After the war was at an end, the states began to extend their commerce abroad, and cover the ocean with their sails and sailors. But Mr. Bull seemed to think the ocean his domain. Somebody—some English poet—had put it into his head that Britannia rules the waves! And, feeling that he was master of the ocean, the old gentleman was very cavalier in his treatment upon the deep of the crafts of other powers. He had peculiar views as to the laws of nations; and, instead of recognizing the codes as unfolded by Grotius, Puffendorf, Vattel, and other authorities, he was disposed rather to be governed by rules of his own making. He was quite unceremonious in his treatment of the commerce of the whole world, and of the American commerce in particular. If, in his war with France, he was in want of sailors, or soldiers, he went aboard of American merchantmen for them. He pretended he was in pursuit of British subjects; but, as by the English laws no subject of Great Britain could legally expatriate himself, and become a citizen of another country, those who had become citizens of the United States were impressed, and frequently those who were American-born. To this the early statesmen of the republic remonstrated; and, although Bull would occasionally qualify his claim and action, he ever bore himself like one above the reach of his injured victim. As Washington before had done, Mr. Adams remonstrated against the impressment of American seamen; but, under the administration of the latter, that practice, with others as unjustifiable in regard to American commerce, was persisted in by the assumed master of the ocean.

No sooner had France become a republic than England, and the monarchies of Europe, undertook to replace the Bourbons upon their throne. The monarchs of Europe were well united in the feeling that it was far from prudent to tolerate a powerful republic in their very midst, and readily embraced the British policy of restoring monarchy to France, let the cost be what it might. But the armies of republics, when their liberties are attacked, are usually brave in war, and fight with an enthusiasm and desperation not often manifested by the soldiers of kings. The result was that France rapidly broke up the alliances against her, and was almost everywhere on the land victorious, having, sometimes, the most of

Europe bound to her policy. While these things were thus progressing, England nearly annihilated the navies of the belligerents, leaving no rival for the commerce of the world but the United States. The manner in which this country profited by its position is clear proof of the wisdom of its administrative policy. The stern and unyielding resolution to maintain an entire neutrality as to the wars of all foreign or transatlantic powers, though at first in opposition to large numbers of very worthy citizens of the United States, proved in the event so eminently judicious, as a policy for this country, that it has ever since, by all statesmen, been adhered to. Moreover, Hamilton was an American Pitt. The ultimate greatness of this country, the extent of its resources, the correct course for it to pursue for the development of its best interests, and its future commercial career, were seen and understood by that statesman better than by most other men of his day. It was fortunate for the country that so penetrating and practical a mind was, at that period, at its command. The rapid growth of commerce for a few years attested this; for it was the astonishment of the world. But the commercial policy of the country will be more particularly considered hereafter.

CHAPTER VI.

JOHN ADAMS' ADMINISTRATION. — HIS PART IN THE ESTABLISHMENT OF THE AMERICAN CONSTITUTIONS. — THE PROVIDENTIALLY FORTUNATE CONCURRENCE OF EVENTS THAT FAVORED THE FREEDOM OF AMERICA, AND THE GROWTH OF HER FREE INSTITUTIONS. — DEFEAT OF THE FEDERALISTS BY THE REPUBLICANS IN 1800. — COMMERCIAL PROSPERITY OF AMERICA DURING THE ADMINISTRATION OF ADAMS. — JEFFERSON'S POLICY AS TO COMMERCE.

The administration of John Adams, which ended in 1800, was not essentially different from that of Washington. At his recommendation the so-called alien and sedition laws were passed, which were used by his enemies much to his disadvantage. They were measures of too little consequence to deserve much consideration, as they indicate nothing in regard to the political principles of Mr. Adams. The laws in question might have been wise, or unwise, without reasonably affecting his standing as a statesman or patriot. But from that day Mr. Adams, and the party supposed to inherit Federal principles, have had arrayed against them all the voters of the country of foreign birth. The neutral policy inaugurated by President Washington was strictly pursued by his successor, whose overtures to France for a commercial treaty were indignantly spurned, and his ministers ordered out of that country. A speck of war with our revolutionary ally, especially on the ocean, took place. In one or two naval encounters our young republic showed a vigor not only respectable, but somewhat significant. Our transatlantic neighbor soon thought better of our friendship, received our ambassadors, and entered into a treaty with us, though based on principles of neutrality.

Mr. Adams, as has before been remarked, was in Europe at the time the United States Constitution was formed; but it should not be forgotten that the framework of that Constitution might almost be claimed by him as of his originating. The constitutions of many of the states were of an earlier origin than that of the United States; and in the more essential principles the latter is unquestionably patterned on the model of some of the former. On occasion of the construction of the state constitutions, which were called for immediately on throwing off the government of the mother country, there was considerable discussion as to the best form for such institutions. Mr. Adams said and did more, perhaps, than any other American upon the subject. His counsels were of great service in Massachusetts, in the formation of her constitution, which was prepared in 1779, and was almost the sole work of his hands; and, in 1776, it seems he was consulted by Virginia, North Carolina, and New Jersey, and submitted to them brief outlines, which were published, and served as the basis for all the state constitutions adopted prior to the adoption of the United States Constitution. The most valuable principles of the English Constitution were incorporated therein. Monarchy and nobility, and privileged classes, were not to be known here, of course; but the great principles of liberty established by our English ancestors were regarded as too valuable to be surrendered at such a crisis. Our fathers were in a situation to prune away the more objectionable parts of the British system; but the whole system itself it would have been madness to cast off. But still, it was considered by French statesmen and republicans as strange that the Americans, in declaring themselves free from the mother country, should imitate her form of government. The letter of M. Turgot to Dr. Price, in 1778, took special exceptions to the wisdom of this step by the Americans; and, as it appears, there were Americans who entertained the same prejudices upon the subject. Those who dissented from the views of Mr. Adams would take the course adopted afterwards by the French republic, — would have only a house of representatives, with no senate, or executive, other, perhaps, than that chosen by such house, — and would have the judiciary annually elected, either by the house or the people. As we look back to those interesting times, and contemplate the condition of this country at the assumption of its independence; behold the entire repudiation of all British authority, whether from without or within — all British officers, and all legal processes authorized by British laws, spurned; and see some three millions of intelligent, industrious, and virtuous freemen engaged in the work of forming for themselves a government, we cannot help feeling the deep debt of gratitude we owe to the founders of our republic. We see that their wisdom, statesmanship, and patriotism, encountered ignorance, prejudice, and foreign intrigue; and it is with mortification that we reflect that for years we have been accustomed, under the influence of party bias, to treat with neglect, and almost contempt, the names of some of the firmest, wisest, and best patriots, that assisted in laying the corner-stone of our great Temple of Liberty.

The establishment of the Independence of the United

States, the adoption of our Constitution, and our subsequent stability and success, have all been very much due to the singular interpositions of fortune. The lover of his country sees the hand of Providence manifested in all its history. But the belief in providential interposition is apt to inspire conceit, and a sense of security based on the favor of Heaven, not compatible with the best interests of the country, and should not be indulged in too far. At the outset, France aided in producing an alienation of these colonies from Great Britain, and then aided them in the establishment of their independence. But when the example of the rights of man, which France had assisted the Americans in setting to the world, was followed in that country, all the monarchies of Europe were alarmed, and combined their arms to restore the Bourbons to their throne; as it seemed to be solemnly resolved by them all that a republic in the heart of Europe could by no possibility be tolerated. Had the monarchs of Europe been immediately successful in their attempt to crush out republicanism in France, they would have been in a situation to direct attention to the institutions of the United States. That European despots have ever looked with dread upon the successful example of republicanism in America, is but too well known; and that those rulers have ever desired, and still do desire, the subversion and overthrow of our present system, no one can doubt; but fortune has been the favorer of the United States to an extent unparalleled in the history of the world. It will be recollected that the birth of the constitutional government of the United States, and the breaking out of the French Revolution, were simultaneous events; they both occurred in 1789. The occupation of Europe from that date until the fall of Bonaparte, in 1815, is well known. To protract the controversy which engaged the European crowned heads, the American is disposed to think that Providence raised up Napoleon Bonaparte, as, under the shelter of those European contests, America grew up to a stature and strength that rendered her safe from at least the arms of foreign powers. Europe obtained a general peace in 1815; but the long, bloody, and devastating wars, which had led to that peace, left the European governments in no situation to undertake a crusade against a republic some three or four thousand miles away. Furthermore, the commerce of Europe, saving what was in the hands of England, had been mostly annihilated, and England herself was so overwhelmingly burdened with debt, incurred in her long struggle with Napoleon, and her manufacturing and commercial interests so prostrated by loss of American trade, that she was quite ready and willing to adjust her differences with the United States, and that on no unfavorable terms for this country.

At the outset of our Union the wars of combined Europe against France produced much excitement in this country; but the firm position of neutrality taken by the Federal party, and maintained in spite of popular clamor, was the dictate of the soundest wisdom, and, beyond all controversy, proved the salvation of the United States. The Federalists and Republicans, under the administration of the first presidents, were divided more upon questions of the foreign policy of this country than upon domestic questions. Many of those measures adopted by the Federalists while in power, were continued by the Republicans after their ascendency, showing that the latter were not entirely blinded, by passion and prejudice, to whatever, in the policy of the former, experience had demonstrated to be wise and useful. And, since those days, the two great parties existing in the country have constantly had an influence upon each other, which time has always been certain to demonstrate. That this is so is the most encouraging feature of modern politics. It encourages an individual to persevere in his adhesion to the minority. There is no patriotism in the politician who seeks rather the ascendency of his party than the promulgation and establishment of correct political principles ; and he who sides with a minority, if that minority is intelligent, virtuous, and conservative, renders far greater service to his country than the more popular politician who, by the arts of the demagogue, obtains political power.

The Federalists were, in 1800, defeated by the Republicans ; and in March, 1801, Thomas Jefferson, the father of American Democracy, was inaugurated President of the United States. But, in looking back upon the administration of the Federal party, although disposed to hail the ascendency of the Democracy as of essential importance to the cause of liberty, we are obliged to confess that those Federalists were really the fathers of our institutions, and that to them we are indebted for the establishment of that policy which has saved our country from the toils of foreign powers, and rendered it prosperous beyond precedent in the history of nations. The commercial policy of the Federal administration was, notwithstanding their hostility thereto up to a late date, finally adopted by the Democracy. The Democracy at last embraced that policy as the result of the teachings of experience ; but the Federalists inaugurated it as the suggestions of far-seeing wisdom. This was no particular disparagement to the leading Democratic politicians. Neither Grenville nor Lord North could, with Pitt, foresee the advancing commercial greatness of England; nor was it strange that Jefferson failed to anticipate, with Hamilton and Adams, the splendid commercial career of this country. In fact, no one, at the outset of the United States government, was prepared for the extraordinary prosperity which so soon ensued, because no statesman could have anticipated it, without foreseeing the protracted European wars to which it was in a great measure attributable. The Federal administration departed with the eighteenth century, — a century which had witnessed great changes among the nations of the west. At the commencement of that century England had but faintly begun to unfold her energies, and had given but few of the signs of greatness to which she was destined. It was more than fifty years — that is, near the middle of the eighteenth century — before Europe began to look with wonder upon the growing importance of their British neighbor, and tremble with apprehensions of her extensive colonies and fast increasing commerce. At the commencement of that century her whole exports did not annually exceed the value of twenty millions of dollars, — scarcely exceeding the amount annually sent to the American colonies alone at the breaking out of the American Revolution. During the revolutionary period, commerce with the rebellious colonies was, of course, suspended; but, after the treaty of peace, trade began to revive, and its extension, by both the mother country and the states, was unexampled in the history of the western powers. The commerce of almost the whole world was thrown into the hands of England and the United States, and the exports of the latter reached, during the administration of the last of the Federalists (Adams), the amount of about ninety millions of dollars per annum. That this commerce was the result of the peculiar situation of the affairs of Europe, and not the healthy development of the natural course of events, and was, in the nature of things, to be temporary, should not be overlooked, although this was not considered by many Americans, when, after a short period of enjoyment of that trade, this country was compelled to relinquish it entirely, for a season, to vindicate its rights upon the ocean. After the general peace of 1815, it was many years before the commerce of the United States became as extended as it had been prior to the system of non-intercourse forced upon this country by the aggressions of England, under the administration of Jefferson. But that peculiar period of commercial prosperity was a golden era for New England. As the leading Federal politicians were New England men, it was natural that that party should be devoted to the commercial interests of the country. Canals, and railroads, and western emigration, had not at that time rendered New York city the great emporium of the United States that a later period has found her. England looked with no complacency upon the ubiquity of American commerce, and her aggressions upon it never ceased, from the peace of 1783 until the peace of 1815. It was charged by the Republicans upon the Federalists that, for the sake of enjoying those rich commercial harvests, they were too much disposed to submit to British outrages, and pocket their affronts. The suspected partiality of the Federalists for England seriously affected the minds of the masses of the American people, and contributed more than perhaps anything else to throw them out of power. Mr. Jefferson was a statesman of another stamp. It was not his opinion that the highest interests of this country were to consist in commerce ; and, perhaps, he did not accord to the commercial policy of the country sufficient importance. But, if the Republicans accused the Federalists of inclining to the interests of England, the Federalists, on the other hand, appeared perfectly sure that the Republicans were for espousing the cause of France. Both parties were, undoubtedly, too jealous of each other ; and, although the true interests of the country were at the hearts of both, they carried their jealousies too far. Still, although profoundly impressed with the value and worth of those noble old Federalists, the candid American of the present day will, on the whole, say that, all things considered, the ascendency of the Republicans was, in the end, of essential importance to the country.

CHAPTER VII.

JEFFERSON'S ADMINISTRATION AND CONSERVATISM. — REFLECTIONS ON THE DOCTRINE OF INSTRUCTION. — FOREIGN INTRIGUES IN REGARD TO AMERICA. — EUROPEAN NATIONS DESIRED HER INDEPENDENCE OUT OF FEAR FOR THE INCREASING POWER OF ENGLAND, AND WERE OPPOSED TO THE PERMANENCE OF REPUBLICAN INSTITUTIONS HERE OUT OF FEAR OF THE EXAMPLE. — REASONS WHY AMERICA HAS BEEN EXEMPT FROM EUROPEAN INTERFERENCE. — THAT THE PERMANENCY OF REPUBLICANISM HERE MUST EVENTUALLY SUBVERT MONARCHY IN EUROPE FELT TO BE CERTAIN. — REPUBLICANISM IN AMERICA ONLY TO BE PRESERVED BY UNION. — FOREIGNERS WILL SOONER SEE US BROKEN IN PIECES BY LEAVING US ALONE, THAN ATTEMPTING OUR DESTRUCTION BY FORCE.

The success of the Republicans in the election of Thomas Jefferson was a triumph over no mean and insignificant party, or one that would be likely to submit tamely to defeat, and ground arms after the first repulse. Parties in those days were not without their ultra elements. There was Jacobinism in the Republican ranks prior to Jefferson's election, and in the Federal party afterwards. Those Federalists who had with triumphant joy seen the adoption of the Constitution, were scarcely consolable after the defeat of their favorite party. The Federalists numbered in their ranks many of the wealthy of the land, and embraced many men of talent and popular note. A large share of the presses of the country, with a great majority of the pulpits, were in the Federal influence; and as the triumph of Federalism was considered absolutely indispensable for the safety of the government, of course the most extraordinary zeal was infused into the politics of those days. Much occurred at the outset of this government, which was thought calculated to defeat the hopes of the patriot as to its durability. Unfortunately, certain portions of New England, in the overthrow of Federalism, conceived that they had been wronged, and that the triumphant party was one necessarily arrayed against their rights and interests. The defeat of the Federal party, in 1800, wrought a change upon its temper, tactics, and policy. All the Federalists that, under Washington and Adams, belonged to that party, did not continue to adhere to its ranks in subsequent days. The times were soon changed, and men were changed with them. Among the Federalists, as well as among the Republicans, there were conservatives and ultraists. It appeared that the Federalists out of power did not talk as they had acted in power; and many conservative Federalists were but too elated to discover that the Republicans in power did not act as they had talked while out. It is natural enough, perhaps, that ambitious politicians should, in order to be elevated to office, sometimes in defiance of their better judgment, pander to the ignorance and prejudices of the people, and appear to encourage views and measures that they would be sorry to uphold when in power. It is characteristic of the fanatical leaders of a fanatical party to practise and preach the same political doctrines, because their madness is not assumed, and has no method in it. Occasionally a politician will be of so exalted a character as to scorn to be seen appealing to the prejudices of the masses; but such have always been scarce, and daily grow more so.

During the revolutionary period men were selected for office less on account of any peculiar views as to political measures, than for their known ability and integrity. Representatives were allowed to take their places in the Congress, and act their impartial judgment after mutual discussions with their associates, and were not bound at all events to bow in obedience to the local prejudices of their constituents. This high character of revolutionary politics soon disappeared among the most of our legislators; and of late years, instead of the ablest men, — those most noted for wisdom and virtue, — men of an inferior grade, both as to talents and morals, have too often been selected by the people as their representatives. These the people *know* they can trust. They acknowledge that others are of superior ability, wisdom and experience, and of well-established moral character; but such have not manifested sufficient zeal in the popular cause — are not regarded as entirely reliable on questions exceedingly dear to the masses. The self-esteem of the simplest clown will not permit him to entertain for a moment the suspicion that he has been duped; and the thought that he is deceived by an artful and wordy leader can never enter his head. The true worshipper of Joseph Smith can never look upon that impostor as an outsider views him. The impositions of Mahomet are none the less certain because no worshipper of him can possibly work himself into the belief that his prophet was not what he professed to be. Political partisanship inspires much of this insane man-worship, and people are exceedingly apt, especially when religious views enter at all into political questions, to adhere to their champions less on account of their real virtues and merits, than on account of the same feeling or principle of human nature which is at the bottom of every species of idolatry. As long as ignorance remains in the world deceit may continue to be practised, and the extent and success of that practice will be in proportion to the extent of the ignorance. Universal and infallible wisdom can never prevail. However mortifying the reflection, it is perfectly safe to say that no section, no congressional district in the United States, contains a population divinely perfect, or a people not liable to error, and whose minds are wholly unobscured by ignorance. From the best district no honorable man would wish to accept the station of representative, and consent to act in no respect saving in accordance with the views of his people. By thus doing he would acknowledge himself the slave of the ignorance and prejudices of his constituents. The true theory of republican government should leave the representative entirely free to act, after thorough discussion and mature deliberation, as his best judgment shall dictate; for what is the use of congressional discussions, if each representative is to receive imperative instructions at home? On account of this practice of requiring obedience in representatives to local prejudices, the men of the land most worthy of office are excluded therefrom. No person truly worthy of a place in the national legislature would ever so degrade and stultify himself as to accept it, subject to such slavish conditions. But there are enough ever willing to flatter the multitude, and inspire the masses with a desire to have their wills carried out; and when this desire has been aroused into a strong passion, none but the *surest* instruments for the work will be trusted. If people were not infatuated,—

were not blinded as by a species of madness, — they would, on a moment's reflection, see the folly and danger of such a system of political action, and at once return to the practice of the purer days of the republic, when men of known virtue and talents were, unshackled, selected for office. The Union was formed by votes, and by votes it will be destroyed, if ever destroyed at all. Without the purer species of representation alluded to, it would not have been formed; and how long it may be preserved under the system based on local prejudices and sectional animosities, must depend much upon circumstances.

America has been as favorable a theatre for the experiment of a republican government as could be wished. Providence in every particular has seemed to favor this republican enterprise. If the experiment shall prove a failure, it will be on account of the fault of the American people alone, as the great Ruler of human events appears to have so adjusted the affairs of the external world as to leave this country, from the dawn of its independence, entirely free to pursue its own course unmolested. Monarchy throughout the world has dreaded our experiment, but has been unable to avoid it. The independence of the colonies, at the time of their rebellion, was thought to be of vital importance, and a highly desirable object to the crowns of Europe, as it would be the destruction of one of the wings of English commerce; but no crown of Europe desired the new-born states to become a republic. But what, under the circumstances, could be done? The attempt of France to follow our example they did resist; but before that labor was entirely off their hands, America had become a great and powerful nation, and had shown herself the second naval power on earth. It is true some few faint efforts were made to shape the character of the institutions of the United States. At the establishment of independence, European intrigue was for a while visible. Some of the leading Americans were induced to think a monarchical government for this country was necessary; and by such, and by some of the foreign commanders sent over by France to aid in the struggle, Washington was invited to establish a monarchy, and assume a crown. But the effort scarcely produced a momentary ripple on the current of events in this country. Afterwards, during the commercial difficulties between the United States and England, the latter made a direct effort to bring about a disunion of the states, and it is well known that England, as well as the monarchies generally throughout Europe, desires the failure of the republican form of government in America. But England and European monarchs have not been able to look two ways at once. The East has commanded their most anxious attention. If the eyes of England and Western Europe have been turned to the West, it was necessarily only for a momentary glance, as the East has ever been the object of their utmost solicitude and concern. That great Asiatico-European power, Russia, has, from the first dawning of civilization in America, stood behind Europe like a huge giant, ready, at so favorable a moment as an embroilment of the latter with this country would afford, to extend her empire to the Mediterranean. Russia, the most despotic power in the world, has ever seen the growth of the American government with unfeigned pleasure, republican though it be. In America the Czar has constantly seen a balance to European power, and looks to a war between her and the powers of Western Europe for an opportunity to consummate the manifest destiny of Russia. Consequently, Russia has not been a swift party to the many-headed European treaties, quintuple or otherwise called, created for the purpose of carrying out European policy in regard to America. It has been a darling endeavor of the statesmen of England and Europe, for some years past, to bring Russia into a general alliance for the promotion of certain European views ; but her policy has never been considered as entirely identical with that of royalty in the West. She is so situated as to render the example of American freedom of but little concern to her, as slight must be the impression it can ever make upon her Sclavonic and other barbaric hordes. The Russian emperors have for a long time looked down upon the key of the world, — the city of Constantine, — the present possession of the declining Turkish power, — as a prize marked by destiny for their acquisition.

The late Czar Nicholas, after well weighing the powers of Western Europe, came to the conclusion that he could realize the traditional destiny of Russia — could, despite all the combinations possible to be brought against him, take a step which must almost immediately change materially the affairs of the world ; but the attempt only demonstrated the settled policy of the Western powers as to Eastern politics. The Crimean war was expensive and bloody, and was curiously terminated by the peace of Paris. The young Emperor Alexander, on the death of his father Nicholas in the midst of the war, undoubtedly found the undertaking of that father too gigantic for his abilities and resources, and was obliged to yield to the superior powers arrayed against him. But has he relinquished the long-cherished ambition of Russia? The discussions of the treaty of Paris were secret, and its theory or philosophy can only be inferred. It was discussed after Austria, in the affair of Kosta, had been affronted by the United States, and an embroilment of the latter with England was pointing to war, on account of the enlistment controversy. All we know is that a peace with Russia was concluded on most favorable terms; England and France paying their own expenses incurred in resisting the aggressions of the former; and, apparently as a consideration therefor, that power became a party to a general European alliance. Without the cordial union of Russia with Europe, America has nothing to apprehend from European interference; with it, she has nothing to fear so long as united. All the world combined could not overthrow republicanism in the United States, should perfect union exist. Therefore, it would be well for Americans not to neglect their situation. Europe and America confront each other, a broad battle-field being spread out between them. The governments as now prevailing in them cannot endure. The continuance of republican institutions in America must prove the subversion of monarchy in Europe. This result is as certain as time is to endure, and it is not to be doubted that Russia has at last been made to perceive it as a truth of importance even to her. Russia, though heretofore a friend to far-off republican America, could not endure republicanism so near as Hungary, and, by quenching the Hungarian republic, united with herself, in close bonds, that firm and unalterable friend of hers, the house of Austria; and Austria, especially after the Kosta and Hulsemann affairs, would be a warm advocate for a closer union of all monarchies for defence against the spread of republicanism. In fact, young as America was, when Hungary was crushed by the combined arms of two powerful despots, she was not easily restrained from reaching forth a delivering hand. Had our country been a half or a whole century older, with a population of one or two hundred millions of freemen, and with a navy in keeping with our population and resources, we could, without trouble, have seen fair play in Hungary's struggle with the house of Hapsburg. The day is at hand when the nations of the world will be obliged to bow in submission to the will of America, and free institutions will flourish through the encoúragement of the great American republic. It will be so, or, through the agency of disunion and civil war, the arms of European monarchs shall crush out republicanism in this country, and despotism be again made universal.

But this digression proceeds from the current of thought suggested by the statement that the continuance of free institutions is dependent on the people of this country themselves, and that from the earliest period of our history, external and internal circumstances have, under Providence, been exceedingly favorable for their development.

The consolidation of our Union was a difficult work. It is not yet complete. Its success is differently regarded by different persons. Its utility and beneficence, when looked down upon from some higher sphere, must be dazzlingly conspicuous ; the American Union must by all impartial and benevolent minds be pronounced the greatest achievement, in the cause of humanity and human progress, that has ever been accomplished by mortal hands. It is the day-star of Freedom throughout the earth, and the asylum for the oppressed of all nations. It is daily, throughout the world, the first and last thought of by down-trodden men; and by night, in their dreams, the magnificent temple of American Freedom breaks upon their eyes as a vision of Paradise. But still the Union may have its faults. It may work unequally in some instances. The government of the Union may not be what the most refined theoretical moralist would prefer, and the legislation under it may occasionally seem unjust and oppressive to portions of the people; but how little should such considerations weigh in the mind of the patriot when the value of the Union itself is considered!

CHAPTER VIII.

FEDERAL PRINCIPLES OF NEUTRALITY CONTINUED BY JEFFERSON. — HE WAS CHARGED WITH PARTIALITY FOR FRANCE. — PARTY SPIRIT OF THOSE DAYS. — THE PURCHASE OF LOUISIANA. — RESISTANCE OF BRITISH AGGRESSIONS. — VIOLENT OPPOSITION TO THE ADMINISTRATION IN NEW ENGLAND. — HOSTILITY OF THE NORTH TO THE SOUTH MANIFESTED. — ANTI-SLAVERY FEELING IN NEW ENGLAND IN 1796. — VINDICTIVE SPIRIT OF NORTHERN PHILANTHROPISTS AT THE PERIOD OF THE FORMATION OF THE GOVERNMENT. — WHAT THE SOUTH, UNDER THE CIRCUMSTANCES, OUGHT TO BE TOLERATED IN ATTEMPTING. — COMPROMISES IN THE CONSTITUTION IN REGARD TO SLAVERY. — ANTI-SLAVERY IN NEW ENGLAND BORROWED FROM THE DESIGNING ENEMIES OF OUR COUNTRY IN OLD ENGLAND. — ENGLAND, ON FAILING TO ENSLAVE OUR FOREFATHERS, AT ONCE COMMENCED TEACHING THEM THE PRINCIPLES OF NEGRO FREEDOM AND EQUALITY. — HER OBJECT IN THIS. — EFFECT OF HER WRITERS ON AMERICANS. — ABOLITION OF THE SLAVE-TRADE, IT WAS THOUGHT, WOULD PUT AN END TO SLAVERY IN THE UNITED STATES, AND RENDER THE CULTIVATION OF COTTON IN THE EAST INDIES PROFITABLE, ETC.

JEFFERSON, as is well known, was not elected to the presidency the first time by the people. He and Aaron Burr having had an equal number of votes, the election was carried into the House of Representatives. The selection was limited to Jefferson and Burr, though, of course, both Republicans. The Federalists, for reasons better attributed to party spirit than anything else, sustained Burr; and, as there were other candidates, many ballotings were required before an election took place. We are told that the excitement was great, as party spirit ran high. The course taken by Burr, in permitting himself to be used by the Federalists in opposition to Mr. Jefferson, rendered him unpopular with the Republicans, and from that time, although he had before been a distinguished patriot, holding responsible commands in the revolutionary army, arising to the vice-presidency, with fair prospects of ultimately reaching the presidency, he took a downward career, and finally became an object of general reproach, if not of infamy. His duel with Hamilton, his fillibuster enterprise against Mexico, and his libertinism, are so inseparably connected with his memory, that his name scarcely ever recalls pleasant associations.

Of Mr. Jefferson's administration it is not important here to speak further than necessary to show the principal distinctive political issues that from time to time existed between the Republican and Federal parties. The repeal by his administration of Mr. Adams' judiciary law, and of the alien and sedition laws, so called, needs no comment, as those laws were never magnified into the dignity of measures. Their agitation ceased with his first election. The purchase of Louisiana by Mr. Jefferson, although it caused much noise at the time, may be placed in the same category. It is true he was much censured for the act, as one in defiance of constitutional authority; but, right or wrong, the thing was irremediable. The greatest cause of objection to Mr. Jefferson, on the part of the Federalists, was his alleged indifference or hostility to commercial interests, and his general views in regard to the foreign policy of the country. It was insisted that he was a favorer of the French Revolution, and an enemy of England. Probably the true admirer of Mr. Jefferson at this day would claim in his behalf some degree of truth in both of those positions; but as to whether his feelings in favor of France and against England were carried to a censurable point while president, remains a question for the decision of the candid historian. It would be hard to establish this to the satisfaction of a Jeffersonian Democrat at the present day. When we look back upon his administration, we cannot, so far as the foreign policy of the nation was concerned, help observing in it with pleasure much of the conservatism exhibited in the preceding administrations of Washington and Adams, as if inspired by their illustrious examples. But Mr. Jefferson had obstacles to encounter not experienced by his predecessors, and met them in such a manner as appeared to him the most advisable. His resistance of British aggressions, as well as that continued by Mr. Madison, produced an astonishing degree of opposition and excitement in portions of the country, and came near, as thought by some, producing a dismemberment of the Union. The seat of this excitement and opposition was New England. Massachusetts, that has been more benefited by the Union than any of the states, accepted it with reluctance. The United States Constitution, when submitted to her convention of delegates, was only adopted through the strenuous exertions of her popular governor, Hancock, and that by a very slight majority. The exact feelings of all the New England people in regard to forming the Union it would be vain to endeavor to portray; but it is very certain that when the system, as adopted, was proposed, many bugbears arose in the minds of the people to incline them to recoil from it. The leading men of those days saw clearer into the measure than the masses did, and, as the most eminent men in the country then had great weight with the people, their influence secured its adoption. But it was not natural that the Puritans of New England should find their hearts cleaving with very great fondness to their ancient persecutors, their Church of England neighbors in the South. And, more than this, the manners, habits and customs, of the South were not in accordance with New England sentiments. The South, too, abounded in slavery. The opposition to the South on account of her slavery institutions sprung up astonishingly quick, considering the North had but so recently themselves reformed in that matter. But so we believe it ever is; towards those who practise vice the reformed are always less tolerant than those who were never tainted with it. An inveteracy towards the South, as such, soon manifested itself in noble New England, and views and feelings were exhibited far from creditable to this, in many respects, most interesting portion of the earth. As subsequent events fortunately proved, the illiberal feelings alluded to were at the time limited to but a small portion of the New England people; but it was a portion that has since made itself felt, and during the last sixty years has promulgated them but too successfully, especially in the North. That portion was the most bitter faction that assailed the administration of Mr. Jefferson; and, as a specimen of their spirit, take the following from a leading New England journal which was published before Mr. Jefferson's election to the presidency: "Negroes are, in all respects, except in regard to life and death, the cattle of the citizens of the Southern States. If they were good for food, the probability is, that even the power of destroying their lives would be enjoyed by their owners, as fully as it is over the lives of their cattle. It cannot be that their laws prohibit the owners from killing their slaves because those slaves are human beings, or because it is a moral evil to destroy them. If that were the case, how can they justify their being treated, in all respects, like brutes? for it is in this point of view alone that negroes in the Southern States are considered in fact as different from cattle. They are bought and sold — they are fed or kept hungry — they are clothed or reduced to nakedness — they are beaten, turned out to the fury of the elements, and torn from their dearest connections, with as little remorse as if they were beasts of the field."

Many of the grounds of opposition to the Democratic party have, since Jefferson's day, become obsolete; but as the hostility founded on sectional dislike, such as is evinced in the foregoing extract, has continued and constantly increased till the present time, and has ever formed an element in the party politics of the country, and was intimately connected with the fate of the late Whig party, it will be necessary to consider it a little more in detail. The sentence quoted above was published before New England had been encroached upon by the slave power. It was published, in connection with a vast amount of similar matter, about the close of Washington's administration, which must convince the candid mind that, at the outset, the abuse of Southern society and Southern institutions by New England people, was not and could not have been in retaliation for what in later days has been termed "Southern aggressions." In what, during the administrations of Washington and John Adams, had the South misused the North? But still we see at that time influential New England journals characterizing their Southern neighbors as fiends. At that time even Louisiana and Florida had not been purchased, which might, as encroachments of the slave power, have been interposed as a justification. Candor must acknowledge that the sectional warfare between the North and South originated in the former, as no historian can discover an excuse for such feelings as were manifested by such language as we have quoted. It is right that we of New England should consider this fairly; because, if it be true in fact that we were the first to commence a crusade against the institutions and people of the South; if we were the first to raise a fratricidal hand in sectional warfare; if we were the first to arouse jealousy and hatred between the two sections of the country; we should look to it well that our over-zealous humanity — to give the motive no worse a name — may not prove the ruin of our country. Modern expressions of Northern men and women against the South cannot well be more bitter and irritating than those used in New England in 1796; but they are now more abundant, being found and heard everywhere. But in these later days the unmitigated hatred (no stronger, however, than entertained by many in '96) indulged by vast numbers in the North towards the South, is excused by the plea that the South is and has been scheming to extend her institutions. Northern people are perhaps a little too incautious in accepting such an excuse for entertaining unfair and unfriendly feelings towards their Southern neighbors. We have a right to hate and detest slavery, and should belie our natures were we not to do so; but to do injustice to those unfortunately afflicted with the charge of African slaves, were to render us worse than the slaveholders themselves. We are proud to think that New England has purer morals and religion than any other part of the world. For intelligence, virtue, and religion, we are unexcelled. It therefore becomes us, the first thing we do, to see that we are just. Let us take it for granted that the South is somewhat benighted; that her religion is far from the genuine stamp; that her morals are far inferior to those of New England; still, is it becoming or morally right in us to bring railing accusations against them? — to treat them worse than a Christian spirit would a fiend? When divested of our prejudice and excitement, and reason and common sense assume the ascendency, we must look at the matter in a different light. For their unfortunate institution no one pretends they are to blame. They are indebted for it to England and New England, without whose capital, sailors and ships, Southern slavery had never existed. For their ignorance we should pity them, and send them our schoolmasters, who in happy years past have ever found a cordial reception everywhere in the South. For their bad morals, and incorrect religion, we should extend our heartfelt sympathies, and do all in our power, by prayers in their behalf, and by setting them perfect Christian examples, to win them from the error of their ways. The good Christian, the judicious missionary, never attempts to convert and reform the victim of error by violent denunciations. If it be true that of late years the South has been anxious to increase the number of slave states, is it just to say that her object in so doing is to wrest from the North any of her rights? Has the South, except in multiplying slave states, ever been seen infringing upon Northern rights? It is not pretended. Then, would it be any stretch of liberality on our part to make this allowance for her; viz., that she, from the earliest period of our government, witnessing the commencement of a fierce crusade against her and her institutions, thought it, as a matter of safety, — of self-protection against growing Northern prejudices, — quite necessary for her to have the ascendency in, at least, one branch of the national government? That, by increasing slave states, the South could expect to get the whole government into her hands, none but the most unlettered and simple-minded ever for a moment supposed. The great majority of the people are and ever must be in the free states; and, without a majority in the Senate, the South must always be at the mercy of the North. That she should be reluctant to trust to the sentiment of the North, of which she has personally witnessed so poor examples, no one is surprised; and, under the circumstances, he must be a harsh judge of human actions, who would much censure the South for the efforts she has made to secure some check upon what she feels she is destined to experience of Northern aggressions. Of course, we shall never trample upon her rights, nor treat her otherwise than with justice and kindness; but human nature is known to be an uncertain law, and we should not be surprised to find that our neighbors in the South desire a surer guaranty of their rights. We denounce the South violently because she has gained several states by the Louisiana purchase, and by the Mexican war. Some of them were free states; more of them slave. Allowing all that is charged against her, in regard to these acquisitions, to be true, should the strong, powerful, and magnanimous North treasure it up as a cause of hostility towards her? We must force ourselves to decide candidly these questions, or we shall ere long find we have no common country under the protection of whose strong arm we can quarrel with one another. That the South should struggle for the preservation of political power we should expect; but, as that struggle ever has been and ever must be vain, we should witness it with feelings of sympathy; and, when we bear the victories from her less successful hand, we should treat her with tenderness as an unfortunate rival. To exult over a fallen foe, and heap upon him opprobrious epithets, is characteristic of the warfare of demons, and not at all becoming the sons of New England. It is not disputed that the slave states have been increased by the acquisition of territory by our government; but whether or not the North has not more profited by that increase of territory than any other section, is, to say the least, an open question. Moreover, in our fury towards the South, we forget that all the free states formed out of the north-western territory — the pride and strength of our country — were the gift of Virginia. That noble state gave them to the Union, and voluntarily devoted them to freedom. Why should we forget this while nursing our hatred towards that Section?

We have seen that early, in New England, the hatred of the South, among some classes, was bitter in the extreme. It vented itself in denunciations of slavery. The slave controversy was more or less agitated at the formation of the Confederation, and then again at the adoption of the Constitution. At those dates, however, the bearing of slavery upon the ratio of representation occasioned the most difficulty. The bulk of the slaves were in the South, as many for that market had been sold by Northern States preparatory to acts of emancipation. The representation was to be according to the population, there being one representative to a certain specified number of people. In the enumeration, as a basis of representation, every living being in human form who was a citizen was to be counted: old and young; men, women, and children; white, red, and black; and inmates of asylums and prisons. There was to be no exception — all human beings were to be counted. The South saw no reason for exempting their slaves from the enumeration; but the North objected. That the slaves should form a basis of representation, was conceded; but the framers of the Constitution would not recognize them as equal to whites, and it was provided that in their enumeration two-fifths should be thrown out, leaving three-fifths of the slaves to be included with the free, in establishing the basis for representation and taxation. The limitation of course was against the South; but she surrendered the point out of a compromising spirit. But the world saw, from the discussions on the subject, that slavery was eventually to become an element of discord in the United States. By recurrence to unerring guides it will be found that the anti-slavery outcry in New England was but the echo from a shriek for freedom by liberty-loving Old England. Wilberforce and his coädjutors commenced their labors in the anti-slavery cause just at the period of the adoption of the United States Constitution. It was about that period that Parliament, under the Wilberforce movement, began to agitate the abolition of the slave-trade; and the speeches of British orators, the books and essays of British authors, and the songs of British poets, vividly portraying the foul sin of slavery, were instantly reproduced, perused, and wept over, in

New England. Cowper's spirited poem, which came forth at that period, no doubt inspired millions of hearts with hatred of slavery. Our own early sentiments of hostility to human bondage were awakened and fixed by that touching production. It was not easy to induce the British government to give up the slave-trade, and emancipate her slaves; but still it was finally accomplished. The labors of Wilberforce and Clarkson, in those enterprises, are familiar to the world; but these philanthropists alone would never have accomplished much, had not their efforts been in accordance with what was conceived to be the policy of the government. Pitt favored the abolishment of the slave-trade; but success was more than even he could accomplish. Fox undertook it, and his effort was crowned with success. But it must not be taken for granted at once that humanity alone was England's motive for her action in regard to slavery. It would have been a ridiculous inconsistency for the nation that had just failed in an effort to enslave our forefathers in America, and was at the time employed in reducing republican France to its former feudal bonds, to thus interest herself in the establishment of the freedom of African negroes, purely on the score of humanity. The fact is, by her keenest-sighted public men the inhumanity of the act was foreseen, and by subsequent events has been proved. The British statesmen were obliged to resort to other arguments before their measures in regard to their slaves could be brought about. England considered that her material interests were involved in the measure; but whether they were or not is not perhaps yet fully determined. The abolition of the slave-trade did not seriously affect the production of our great cotton staple, for which England is dependent on us; and consequently their slaves in the islands off our southern coasts were manumitted. Negroes, however, are not Anglo-Saxons. The enfranchisement of those in the West Indies has not as yet imparted the slightest spark of the spirit of freedom to the negroes in our Southern States; and, so long as our cotton plantations are worked by African slaves, Great Britain can never hope to compete with us in the production of the raw material. Notwithstanding the intrigues and efforts of the British court to prevent the consummation of our Union, and their studied designs of alienating the people of the Northern and Southern sections of the country from each other with a view of producing a separation; and notwithstanding the mission of her special agent a short time afterwards sent through New England to seduce her from the Union; all such machinations have as yet resulted in nothing equal to the hopes of that scheming and ambitious power. Well indeed might England, in 1787 and 1788, essay her intrigues and insidious influence to accomplish what she so signally failed ten years before to accomplish with the force of arms. The division and separation of the United States was at an early day of the Revolution a favorite project of the British cabinet, and two large armies were put in motion for its accomplishment. One was to proceed up the Hudson to meet a large force under Burgoyne, who moved down Lake Champlain from Canada. The Green Mountain boys happened at that moment to be strongly in favor of union, and merrily enough escorted Burgoyne's army through New England to its music; that is, to the tune of Yankee Doodle. The battle of Bennington checked Burgoyne's army and led to his surrender; and in all human probability the success of the great revolutionary struggle turned upon that event. The success of the Burgoyne expedition must have overthrown the American cause, and the fate of that expedition was settled by the Vermonters. At that day, British sentiments were not particularly regarded amongst the Green Mountains. It is true, Vermont borrowed her inhabitants from Massachusetts and Connecticut, but did not at first take along the exalted humanitarian feelings of those colonies. Their love of liberty and justice was not excelled anywhere; but we are sorry to say that the original settlers of the Green Mountains, of whom Ethan Allen was a type, had not that regard for sacred things that was peculiar to the Atlantic colonies. Their disregard of Sabbath and sanctuary privileges, and their rough, uncouth, and somewhat profane, method of speech, would have rendered them outlaws in the more religious states of Massachusetts and Connecticut. But these Green Mountain boys, nevertheless, loved freedom and contemned vice and crime; and when King George attempted to separate them from their Southern brethren by a fence of bayonets, they raised at Bennington a shout of defiance which was soon echoed by the Virginians from Yorktown. But the rough and unpolished manners of these boys have been much improved upon by their children, and the records of the state will now show the Vermonters the most Christian and virtuous people on earth. The reader, if he has doubts, will please examine the statute-books, and these will show a morality unparalleled. Horse-racing and gambling are prohibited; theatrical and circus and all other kinds of shows are forbidden. Lotteries are dug up root and branch. Of course, no Vermonter ever sees a theatrical exhibition, go where he may, or ever pays a cent for lottery tickets. Sabbath-breaking, and profane swearing are both visited with penalties ; and, as a prosecution for either was never known in the state, it follows as a matter of certainty that such offences have never been committed. Rumselling is punished in the severest manner, and may be considered as forever at an end. And slavery! her statute-books are sprinkled all over with acts in denunciation of it. Vermont has always had a wholesome horror of slavery, and, so far as sin may be involved in the system, nobody can doubt but her skirts are clean from it. It has ever been objected to New England, by foreigners, that it abounds too much in cant. But the goodness of the Vermonters of later times is not in *profession* merely ; any one can look into their laws and see that all their excellences are carried out. That is the right way. A reform never becomes *un fait accompli,* until it finds its way into the statute-book. When such movements are found thus engrossed, it is a sure sign that the reformer has himself been in the legislature, and the accomplishment of his work can be relied on. But perhaps this is somewhat digressive. The writer alludes to these things to show that his native state, though in early times distinguished for rather rough settlers, is not now, in all moral reforms, behind the best state in New England. Of course, we would not claim that none of the leaven of unrighteousness, which originally abounded in the state, now remains ; because there are a few of us who have yet veneration for the somewhat antiquated and out-of-fashion institutions of our ancestors, and are rather a clog upon the progressive morality of the present age. Of such it is no less than fair to remark that our compulsory piety exists only by force of local law, and would not, probably, be recognized beyond the limits of the states in which such laws prevail.

CHAPTER IX.

FACTIOUSNESS OF THE FEDERAL PARTY, AND ITS OPPOSITION TO THE WAR-MEASURES, CAUSE OF ITS RUIN. — ATTEMPT OF ENGLAND TO DESTROY AMERICAN COMMERCE. — IMPRESSMENT OF SEAMEN AND THEIR TREATMENT. — ORDERS IN COUNCIL AND FRENCH DECREES. — BLOCKADE. — DAMAGE TO AMERICAN COMMERCE. — FRENCH AND BRITISH PARTIES IN THE U. S. — AMERICAN COMMERCE IN THE NORTH. — THE CHESAPEAKE AFFAIR. — EMBARRASSING CONDITION OF THE GOVERNMENT. — JEFFERSON'S COURSE, ETC.

THE Federal party never recovered from its defeat in 1800. Its dignity, propriety, and conservatism, never appeared so prominent after that event as before. In endeavoring to regain its lost ascendency, its efforts often became factious, and the judgment, the deliberate judgment, of the American people was finally pronounced against it. It would be a mistake, however, to suppose that that party did not embrace in its ranks some of the finest minds and purest patriots of the land; nor must it be concluded that political perfection was the property of the successful party. The Whig party sprung from the ashes of the old Federal party, and succeeded it as the opposition of the Democracy; but, before the nativity of the Whig party, there had been a change of times from the days of Jefferson, and a change in the situation and politics of the country. The Whigs, in fact, inherited no more of the party measures of the Federalists than they did of the Republicans; indeed, some of the leading Whigs had been Republicans, and many of the Democratic party formerly belonged to the Federal party.) The great measure by which the prospects of the Federalists were forever destroyed, was the war with England of 1812. Their fierce and factious opposition to that measure, and to the restrictive measures of Jefferson's administration preceding the war, proved fatal to the hopes of Federalism, and was the means of establishing the ascendency of the Democracy for half a century. It will be necessary to take a hurried view of the causes of that war which had such potent influences on the politics of the country.

The aptitude of America for commercial enterprises was early discovered by England, and the enterprising character of American sailors was beautifully noticed by Burke. On the establishment of independence, our merchant vessels began to cover the ocean. The establishment of a navy was one of the patriotic accomplishments of the administration of John Adams, for which Democrats ought to venerate and love his memory; for to that navy were they indebted for the glory of the war that has given them such a permanent hold upon the affections of the American people. But our commerce, from its dawn, was pounced upon by England. She rode the seas triumphant, and proclaimed and felt herself their mistress. The raging European wars had soon resulted in the destruction of all the commerce of Europe, and England and America were doing the carrying-trade for the world. The promising aspect of American commerce was not favorably regarded by Britain.

It happened that, in prosecuting her wars with France, the British were constantly in great need of sailors and soldiers. Her method, on extraordinary occasions, of replenishing her navy, was by impressment. A naval officer with marines would go on land, and seize upon able-bodied men, and carry them away on board of ship, and compel them to serve, perhaps for years, before they were again permitted to visit their homes. Men-of-war would also board merchant vessels for the same purpose. Immediately after the establishment of our independence, Great Britain commenced impressing men from the United States merchant ships, wherever found upon the ocean. They did this under the pretence that they intended to impress British subjects only; but the impressing officer having nothing to guide him but his discretion, and as at the time both America and her navy were regarded with contempt, it was often, nay, almost always the case, that more or less of American citizens were impressed. It was a maxim of the British law, "Once a subject, always a subject." The right of a citizen to expatriate himself, and become the citizen of another country, was not recognized by the laws of England. Consequently those American citizens depending upon naturalization for exemption from impressment, were uniformly seized by the impressing officers. The result was that citizens of foreign birth withdrew from our commercial service, much to its injury. These impressments continued up to the war of 1812, and many were the Americans forced to fight British battles against countries at peace with the United States. Not only this, but when war ensued between Great Britain and the United States, American citizens were forced, under the lash, and threats of death, to do battle against their own country. The number of impressments can never be accurately ascertained ; but it amounted to many thousands. The Java and Guerriere, when taken by our navy, had aboard of them many Americans who had been pressed into service against their country ; and the British navy everywhere abounded in impressed American seamen. Some American authorities at one time estimated the whole number of impressments as high as fourteen thousand ; and the number of native-born Americans in this manner dragged into the service of England was very large. Of course, our agents, consuls, and ministers, in the various parts of the British empire, exerted themselves in behalf of the impressed, and procured many discharges ; but these discharges were after great delay, and many hardships endured by the wronged citizen ; and, as ascertained at the close of the war, there were many who had been forced to drag out slavery in the British fleets until the war closed.

At that day, Britain was not disposed to look very graciously upon this young republic. She was an ancient and haughty monarchy, and the United States were thought a little upstart of a government, for which her arrogance should have but little respect. The treatment of Americans thus impressed by British naval officers was haughty and cruel. No greater indignity could be offered any country than to thus impress her citizens, and force them to bear arms against her. It was not only an outrage upon the rights of the individual under the laws of nations, but was also a gross outrage upon humanity, and could only be perpetrated by senseless tyrants. After war was declared against

England by the United States, the American sailors thus impressed begged to be excused from serving against their own country, and claimed to be treated as prisoners of war; but such applications were answered with irons and the lash. Authenticated cases of the kind were at the time established. Perhaps all British officers did not carry their contempt of the rights of Americans so far as this; but many did. The impressments of American seamen were continual, notorious, and brutal in manner. Many instances of the kind were certified by authentic proof. Among others, we read of the impressment and conveyance on board of the British man-of-war Brunswick, during the administration of John Adams, of Eliphalet Ladd, John Eddes, and others. One of the press-gang, with a drawn sword, cut Ladd on the forehead, and made a wound of three inches. Eddes, for claiming to be an American citizen, was whipped with a rope's end until his back was bruised from his shoulders to his hips. Neither to Eddes nor to Ladd was any surgical aid allowed, and the sufferings subsequently experienced from their wounds was most intense. William Savage, impressed at the same time with Ladd and Eddes, was severely beaten by the boatswain's mate, who doubled a rope of about three inches and a half thick, and plied it to his neck, back, face, head, and stomach, until the mate was exhausted, when he gave the rope to one of the marines, who applied upwards of a hundred blows. Savage was awfully mangled, externally and internally, the infliction being followed with raising of blood. His cruel treatment was for his persistence in claiming to be an American citizen. The case of Isaac Clarke was touching; he was of Salem, Massachusetts. Many of the impressed were of that state. Clarke was impressed from the ship Jane, off Norfolk, by the British ship Porcupine, and presented the commander with his protection from a United States custom-house. The paper was torn in pieces before his eyes with angry oaths, and he was commanded to duty. On Clarke's remonstrating, he was put into irons, and the next morning given two dozen lashes. He was then again put in irons, and kept on one biscuit and a pint of water for twenty-four hours. In this manner he was treated for a week, when he was asked by the commander if he would do his duty. On refusal, he was stripped, and again given two dozen lashes, and kept another week on the former allowance. Being then once more interrogated if he would go to work, Clarke insisted on his rights as an American citizen; whereupon the commander told him he should be punished until willing to submit, and ordered a repetition of the two dozen lashes, and that a very heavy iron chain be put around his neck, and fastened to a ring-bolt in the deck, and that no person should speak to him, or give him anything to eat or drink, saving the before-mentioned allowance, until he should consent to go to work. In that manner he remained nine weeks, and was so completely exhausted by hunger and thirst as to be obliged to yield. Clarke remained enslaved in the British service for upwards of two years. These cases are given as specimens, as no American citizen was impressed without the like or worse usage. But the United States at that time was in her infancy, and properly enough stood in awe of the greatest naval power in the world. The cabinet and admiralty courts of England were constantly beset by American agents and ministers; but that power with fair pretences amused our officials, and moved on in her career of indifference as to our rights. Mr. Jefferson, when Secretary of State under Washington's administration, commenced remonstrances to the British court against impressments, insisting on the manly rule that "the vessel being American shall be evidence that the seamen on board her are such." But what course to take was an embarrassing question for this country. We had no army, and our navy was in its infancy. Remonstrance and negotiation were resorted to, but to no satisfactory effect. It was universally felt in America that impressments were wrong; but people were divided in opinion as to how long efforts for a peaceable settlement of the question, in lieu of a resort to arms, should be continued. As England was at war with France, the question as to making war on the former drew into it the merits of the struggle between those two powers. The result was that those who were for making war on England were charged with being partisans of France; and those in favor of submitting to English aggressions were denounced as hostile to the efforts of France to establish freedom.

But Great Britain did not limit her disregard of the rights of the young republic to the free appropriation of her sailors. While England and France were at war, America, being a neutral country, was entitled to carry on her commerce with both, saving in contraband articles; that is, in implements and munitions of war. America could not only convey her own produce and manufactures to the markets of those countries, but she could likewise carry the goods of other countries, and those obtained from their colonies, to them. After

Europe became involved in a general war, the carrying-trade of the United States increased with wonderful rapidity. The whole exports of this country, foreign and domestic, during the years 1803, '4, '5 and '6, amounted to upwards of three hundred and thirty millions of dollars. This rapid growth of our commerce excited in our haughty neighbor fearful forebodings, and it was seen that something must be done to give it a check. Accordingly, in 1793, commenced the issue of that series of orders in council intended for the overthrow of American commerce. The order of that year directed all ships of war and privateers to seize all ships laden with goods, the produce of any colony belonging to France, or carrying provisions or other supplies for the use of such colonies, and to bring the same with their cargoes to legal adjudication in the courts of admiralty. This order was in direct violation of international law, and in opposition to repeated decisions of British courts of admiralty; and what rendered it more unjust was the fact that it was issued with secrecy, evincing on the part of England a decided disposition to plunder. American merchants suffered largely by this order, which caused indignation amongst all parties in the United States. Such an act at this day would not be tolerated a moment.

But the British orders in council of May 16th, 1806, were a still stronger blow aimed at the rights of neutrals, of which the United States were the principal, and nearly the only one. It was the famous order for blockading the whole coasts of Germany, Holland, and France! It is well understood that, by the law of nations, when two powers are at war they are respectively invested with certain rights and privileges in regard to neutrals which they do not possess in time of peace. The right of blockade is one of these rights; the right of search another. The latter mentioned right allows the vessel-of-war of a belligerent to visit the trading vessels of neutrals dealing with her enemy, to see if they have aboard any contraband articles. A declaration of blockade, when made by a belligerent of his enemy's ports or harbors, is a prohibition to all the world from entering into them for purposes of commerce; and, when properly made, and under the proper circumstances, all the world is bound to regard it. If, after the regular blockade of a port, a neutral vessel enters, it is liable to seizure; and, if seized, is forfeited. But, to render a declaration of blockade justifiable and regular, it must proceed from the right authority, be publicly made, and maintained with sufficient blockading force. In this respect, the laws of nations require that, in order to render the communication with any such place unlawful to a neutral, the blockading force must be actually present, investing it, and with sufficient power to render such communication with it hazardous. But think of the British order of blockade of the whole coast of Europe from the Elbe to Brest! — nearly a thousand miles! All the navies in the world would have been insufficient to properly invest, as by blockade, so extensive a coast; and yet, under the shadow of that order, Great Britain claimed the right, and exercised the privilege, of seizing upon every merchant ship that had traded upon those tabooed coasts, and made free plunder of them! It was no more nor less than the assumed right of England, by virtue of her own sovereign will and power, to forbid all nations of the earth from trading with her enemy. It was a decree made when American commerce had, prior to the war, reached its highest point, and was intended to drive it from the ocean.

At the time this extraordinary order in council, which was aimed at the commerce of America, and designed for the benefit of that of England, appeared, Napoleon was at Berlin. Western Europe at the time was pretty much under the control of that extraordinary genius. Bonaparte had excluded British goods from the country between the points that bounded the blockade, in retaliation for which, or to force her own wares into those countries, the declaration of blockade was made by England. Immediately, however, on receiving notice of the order of the British government, Napoleon issued what has been called the Berlin decree, blockading the British Isles! A decree no doubt intended as a slur upon the British orders in council, as he had no means of executing it. The spirit of those orders and decrees was well understood at the time by the Americans, as by the English order their commerce was foully invaded, while by the French decree they received no injury at all. It was clear enough that American commerce, and not solely the injury of France, was aimed at by that high-handed measure.

To pass over the millions of dollars' damage done to American commerce by these British orders in council, —and not stopping to consider the indignation of the Americans, their attempts at obtaining redress, and the sayings and doings of the American apologists for the course of Great Britain,—we will pursue the conduct of that power a little further. In passing, perhaps a word is due to the apologists for Great Britain. There were not many Americans that attempted to justify her acts fully; but many who were disposed to extenuate and submit to them. It must not be forgotten that America has always read European history, and studied its politics, through British spectacles. This country received its prevailing opinions of the French Revolution, and of Napoleon Bonaparte, from British writers; and it is now known that those writers were either the voluntary or subsidized champions of the British government. New England, taking the character of Napoleon from England, could not but feel the deepest anxiety for his overthrow, as he had been pictured a monster of passion, vice, and atheism. So abhorrent were French infidelity and sensuality made to appear to Americans, that many enlisted their feelings deeply in the cause of England and her allies, and were quite innocently seduced into the belief that the orders in council were necessary instrumentalities for the overthrow of Napoleon. Not a few of our people thought we ought to make common cause with England against her enemy; and, of course, such were not disposed to find fault with any necessary step taken by that government, if thought to be taken solely for the purpose alleged, although it might conflict somewhat with American interests. The fact is, the simplicity and sincerity of such Americans rendered them the easy dupes of British duplicity. England has ever been a loud preacher, and her fortune has depended much on the fact that quite a large portion of the world is governed solely by preaching. If satisfied that this is right, there are multitudes who never inquire further, or take the trouble to ascertain whether the preacher's language is hypocritical or sincere. But England, finding her will and pleasure to be the only code of laws necessary for her to observe on the ocean; that, do what she might, her acts would not only be acquiesced in by this country, but apologized for by many of our people; that, since the triumph here of the party charged with French views and principles, a strong feeling of disaffection had sprung up between two portions of the country, the northern portion becoming warmly English in their sympathies; and finding, in short, that there was a probability that, by playing upon that sectional feeling, and endeavoring to bring the Democratic administration into disgrace, an entire separation of the states might probably be effected, she carried her insolence and audacity so far as soon to arouse the indignation of the whole country to the highest pitch. On the twenty-second of June, 1807, upon our own coasts, off Norfolk, the British vessel Leopard attacked the American frigate Chesapeake, killing three men, and wounding many, and took from her four men, one of whom was tried and hanged as a deserter, and the others retained some five years before they obtained their freedom. An instance of a more wilful and insolent disregard of a nation's rights is scarcely to be found in history. The commander who perpetrated the act was guilty of a high crime,— was truly guilty of murder,— and should have been properly punished. But in the British navy a feeling of contempt for American rights was prevalent, and the overbearing and haughty conduct of British officers was everywhere encountered by American naval officers. The affair of the Chesapeake was the fruit of the long-growing contempt of British lordlings for American pretensions. The act itself, as well as the manner it was dealt with by England, spoke volumes. It is true the British government disavowed it; but, instead of punishing the offender, he was rewarded. As a matter of form, and to give the appearance of censure, he was removed from the station he then occupied, but was placed in a more desirable one.

The measures taken by Mr. Jefferson in resistance to British aggressions were at the time violently denounced, and, perhaps, were not the wisest that could possibly have been taken ; but what better course, under all the circumstances, could have been pursued, would be hard to discover. As for war with England, the thought was considered, even by the Federalists, as ridiculous. Without granting that war should have at once been declared, no measures better than those taken by Jefferson could possibly have been resorted to. The first step, after the attack on the Chesapeake, taken by Mr. Jefferson, was the issue of a proclamation requiring all armed vessels commissioned by Great Britain, then within the waters or harbors of the United States, to leave immediately, and forbidding the future entrance of such vessels into the same. This proclamation was made July 2d, 1807. During that year intense excitement pervaded the country. England was powerful, and daily increasing in power, acquiring immense gains by her commerce, and by what she plundered from other nations. But the commerce of the United States was not yet annihilated, nor was this country bullied into a partial position in regard to the European controversy. It seemed to be expected by England that America would resent the Berlin decree of Napoleon, although as to us it proved an entire nullity. That American commerce, and not solely the design of affecting France, formed the objects of the orders in council, was apparent from the order of November 11th, 1807, if never before. A reason for this order was the complaint that the United States had acquiesced in the Berlin decree. The last-mentioned order declared that all vessels bound to France or any of her dependencies, or any port from which British vessels were excluded, and all vessels bearing French consular certificates of origin of cargo, should be liable to seizure and forfeiture! The weight of all these orders fell with crushing effect upon this country. They were commercial in their objects. France had no navy that durst appear upon the ocean; and Napoleon, though he could issue retaliatory decrees, could not stretch his arm beyond the coast. They were decrees, *et preterea nihil.* His Milan decree was in answer to the orders of November 11th, 1807; but Napoleon, though omnipotent on land, had no power to enforce his decrees upon the ocean. Immediately after the orders in council of November 11th, to wit, on the 25th of November, 1807, an additional order was issued to the effect that trade might be permitted between the United States and France, and French dependencies, *on the condition that the vessels engaged in it should enter some British port, pay a transit duty, and take out licenses!* Between the extravagances of the British and French decrees, American commerce was in danger of annihilation. It could not escape falling a victim to either one or the other of these powers; if it escaped Scylla, it was in danger of falling into Charybdis.

CHAPTER X.

THE PROTECTORS OF NEW ENGLAND COMMERCE AND OF THE HONOR OF THE COUNTRY FOUND IN THE SOUTH AND WEST. — THE EMBARGO. — THE ELECTION OF MR. MADISON. — THE DESTRUCTION OF COMMERCE OCCASIONED BY BRITISH ORDERS IN COUNCIL CHARGED TO THE EMBARGO. — RESISTANCE OF THE EMBARGO IN NEW ENGLAND. — STATE RIGHTS AND NULLIFICATION IN MASSACHUSETTS. — JOHN HENRY SENT BY ENGLAND TO FOMENT DISUNION. — HIS DESPATCHES. — THE ERSKINE TREATY. — NON-INTERCOURSE. — COURSE OF ENGLAND.

It is natural for political parties to find fault with each other's acts; and human weakness, which is the attribute of all parties, should not be overlooked in the study of history. New England was the seat of Federalism, and the encroachments of England upon our commerce were peculiarly oppressive to that part of the country. In preventing the people of the United States from enjoying the carrying-trade for the colonies of France and Spain, England aimed a blow at the interests of New England. This was felt to be so. From 1793 up to a late period in the administration of Mr. Jefferson, the leading merchants of the North were loud in their denunciations of England's outrages upon American commerce; but, when the time came for a vindication of the rights of that commerce, it seems quite strange to find that its defenders and champions were the West and South; and that the North was, as a general thing, opposed to the measures taken by the general government for its protection.

The insolent attack upon the Chesapeake by the Leopard, took place on the twenty-second day of June, 1807. Mr. Jefferson called an extra session of Congress on the twenty-sixth day of October; and the remedy by that body devised for the hostilities to American commerce practised by France and England was the embargo, which was intended to wholly suspend all foreign trade. An act to this effect was passed on the twenty-third of December. That the embargo was a necessary and justifiable measure, under the circumstances, no one now would doubt; but that it was continued too long, to the exclusion of other remedies, may be true enough. It was continued until the first of March, 1809, — to the administration of Mr. Madison, — before it was repealed. It was certainly a heavy blow to England, as the United States had become, as a market, almost indispensable to her; but, unfortunately, New England felt that she was also a sore sufferer by the measure.

In the complaints of New England there was thought to be much unfairness. Her commerce, it is true, was prostrated; but how could it exist under the British orders and French decrees? The embargo was the result of these orders and decrees; but, as the fall of our commerce was subsequent to the embargo, many were disposed to limit their vision to that act, and see nothing beyond. Therefore, by many, the ruin of commerce was charged to the embargo, as though it had not been annihilated by England and France. The embargo was laid to save American property and honor. If the country was not in a condition to vindicate its honor

10

upon the ocean, it was resolved to withdraw from that theatre until it could acquire more power, or become enabled to maintain its rights through some other medium. But, allowing the embargo to have been an unjustifiable and impolitic act, still, while it was the law of the land, all parts of the country should have submitted to it. Its evasion should not have been countenanced by upright and moral men. Although all parts of the country conceded to New England the very highest character for virtue, intelligence, and the Christian graces, it was in bitter terms complained of her that she did all she well could, short of civil war, to nullify the acts laying restrictions upon commerce. It is true she pretended that the embargo was unconstitutional; but the uncharitable considered this view taken by her of it only as a pretence. To attempt to throw off allegiance to unpleasant laws, by affecting to consider them unconstitutional, was thought to be disingenuous, as there was a ready legal way of testing that question. Although embargo acts had been passed under the administrations of Washington and Adams, and are clearly within the constitutional power of Congress, the one laid under the administration of Mr. Jefferson was pronounced unconstitutional, and denounced as a high-handed act of tyranny. As the excitement occasioned in the North by the embargo act, and the enforcing act, so called, was extreme, — as the opposition was so violent as to render that measure almost a dead letter in New England, and attract attention abroad, and lead to singular events, — it will be well for the reader to recall more particularly to his memory the spirit of those times. Early in 1809 the people of Boston, in town-meeting assembled, in a memorial to their own legislature, prayed the *interposition of that body* for relief from what was styled an "unconstitutional measure of the general government." It was not probably a *personal* liberty bill then contemplated by the memorialists, but a bill to free them from all restraints in their pursuit of happiness. During the pendency of the embargo through the year 1808, great intemperance of feeling was manifested in the New England States. It was thought, at home and abroad, that the country was verging to a separation, as the Northern States charged the Southern ones with being the enemies of their prosperity. For instance, as a specimen of the expressions of Northern people upon the subject, the Boston *Repertory* said: "We know, if the embargo be not removed, our citizens will ere long set it at defiance. It behooves us to speak; for strike we must, if speaking does not answer." Mr. Hillhouse, a United States senator, in a speech upon the subject, said: "In my mind the present crisis excites the most serious apprehension. A storm seems to be gathering, which portends, not a tempest on the ocean, but domestic convulsions! However painful the task, a sense of duty calls upon me to raise my voice against the bill. I feel myself bound in conscience to declare, *lest the blood of those who shall fall in the execution of this measure may lie on my head,* that I consider this to be an act which directs a mortal blow at the liberties of my country; an act containing unconstitutional provisions, to which the people are not bound to submit, and to which, in my opinion, they will not submit."

The Boston *Centinel*, of September, 1808, said: "This perpetual embargo being unconstitutional, every man will perceive that he is not bound to regard it. If the petitions do not produce a removal of the embargo, the people ought immediately to assume a higher tone. The State of Massachusetts has a duty to assume. This state is still sovereign and independent." The Boston *Gazette*, of the same period, said: "It is better to suffer the amputation of a limb, than to lose the whole body. We must prepare for the operation. Wherefore, then, is New England asleep? Wherefore does she submit to the oppression of enemies in the South? Have we no Moses, who is inspired by the God of our fathers, and will lead us out of Egypt?"

But the mission of a British emissary, John Henry, will perhaps show, as well as the above extracts, the dangerous point to which party prejudices had spurred many Northern people. The embargo had produced great suffering in England, and was the first blow, after the peace of '83, that had had any tendency to bring that overbearing power to her senses. The American trade was a vital spot in the British system. Unfortunately for Britain, she was dependent on the United States, and was taught, by the struggles ending with the last war, that she had everything to lose, and nothing to gain, by ruptures with this country. The embargo impaired her revenues, shut her manufactories, and threw thousands of her people out of employ, a charge upon the kingdom as paupers. It was then she attempted, and, to a considerable extent, with success, to carry on trade with the American people in defiance of the laws, and even resorted to an open encouragement of smuggling; but, despite all such efforts, she found that American trade was a consideration that of itself would command a respect for American rights. Impressed with this fact, early in 1809, Mr. Erskine was sent over with powers to arrange matters with Mr. Madison's administration, on a satisfactory basis. Mr. Erskine arrived at the seat of government not many days after Mr. Madison's inauguration, approached his cabinet with old-fashioned, straight-forward English professions of good-will and honesty, and a settlement of the difficulties then pending was at once agreed upon. The basis for a treaty was settled on the 17th of April, 1809. Trade with England was to be restored, and she was to restore to freedom the Americans taken from the Chesapeake, make satisfaction for that outrage, and rescind her orders in council of 1807. The entire cordiality with which Mr. Madison met the British overtures took the Federalists by surprise, as they had supposed his administration was to be but a bureau of the French emperor's government, and subject to the imperial will. The Federal and Republican parties were both too jealous of each other, and scarcely ever did each other justice. But, unfortunately for the success of the Erskine negotiation, the violent sectional demonstrations of New England in 1808 had attracted the attention of the British; and, at the same time that Mr. Erskine was despatched to the seat of the United States government, Governor-General Craig, of Canada, sent into New England an emissary, by the name of John Henry, to make observations, and report the prospects, in case the American foreign difficulties should be continued, of a division of the Union. Mr. Henry went first to Burlington, Vermont, then to Windsor, and passed through New Hampshire to Boston, Massachusetts, where he remained some two or three months. From these places he transmitted to his employer, the Governor-General of Canada, twelve despatches, in which he pretended to set forth truly the political situation of New England, the state of her feelings as to the national government, and the part she would act in event of a war with England. From Burlington, February 14th, 1809, he wrote: "I learn that the governor of this state is now visiting the towns in the northern section of it, and makes no secret of his determination, as commander-in-chief of the militia, to refuse obedience to any command from the general government which can tend to interrupt the good understanding that prevails between the citizens of Vermont and his majesty's subjects in Canada. It is further intimated that, in case of a war, he will use his influence to preserve this state neutral, and resist, with all the force he can command, any attempt to make it a party. I need not add that, if these resolutions are carried into effect, the State of Vermont may be considered as an ally of Great Britain." However, when Mr. Henry reached the eastern side of the state, where there were more Democrats, his opinion, as expressed above, was somewhat modified. His first despatch from Boston was under date of March fifth. A few extracts from his various letters will show their general tenor and scope. In that of March thirteenth, from Boston, he said: "You will perceive, from the accounts that will reach you in the public papers, that the Federalists of the Northern States have succeeded in making the Congress believe that, with such an opposition as they would make to the general government, a war must be confined to their own territory, and might be even too much for that government to sustain. * * * To bring about a separation of the states, under distinct and independent governments, is an affair of more uncertainty, and, however desirable, *cannot be effected but by* *a series of acts, and a long-continued policy tending to irritate the Southern and conciliate the Northern people.* The former are an agricultural, and the latter a commercial people. The mode of cherishing and depressing either is too obvious to require illustration. This, I am aware, is an object of much interest in Great Britain, as it would forever secure the integrity of his majesty's possessions on this continent, and make the two governments, or whatever number the present confederacy might form into, as useful and as much subject to the influence of Great Britain as her colonies can be rendered." In his other letter, from the same place, Mr. Henry, among other things, said: "*It should be the peculiar care of Great Britain to foster divisions between the North and South,* and, by succeeding in this, she may carry into effect her own projects in Europe, with a total disregard of the resentments of the Democrats in this country." * * * "A war would produce an incurable alienation of the Eastern States, and bring the whole country in subordination to the interests of England, whose navy would prescribe and enforce the terms upon which the commercial states should carry, and the agricultural states export, their surplus produce. All this is as well known to the Democrats as to the other party; therefore they will avoid a war, at least until the whole nation is unanimous for it. Still, when we consider of what materials the government is formed, it is impossible to speak with any certainty of their measures." After the Erskine negotiation, under date of May twenty-fifth, he wrote: "The unexpected change that has taken place in the feelings of political men in this country, in consequence of Mr. Madison's prompt acceptance of the friendly proposals of Great Britain, has caused a temporary suspension of the conflict of parties. * * * I beg leave to suggest that, in the present state of things in this country, my presence can contribute very little to the interests of Great Britain. *If Mr. Erskine be sanctioned*, in all he has conceded, by his majesty's ministers, it is unnecessary for me, as indeed it would be unavailing, to make any attempt to carry into effect the *original purposes of my mission.*"

The papers of Mr. Henry were transmitted to the British cabinet about the same time that the Erskine treaty was sent forward, and the result was that the British government refused to ratify the treaty, and alleged that Mr. Erskine had exceeded his instructions! The cause of the rejection of the Erskine treaty was at the time incomprehensible to Americans. The Federalists concluded that Mr. Erskine had really transcended his authority, and not a few of them condemned Mr. Madison severely for entering into a treaty that, on its face, ought to have apprized him that the minister could not have been acting within the scope of his authority! But, as Mr. Henry regarded his mission not a very honorable one, he claimed of his government more than ordinary compensation. As the ministry did not readily accede to his demands, he got into a passion, and, for a liberal compensation, placed all his papers, including his correspondence with members of the British cabinet, in the hands of our government, and they were laid before Congress, March, 1812, and published and circulated in the country. In those days the Henry papers were used by many Democrats to show that the Federal party was a disunion party; but that could never have been justly said of it. The most that reasonable opponents could say in the matter, would be that, as disclosed by the papers, sectional prejudices of so serious a character were maturing, as finally to lead to an irreconcilable alienation of the Northern from the Southern portion of the country. Happily for our country, subsequent events soon extirpated the causes of disaffection growing out of our foreign relations, although the repudiation of the Erskine arrangement again plunged us into difficulties, and revived party animosities with renewed vigor. But the principal reason for alluding to the Henry mission here is to show the policy of Britain, at that time, with regard to this country, and to exhibit what her feelings and views then were, and, from the nature of things, always must be, towards us.

The non-intercourse act expired in May, 1810, when our government made propositions to both of the belligerents, that if either would revoke its hostile edicts that act should be revived and enforced against the other. Accordingly, the French minister of state informed the American envoy that the Berlin and Milan decrees were revoked, to take effect from the first day of the succeeding November, and proclamation was made by President Madison accordingly. As Great Britain had professed a willingness to repeal her orders whenever France should revoke her decrees, she was now called upon to fulfil her promise; but, for various reasons discussed in the histories of those times, she refused, and continued to prey on the American commerce. She stationed ships of war before the principal harbors of the United States, to board and search the American merchantmen departing or returning, and many of them were sent off to British ports as legal prizes. Many impressments were made, and the contempt manifested by British naval commanders, on all occasions, for the republican flag, was, perhaps, the natural result of the long-continued patience with which this country had submitted to aggression and insult.

CHAPTER XI.

ENGLAND COÖPERATED WITH NEW ENGLAND TO RENDER THE ADMINISTRATION OF THE REPUBLICANS ODIOUS. — ENORMOUS LOSSES TO AMERICAN COMMERCE. — WAR DECLARED JUNE 18, 1812. — COURSE OF THE FEDERALISTS. — MEN OF THE TWELFTH CONGRESS. — CRAWFORD, CALHOUN, RANDOLPH, CLAY, ETC.

THE Americans had submitted to the aggressions of Britain, and the outrages of France, until endurance ceased to be a virtue, and until their submission began to cover the country with dishonor. Since the commencement of the obnoxious orders in council, Great Britain had captured nearly a thousand American merchant vessels, with their valuable cargoes, and had impressed thousands of our seamen. The injury inflicted upon our commerce was immense. The severest losses fell upon the commercial part of the country ; but, as the course taken by England was fast rendering the administration odious, the North opposed all retaliatory measures towards that power ; and, from what has been shown, it appears that the government saw that, if war should be resorted to, it would have to be carried on in opposition to Northern sentiment, and perhaps at the peril of the Union. Like Mr. Jefferson, Mr. Madison was disinclined to war. Everything in his power was done to obviate a resort to a measure which seemed destined to encounter the fiercest opposition of a large, powerful, and respectable portion of the country. England saw the perplexity of the Democratic administration, and detached to our coasts as many vessels-of-war as she could possibly spare, on purpose to annoy and harass our trade, and goad our government to a step which should prove its ruin.

Early in November, 1811, Congress was assembled, and Mr. Madison, in a brief message, set forth the state of our difficulties with England and France, and called the attention of the Congress to some measures, preparatory to a war, but not absolutely implying its necessity. Congress continued in session until the 6th day of July, 1812, and, on the 18th day of June, passed the act declaring war with Great Britain. Many other acts touching the navy, army, &c., were also passed during the session; but the act declaring war was the one that excited the greatest party feeling. Most of the preparatory measures, as they were called, — measures increasing the navy and army, and placing the country in a warlike attitude, — were voted for by members of all parties. For this, the Federalists were afterwards accused of duplicity. It was said that the Federalists did not believe that the Democrats dared venture on a war with England, and that for a long time they were accustomed to taunt the administration party with cowardice and pusillanimity. Josiah Quincy, a member from Massachusetts, it is reported, said that the Democrats "could not be kicked into war." Hence, it was charged against the Federalists in Congress that they sustained all the preparatory measures, under expectation that the war would not be declared, and that thus additional odium would fall upon the administration party. But perhaps fairness would concede that one opposed to the act of war, under the circumstances, might deem it prudent to place the country in a position more likely to command the respect of other nations.

The Twelfth Congress contained many able men. Twenty years had wrought quite a change in the aspects of the two parties in Congress. If in the earlier Congresses the Federal party contained the most talent, in the Twelfth Congress the advantage, on the score of ability, was decidedly with the Republicans. Messrs. Lloyd of Massachusetts, Giles of Virginia, and Crawford of Georgia, were prominent men in the Senate, the first of whom was Federal, and the two last were Republicans. William H. Crawford was a native of Virginia, but was removed to Georgia when quite a child. He was born to poverty, and arose in the world by his energies, and by the power of his talents. He was admitted to the bar in 1798, and in 1803 was elected to the Georgia Legislature. He became a United States senator in 1807, which position he occupied until appointed by Madison Minister to France in 1813. On his return from France, he was for a short time Secretary of War, and in 1817 was appointed Secretary of the Treasury, which place he held during Mr. Monroe's administration. He was regarded as one of the soundest statesmen of his time, and in 1824 was supported by a large party as a candidate for the presidency. Mr. Crawford was a man of extraordinary height and size, and said to have been in manner awkward and ungraceful. His integrity and high moral character, his firmness, decision and superior judgment, accompanied with boldness, inspired respect and confidence. He was a Republican, and in favor of the war measure. In fact, he was opposed to the embargo, and in favor of an immediate resort to war, on occasion of England's first outrages upon our commerce. John C. Calhoun was, during the Twelfth Congress, a member of the lower house, and, as chairman of the committee on foreign affairs, made an able report, setting forth a history of British aggressions and insolence, and recommended an appeal to arms. Mr. Calhoun's subsequent life is well known. Langdon Cheeves and William Lowndes were two members of the House from South Carolina, of much more than ordinary ability. They, as well as the most of the Southern members, were in favor of war with England, and their speeches on record in the proceedings of Congress are lasting memorials of their statesmanship and patriotism. It will be recollected that Felix Grundy, of Tennessee, was also a Republican member of the House during that Congress, as well as the talented Nathaniel Macon, of North Carolina, the singular John Randolph, of Virginia, the valorous Richard M. Johnson, of Tecumseh memory, of Kentucky, and likewise the brilliant Henry Clay, of the last-mentioned state. However, although Randolph commenced and closed life as a Democrat, he opposed the restrictive measures of Jefferson, and the war measure of Madison, with fanatical energy. He was at the time about forty years of age, having been born in 1773. He entered Congress in 1799, and, saving a short interval while he occupied a place in the Senate, he continued a member of the House thirty years. For energy, for wit, for sarcasm, for invective, perhaps the House has never had his equal. He was a man of peculiar notions and feelings, and was as inaccessible, saving on his "right side," as a porcupine. When enlisted, his sympathies were perhaps as remarkable as his prejudices. His speeches always commanded attention, and were frequently listened to with deep interest. He was a man of much reading, great originality of thought and expression, and entirely *sui generis* in manner and style. Although possessing great energy, much information, and remarkable vigor of intellect, his judgment was never considered reliable. He lacked that balance of mind, and those commanding reasoning organs, which bestow upon their possessor a sound judgment.

Mr. Randolph continued a warm supporter of Jefferson, until the introduction of a non-intercourse resolution in 1806; from which period, until after the settlement of our foreign difficulties, he opposed the principal measures of the administration. He seemed almost a monomaniac in regard to England. France and the French emperor he looked upon with the impatience of the deepest hatred; and England he admired as the champion of civilization. When war was talked of, his indignation at the mention of such a measure was not exceeded by that of Mr. Quincy. The power of Britain, with her thousand ships-of-war, was paraded before congressional audiences in terrible contrast with America and some ten or dozen ill-appointed vessels. The fact, too, that the United States had been for years at peace, and had no army, no discipline, no material at hand, while England had navies, disciplined and veteran armies, and all the appliances of war at her ready command, was enlarged upon, and dreadful consequences predicted in case this country should presume to embark in a war with the mistress of the ocean.

That the United States, at that period, was in an embarrassed and critical situation, and needed wise and patriotic counsels, and a firm and resolute hand, to direct her, is very evident. Mr. Madison was a fine civilian, but involuntarily shuddered at the idea, under the adverse state of things then existing, of involving his country in a conflict with England. The members of his cabinet felt the necessity of some bold movement, and his supporters, in both houses, saw that a war was necessary, and that there could be no honorable escape. Fortunately there was in the Congress of 1811 and '12 a young statesman whose spirit was equal to the occasion. Henry Clay, then about thirty-four years of age, was a member of the House. His superiority was at once recognized, and instinctively felt by all; the speaker's chair was accorded to him. Mr. Clay has been too well known throughout the world, since those days, to render any account of him here necessary. He was a rare man; he had a rare mission; and his life and services have been of inestimable importance to his country. He was born during the Revolution — in 1777 — a year of stirring events in that great drama. In '77 were fought the battles of Princeton, Bennington, Brandywine, Germantown, Stillwater and Saratoga; and a child born and cradled amidst such scenes should be expected to acquire some of the spirit peculiar to them. But Henry Clay was the poor son of a poor Virginia widow, drawing his life from the humblest origin. His story is told in a word. He was indebted to his genius and high spirit for all. In childhood, we see him neglected, in ragged garments riding to mill on horseback, and hear applied to him, as characteristic of all that was observed in regard to him, the title of "The Mill-boy of the Slashes." At an early age, on the marriage of his widowed mother, the humble home, in the care of which he had done his juvenile part, was removed from him, and he entered the great world to pursue his destiny.

He became a clerk in a store; then an amanuensis for a judge; and then a clerk and student in a law-office. At twenty, or thereabouts, we see him, destitute, friendless, and entirely unknown, wending his way into the then new State of Kentucky, and opening a law-office at Lexington. An ambitious and noble soul, an aspiring genius, a high-toned and chivalrous spirit, an open and generous heart, we begin to sympathize with him, and thank Heaven that some good angel guided his steps to the kindly and magnanimous borders of old Kentucky. On seeing him on Kentucky ground, our apprehensions for his welfare vanish, for in the care of Kentuckians, we know he is safe.

But, if the reader will still pursue the vision, he will see the powers of young Harry unfolding, and behold Kentucky taking him to her heart, where he will ever rest. Egypt may forget her kings, and the dust of mummied monarchs may be scattered from decaying pryramids; but Kentucky will never cease to hold the name of her beloved Clay in fond remembrance. With no education but that drawn from nature, and intercourse with others, it was surprising to behold with what marvellous effect Henry Clay could wield the minds and affections of men. He was tall, and possessed a commanding figure. Although his features were not the most comely, he had an eye that ever spoke with a power scarcely excelled by a thrilling and most musical voice. When excited, his whole soul went forth in looks, voice and action; and his emotions were so correct and natural that he was not human that could resist them. He was a natural orator. He was no hair-splitting logician; no dresser up of wordy harangues; no school rhetorician; but to him words were things, and his ideas were stirring realities, inspired by the senses rather than by a refined imagination. His knowledge of men was easily acquired, and extraordinary. No man was sufficiently dark and subtle to hide his motives under a guise that the eagle eye of Clay could not penetrate. He could read human character at a glance; and, as he read, forth went, in speech and action, the treasure of his discoveries. As no man could wear a mask before him, he wore none himself. He had no concealments, no tortuous intrigues, no finesse; truth and right were the great passions of his soul, and the convictions of conscience were at all times, in all places, and under all circumstances, his invariable compass and guide. Hence we see him apparently the creature of impulse. As new facts adduced new ideas of policy, we see him pursuing a new course; and we never see him the slave of opinions. So far from ever being the sycophant of popular feelings, he was often seen bidding them a haughty defiance, and paying a seemingly supercilious disregard to the special instructions of the Legislature on whose will he was dependent for his seat in the United States Senate. His love of country was enthusiastic and boundless. Her honor and interest were his study from an early age. It was singular, indeed, that the great interests of this nation should have been grasped so completely by so young a mind. Undisciplined in the schools as he was, at his first entrance upon public life, his views, for justness, maturity, and practicability, were in advance of those of the first statesmen of the day. Jefferson and Madison, older and more experienced public men than Clay, were, in regard to all the great interests of the country at that time, scarcely his superiors, if his equals. Under the auspices of Clay's public labors, the impracticable domestic and foreign policy of Jefferson was exploded; and it was at least curious to see the young speaker of the Twelfth Congress, by the proper arrangement of the committees, and by his spirit-stirring eloquence, forcing the war measure upon Mr. Madison. Beyond all cavil, Clay was the master-spirit of that Congress; and the justice of his views and course nobody now doubts, although at the time they cost him much angry abuse.

CHAPTER XII.

FEDERAL ASCENDENCY IN NEW ENGLAND AND NEW YORK. — CONDUCT OF THE FEDERALISTS. — PROSECUTION OF THE WAR EMBARRASSED BY THEM. — HARTFORD CONVENTION. — REVERSES AT DETROIT AND ON THE CANADIAN FRONTIER. — THIRTEENTH CONGRESS. — FACTIOUSNESS OF THE FEDERALISTS. — HENRY CLAY'S CASTIGATION OF JOSIAH QUINCY. — WAR CONTINUED. — THE NORTHERN PULPIT. — TRIUMPH OF AMERICAN ARMS, AND THE GLORY OF OUR NAVAL TRIUMPHS. — PEACE OF 1814. — AMERICAN HONOR VINDICATED, AND HER NAME RESPECTED THROUGHOUT THE WORLD.

THE declaration of war gave the Federalists the ascendency in New England, and New York had become opposed to the administration. The election of President took place in 1812, and the Federalists, with many anti-war Republicans, selected Clinton as a peace candidate, to run against Mr. Madison. Mr. Madison, however, was reëlected, and the war, amid unexampled opposition, was waged with vigor. The history of that war is too well known to need recital here. Its commencement was discouraging. The surrender of Hull, at Detroit, early in the campaign, and the ill-success of our troops upon the Canadian borders, excited gloomy apprehensions amongst Republicans, and gave encouragement to the Federalists. The Federalists were so blinded by passion as actually to exult in British victories, and express chagrin at the triumph of American arms. Even the Massachusetts Senate, on the motion of Josiah Quincy, resolved, substantially, that it was improper for a religious people to exult at victories achieved in a war not strictly defensive. The North threw many impediments in the way of the general government, to obstruct its prosecution of the war. The Governor of Massachusetts refused to place the state militia at the disposal of the United States officers, and New England continued her factious opposition to the administration until the close of the war. The celebrated Hartford Convention, however, held in December, 1814, was the most daring and dangerous measure of the Federalists, and was called at the suggestion of the Massachusetts Legislature. The convention was in session a fortnight; but, as their discussions were conducted with closed doors, the exact temper of that body, and the precise ultimate object of its leaders, can only be imagined. There is no person, at the present day, of any party, that approves of the course of the Federalists during the last war; but, although such a convention as that of Hartford was dangerous and highly improper under the circumstances, it should not be charged upon the conventionists, without full proof, that their real object was disunion. Although that body recommended radical changes of the United States Constitution,—changes abrogating almost all its compromises between the North and South, and fundamentally altering it in many respects,—there is no evidence that the recommendation was to be considered a prelude to a revolution. There were many men in the North who ardently desired disunion; but that the Hartford Convention was composed of such, was stoutly denied by the Federalists of those days.

On declaring war, it was thought expedient by government to conquer the Canadas. This project was violently denounced by the Federalists. Learned harangues and essays were delivered to the people, teaching them that government had no constitutional power to force them to march out of the limits of the United States. The effects of such addresses were sorely felt upon the Canadian frontier. A body of American militia under General Van Rensselaer passed over to Queenstown, and in defiance of General Brock's reënforcements, gained and held the British fort. General Van Rensselaer returned for the rear division of the American troops, who, putting themselves upon their constitutional rights, refused to cross the national boundary. The British fort received another reënforcement, and, of the thousand American soldiers who had crossed into Canada, scarcely any effected their escape. A desperate and bloody conflict ensued, in which the British were entirely victorious, under the eyes of the obstinate militia. The affair of Queenstown, following the disgraceful surrender of Hull, and the violent opposition of a large, wealthy, and influential section of the country, rendered the administration of the government by the Republicans extremely embarrassing. In the midst of these calamities and discouraging circumstances, the Thirteenth Congress assembled, and the question of the continuance of the war was discussed with great warmth on both sides. The repeal of her orders in council by Great Britain had given the Federalists a show of reason for insisting that, if left to her own sense of right, she would render the United States justice. No Federalist was more violent in his denunciations of the administration than Josiah Quincy; but the day of Federal power in the halls of the National Legislature was at an end. The assuming and domineering tone of that son of

Massachusetts was properly rebuked. The castigation given him by the thoroughly aroused and indignant Henry Clay was beyond expression severe. That member from Massachusetts must have experienced singular sensations under the delivery by Clay of his immortal speech of January 8th, 1813. It was certainly curious to witness such a masterly vindication of the cause of New England commerce, under such peculiar circumstances. It was said that as Mr. Clay dwelt upon the outrages upon American commerce, as he portrayed the wrongs inflicted upon Massachusetts sailors, as he pictured their capture, impressment into foreign service, and the indifference manifested towards their rights by the American government, — there was scarcely an eye in the house not moistened with tears. And the compliment paid to the American sailors was well deserved, as the result showed.

But in New England the war was regarded by a large party as an abomination. The pulpit was very warm and active in its denunciation of it. Many divines, and some of them quite eminent, pointed to disunion as necessary. One distinguished clergyman said: "The Union has been long since virtually dissolved; and it is full time that this part of the disunited states should take care of itself." Another said: "If, at the present moment, no symptoms of civil war appear, they certainly will soon, unless the courage of the war-party should fail them." And another said: "The Israelites became weary of yielding the fruits of their labor to pamper the splendor of tyrants. They left their political woes. They separated. Where is our Moses?" Such were the expressions of the Gardners, Osgoods, and Parishes, of those days, and indicate what might have been the pulpit at large. In these days it is only the political sermons of our Cheevers, Beechers, and Parkers, that find their way into print; but other divines, though inferior in ability, are by no means inferior in zeal.

Notwithstanding the discouraging commencement of the war, and the unfavorable condition of things for its successful prosecution, it was conducted with brilliant and useful results, and terminated by an honorable peace on the twenty-fourth December, 1814. Before this peace was concluded, Napoleon Bonaparte had fallen, and England became at peace with all the world but the United States; and, when the treaty was signed, some of her veterans were on their way, under Packenham, to immortalize Jackson and his brave soldiers, who encountered them at New Orleans on the eighth of January, 1815, and before, of course, the news of the peace had reached America. But, notwithstanding England had become disencumbered from European contests, and was in a situation to give the United States her undivided attention, she was not disposed to protract the struggle with this country. The eclat with which she had terminated her contest with France enabled her, without a sacrifice of credit, to treat favorably with us, and her condition and true interests required that her controversy with the United States should cease. She was monstrously in debt; the close to her of the American market was more destructive to her people than sword or cannon; and the longer the contest continued, the better prepared the United States became for the war, and more destructive and ruinous it became to England. For the little time it continued results really astonishing were produced. That little navy, first organ ized in 1798 by John Adams, under the fiercest opposition of Jeffersonian republicanism, and afterwards all but annihilated by Jefferson, during his administration, was, as a necessity of this war, resuscitated, not by Madison, but by such spirits as Cheeves, Lowndes, Calhoun, Crawford, Clay, Lloyd, and Quincy; and in two short years, by the unparalleled success of its encounters with the British navy, electrified all Europe. The check for the growing monster of the Isles was discovered. England was no longer the undisputed mistress of the ocean. The names of Lawrence, Decatur, Bainbridge, Perry, McDonough, and others equally brave, were born with the war of 1812, and will forever adorn the American annals. The commanders and sailors had been bred in that merchant service whose wrongs they were proud to avenge; and, since that war, our commerce has not been molested, nor have American seamen been impressed or insulted by the domineering mistress of the ocean. From being the degraded, insulted and despised nation of herb-raising Chinese, "striving for a commerce that she could not protect," and "vaunting an honor she could not maintain," America at once took her stand before the world as a power of first-rate magnitude; and her importance in the events of coming time was at once recognized. Upon the ocean she had not always been triumphant, but had always achieved renown. Her defeats were glorious. The captives and slain of the fatal Chesapeake were wept by the enemy on English soil. But England was amazed, and the world astonished, at the brilliant exploits of our young navy, when it frequently gained victories over superior power and discipline. The haughty presumption of British commanders was at once checked; and, from being the most

12

arrogant and insolent of mortals, they became prudent and respectful. At the opening of the war, but little regard was paid to the presence of an American vessel-of-war; but soon the feeling was changed, and a challenge would not produce an encounter even where the advantage was on the British side. One day, England and France were trampling America under their feet, rendering her an object of pity and contempt to the world; and the next, she was an object of dread to her enemies, and of admiration to the nations of Europe. Mr. Crawford was in Paris, as minister, at the abdication of Napoleon, when the allied powers entered that city. The respect paid to the stars and stripes that waved over his quarters, by the various representatives of the different powers of Europe, was said to have been a matter of great satisfaction to that able and patriotic gentleman; and everywhere, as the American minister, he was treated with marked consideration.

CHAPTER XIII.

THE FEDERAL PARTY ANNIHILATED, BUT THE MEASURES OF THE ANCIENT FEDERALISTS REVIVED. — THE NAVY, THE BANK, AND THE TARIFF. — POLITICS HERETOFORE HAD BEEN BASED ON THE FOREIGN POLICY OF THE COUNTRY; AFTER THE WAR, TURNED MORE ON DOMESTIC POLICY. — INTERNAL IMPROVEMENTS.

It is with nations as it is with men; their prosperity is oftentimes more the result of fortune than the achievement of wisdom. We have but to cast our eyes over the history of any state to discover how slightly its destiny has been shaped by human intelligence. The prominent interests of America, as well as of England, have struggled into existence without the cherishing hand of a fostering government. It is true, these interests, in some instances, have been in a measure protected and encouraged, after their prominence rendered their continuance indispensable; but in the germ they received no sunshine-smiles of favor to promote their growth. "With how little wisdom this world is governed!" was an observation of Chancellor Oxenstiern, and its truth is humiliating. At every great political event we are reminded of the saying, "Man proposes, God disposes;" and how near-sighted do man's views and calculations always turn out in contrast with the results of Providence! The American Revolution was commenced to resist the levy of an illegal tax, with no object, but to avoid that levy, in view; but the establishment of a new nation upon the earth was the result.

The war of 1812 was undertaken to emancipate our commerce from the shackles of British assumption, and resulted in an entire change of the internal and external policy of our country. It was truly said to be our "second war of independence;" and, as the Revolution was more like the struggle of a birth than of a war, the war of 1812 followed as the natural effort attending such natural phenomena. The mother country did not recover from the first labor until after the close of the latter.

The war of 1812 was the crisis in the politics of the United States. It was the extermination of the latter-day Federal party, but the inauguration of the ancient Federal politics. As the Federal party became extinct, original Federal ideas revived. Up to this time parties had been divided principally on questions of foreign policy. Questions of internal policy had been dormant until the passions that originally gave them solution were extinct; so that, when the country was no longer embarrassed with views as to external relations, and domestic measures came uppermost in the minds of politicians, they ceased to be considered as very binding party tests. The establishment of a national bank, under the administration of Washington, as well as of a navy, under Adams, had been violently opposed by the Republicans of Mr. Jefferson's school; but the necessities of the country, as made apparent by the last war with England, taught a new lesson in regard to these measures. There was as yet a lingering remnant of the old Jeffersonian party arrayed against the bank and navy; but the Republican party, as a general thing, had conquered their prejudices in regard to these questions. It is true, when the first charter of the United States Bank expired, in 1811, it was not renewed, but a new charter was granted under the administration of Madison in 1816; and during the war the navy was built up, and has ever continued a living witness of the absurdity of Jefferson's anti-commercial gun-boat system. Langdon Cheeves was the chairman on the naval committee in the Twelfth Congress, who reported in favor of a bill increasing and establishing our navy. Much discussion ensued; but the measure was warmly espoused by the ablest Republicans in the Congress. It was advocated by such men as Lowndes, Crawford, and Clay, Republicans; and Quincy and Lloyd of Massachusetts, Federalists. The old claim that this country was not to excel in commerce; that a powerful navy would lead to monarchy, and was inconsistent with republican institutions; that to sustain a navy, capable of encountering the monstrous naval establishment of England, would incur a charge far superior to all the profits that could ever be realized from the commerce it could protect; were urged by the opponents of the bill. But these objections were all ably answered by its friends, and the policy of establishing and maintaining a naval power, sufficient for the exigencies of our country, was steadily persevered in through that and all future Congresses. The triumph of this measure was perhaps the fruit of the war. The statesmen of that day were led, by the necessities of the case, to see that a powerful naval establishment was indispensable to this country. Those engaged in commerce feared that the charges of sustaining such an institution would fall upon them; and that the agriculturists of the West and South, not engaged in commerce, would be less burthened with the establishment. But the public men of those days were capable of taking more enlarged views of the interests of the country, and they demonstrated that whatever tended to protect and benefit one section, was beneficial to the whole. If the men and money of the North were engaged with their ships in commercial enterprises, it was shown that the West and South were the great staple producers and the consumers of foreign goods, without whose productions, and consumption of imported articles, there could be no commerce. And by the same reasoning those in the South and West who opposed an expensive navy, on the ground that it was to protect the commerce of the North, were taught that without that Northern commerce their productions would be of no value.

The war was also peculiarly well calculated to demonstrate the utility of internal improvements, and of domestic manufactures. Early Republicanism had looked with dread upon manufacturing interests. The English manufacturing cities, with their wretched, half-starved operatives, and squalid aspects, were ever appealed to as examples of this sort of industry, and measures intended for the building up of manufacturing interests were frowned upon by many. But, from his first entrance into public life, Henry Clay became the unwavering advocate of protection to home industry; and the experiences of the last war came in aid of his powerful logic upon the question. The tariff of 1816, immediately following the treaty of peace, was the legitimate fruit of the war, and a return to the farseeing policy of Hamilton. The tariff of 1816 was a tariff for protection; and those who advocated it, did so on the ground of protection. At that day, the leading Democrats, such as Lowndes, Crawford, Calhoun, and Henry Clay, were clear and decided in their views of the propriety of encouraging domestic manufactures, that this country might manufacture for its own consumption, and be independent of foreign supplies. The policy was soundly and auspiciously inaugurated. Massachusetts, and commercial circles in the East, for a long time opposed the measure, fearing that such restrictions on importations would diminish the profits of commerce, which consisted in shipping goods from foreign countries, and selling them here. Commerce was a sweet that the East had then tasted, while manufacturing was but an untried experiment. That, in the protective measure of 1816, the South exercised a sounder policy for New England, than the latter did for herself, is evident enough now; and that the doctrines of that day were conceived in good faith, patriotism, and the true principles of political economy, there is not a particle of doubt. The agitations of party may for a while cause perturbations in a nation's policy; but eventually this country will return to the truly American system of 1816. Saving the factious opposition of the Federalists of the North, and the commercial opposition of the same section to the protective system, there was nothing selfish, narrow, or sectional, in the Congress of 1816, and the domestic policy then inaugurated looked to the best good of each part, by promoting the best good of the whole country. Measures of internal improvement were encouraged by the Democrats of those days, and by no one more ably than by John C. Calhoun; and, although the views of the Democratic party have since changed in regard to these, as well as to the tariff, the sentiments of early times are fast returning. But recently a Democratic congress passed internal improvement bills by a two-thirds vote over the

President's veto ; and it is confidently trusted that the American system of early Democracy will yet triumph as the settled and firm policy of the country. Until that day comes, and until this country so adjusts her measures of internal and foreign policy as to secure and foster all her great interests, she will be but the colony of Europe, and never free from revulsions and commercial disasters, which must periodically afflict all classes, and render industry here subservient to the interests of the Old World. When dispassionately viewed, this is seen by everybody. The statesmen of 1816 were in a favorable point for observation, and this is their recorded testimony. That a country of so vast extent, resources, and advantages, as this, should, through sectional partialities, adapt its measures so as to render it but a tributary to the riches of England, is unpatriotic and ruinous.

CHAPTER XIV.

MR. MONROE ELECTED IN 1816 AND 1820. — EXTINCTION OF PARTY SPIRIT. — MONROE'S CABINET. — REPUBLICANS SUPPORT BANK, INTERNAL IMPROVEMENTS, TARIFF, AND NAVY. — MEASURES OF MR. CLAY. — MR. CRAWFORD'S PRESIDENTIAL EXPECTATIONS. — HENRY CLAY'S. — J. C. CALHOUN'S. — ANDREW JACKSON'S. — TARIFF OF 1816 AND 1824. — SOUTHERN JEALOUSIES, ETC.

THE Federal party had staked its fortunes on opposition to the war, and was ruined. It is true that party had changed much in its leaders, as well as in its measures. There were many of the old Federalists who could not concur in the factious opposition of their party to the administration, and left it for the Republican ranks. Among the most noted of these were Samuel Dexter, Oliver Wolcott, and that sterling old revolutionary patriot, John Adams. At the close of Mr. Madison's administration, the Federal party was effectually silenced — to use a military expression. The presidential contest of 1816 was attended with scarcely any excitement, the Federal party being too small to justify any effort. Rufus King was their candidate, and received the votes of Massachusetts, Connecticut, and Maryland; thirty-four in all. Mr. Madison's Secretary of State, James Monroe, was the Republican candidate, and received the votes of the other sixteen states, making one hundred and eighty-three. Mr. Monroe was, in 1820, almost unanimously reëlected President, there being but one vote cast against him. Connecticut became Republican in 1817, and, in 1819, Maryland, and, in 1823, Massachusetts passed from the hands of the Federalists. Among the members of the cabinet of Mr. Monroe, were John Quincy Adams, Secretary of State; William H. Crawford, Secretary of the Treasury; George Graham, of Virginia, Secretary of War; and William Wirt, Attorney General.

Congress, during Mr. Monroe's administration, was not entirely harmonious upon all questions, nor were the members unanimous in the support of the President. The New England members were more uniformly and constantly his supporters than those from any other section, and on some measures the opposition to the President's views was in the ascendency in Congress. The conflicts and contentions between members were conducted with no design of embarrassing Mr. Monroe's administration; they were either honest differences of opinion as to public measures, or efforts made to influence the succession. The idea that the Federal had become entirely absorbed into the Republican party, and that but one universal party was to rule the country, was not entertained by all the politicians of those days. The Federal party was overthrown; but there were scattered throughout the land a large number of Federalists. Of course they had no expectations of electing a successor to Mr. Monroe. But the leaders of the Republican party were divided on many measures. There was a tendency, on the side of the more radical part of the Democracy, to recede from the liberal policy which had sprung up after the last war. Consequently, during Mr. Monroe's administration, were thoroughly discussed the questions of Bank, Tariff,

Navy, and Internal Improvements; and, as a whole, these measures were embraced by the leading Republicans. All have read the speeches of Henry Clay, and some of the most able of them were made, at this period, on the tariff and internal improvement measures. On the last named measure Mr. Clay, although the ablest Republican in the country, encountered the views of the President with all his ability. Mr. Monroe in his message to Congress took occasion to distinctly lay down his opinions as to the constitutional power of the general government to prosecute works of internal improvement. The state-rights notions of Jefferson and Madison had been against such a power, and Mr. Monroe announced his opinion that Congress had it not; but he regarded such measures of such vast consequence to the country, that he recommended that steps should be taken for the amendment of the Constitution, giving the general government the requisite power.

We have seen that the United States Bank was chartered by the Republican administration. Mr. Crawford had been its champion from the first, and his argument in its favor was what first gave him a national reputation as an able statesman. At first, Mr. Clay had doubted the constitutionality of a United States Bank; but, after the powerful exposition of the question by Mr. Crawford, not only Mr. Clay, but many other Democrats, yielded their doubts, and were afterwards supporters of the measure. Mr. Crawford was an able and influential man, and was the competitor of Mr. Monroe for the nomination for the presidency in 1816, and in the congressional caucus received a respectable share of the votes. His standing had not become impaired at the close of Mr. Monroe's administration. He was one of the contestants for the succession.

According to the practice of those days we are to understand that Mr. Monroe, by appointing John Q. Adams Secretary of State preferred him for a successor to the presidency ; and Mr. Adams was the preference of New England. Mr. Adams was a Republican, as had also been his celebrated father since the administration of Jefferson.

Henry Clay had made a strong impression in the country, and Kentucky, and other Western States, regarded him as a promising candidate for the presidency. He had been a prominent leader of the Republican party for some years, and was unexcelled, for talents and patriotism, by any of its members. His voice had been heard, during Mr. Monroe's administration, in favor of South American and Grecian liberty, in tones that thrilled with enthusiasm the hearts of his countrymen ; and no one had said or done more, to carry through the late war with England, and to establish a system of national policy which should render the country prosperous and independent, than he.

John C. Calhoun, of South Carolina, was also put forward by his state for the succession. Mr. Calhoun, by his war report in the Congress of 1811 and '12, and his speeches supporting the war, the navy, the tariff, and internal improvements, had characterized himself as an able statesman, and an ardent patriot. South Carolina, also, put forward Mr. Loundes for a nomination. Mr. Lowndes was justly prized as a statesman and patriot; but his decease soon ensued.

Tennessee offered for the course Andrew Jackson, a lawyer and captain ; the last man of all mentioned in connection with the office whom a statesman would have selected; and still he possessed elements of greatness for the cabinet as well as for the field of battle. General Jackson had been frequently promoted to high civil offices, such as United States senator, and judge of a high court of justice, and declined to retain the places, on the account, as always supposed, of inexperience and want of fitness for such employments. "His dearest action," many thought, "had been in the tented field." His victory at New Orleans, however, had invested him with a charm, in the eyes of the people, that rendered his aspirations, as the result showed, anything but contemptible.

All of these aspirants (and they were all Democrats) had their friends and supporters in Congress, and doubtless much of the debate, as at the present day, was intended for the eye of the people, rather than to promote the measures under discussion. Even the conduct of Jackson in the Spanish province of Florida was discussed. The British, it was said, had sent emissaries there to incite the Indians to acts of hostility against the Americans. The general was quite arbitrary in his procedure in the premises. He entered Pensacola, where he soon brought the hostile Indians to peace, and rather unceremoniously, so they said, executed a couple of British soldiers that somehow or other fell into his hands. A resolution to censure Jackson was introduced into the House, and warmly supported by Mr. Clay; which fact should not be forgotten in connection with the subsequent conduct of that statesman. Also the Florida treaty, the Texas cession, fortifications, &c., were before Congress; and, prior to the close of Mr. Monroe's term of office, the tariff of 1824 was passed. The tariff of 1816 had been found deficient for the purposes for which it had been intended, and, after a thorough discussion, the tariff of 1824 was enacted. The tariff of 1816 had failed to effect what the act of 1824 accomplished immediately. It was not merely a revenue act, but a tariff strongly protective, and its good effects were at once witnessed in all parts of the country. The curious reader of politics will turn, with some wonder, and read the names of those whose votes stand recorded for and against that act. It was a thoroughly Democratic measure, of course, as Congress at the time had scarcely more than a baker's dozen of Federalists in it. But already had sectional interests begun to show themselves in Congress, and soon national policy had to make way for that of a section. There had been in the North the fiercest, long continued, and most bitter denunciations of the South, her people and institutions. The better part of the Northern people, of course, did not join in this sectional crusade; but the existence in the North of an active and bitter sectional spirit aroused the vigilance of Southern politicians, and at an early day inspired them with apprehensions for the future. The South had not originally been jealous of the North. Virginia bestowed on the Union an empire of territory, and voluntarily consecrated it to freedom. The Union itself was a divine emanation from the heart of Virginia patriots; and on the ascendency of Jefferson and Madison, the general government, cordially supported by the whole South, engaged in a war with England to redress the wrongs and vindicate the rights of Northern seamen. It would indeed be hard, during the early days of the republic, to find an instance where the South, as such, desired, or sought an occasion to trample on the rights of the North, or were the offenders in a sectional controversy. But in the North, unfortunately, there had been rabid haters of the South, and radical disunionists,—those who made no secret of an aggressive spirit towards Southern institutions, — and it was not strange that, witnessing the intemperance of these, the South should in time become aroused to a defence of her peculiar interests.

CHAPTER XV.

ENGLISH POLICY AND PROSPERITY. — NATIONAL INDEPENDENCE. — BRITAIN DEPENDENT ON AMERICA FOR THE RAW MATERIAL FOR HER MANUFACTURES, WITHOUT WHICH HER COMMERCE COULD NOT EXIST. — THIS DEPENDENCE FORCED THE PEACE OF 1814. — HER EFFORTS TO RELIEVE HERSELF. — HER INDIAN COLONIES CANNOT COMPETE WITH SLAVE LABOR IN THE UNITED STATES. — HER ATTEMPTS TO OVERTHROW SLAVERY. — SLAVE-TRADE AND ANTI-SLAVERY. — EFFECT OF HER ANTI-SLAVERY CRUSADE IN THE UNITED STATES —MISSOURI CONTROVERSY. — ANTI-SLAVERY FEELING IN NEW ENGLAND ARTIFICIAL.— SLAVERY A NECESSITY TO THE SOUTH. — THE NEGRO. — NEGRO SERVITUDE AN INSTRUMENTALITY IN THE HANDS OF PROVIDENCE FOR THE CIVILIZATION OF THE WORLD. — EFFECT OF SERVITUDE UPON THE NEGRO. — RIGHT OF CONGRESS TO EXCLUDE A NEW STATE ON ACCOUNT OF ITS TOLERATING SLAVERY, ETC.

England has been taught her policy by experience. It is not to be disputed but that occasionally she has had statesmen capable, by original measures, of developing her interests; but, generally, the commanding importance of her interests has controlled the government, and sometimes in spite of itself. Her prime interests, in former years, were not always readily taken into protection by the reigning power. It was a long while before the feudal lord could busy himself in studying the interests of the merchant and mechanic. But the revolutions of later periods have changed the spirit of the British government. She is now eminently a trading nation — a nation of merchants and mechanics. To promote her trade and manufactures is now one of the first objects of her policy. For this she maintains a large navy, establishes colonies in all parts of the world, and sustains a trafficking friendship with every nation on the earth. The East Indies, embracing quite a share of the inhabitants of the earth, are reduced to her power, purely for the purposes of trade; and the globe is dotted over with her colonies, which consume her fabrics, and give employment to her merchant-ships. Her manufactures are not only used by her colonies; they are also demanded by the whole world, millions on millions of them being annually imported into the United States. Strip England of her manufactories and of her commerce, and her power and importance would at once disappear. The products of her manufactories, in which millions of her people are employed, are enormous. These manufactories are indispensable to her commerce, without which her colonial system, and her whole commercial prosperity, would fall into ruin. Her mechanics must have employment, or the twenty odd millions of people in those small isles would be obliged to devour each other for subsistence. The fabrics manufactured must have a market; and if necessary, in order to force them into China or India, to sacrifice a few thousand soldiers, and a few millions of dollars, the offering is always readily and cheerfully put forth. Her goods are forced into some countries by war, into some by fear, and some are induced to take them by bribery. Her arms are ever ready to place a crown upon the head of a free-trade king in India, and her money to elect a free-trade president in America. The great cardinal principle of modern British policy is to keep her manufactories in employ, and to keep the world abroad an open market for her fabrics.

The works of Providence are inscrutable. We see enough to arouse our curiosity and admiration; but when we think her benign designs in our special behalf are clearly manifest, we are apt almost always suddenly, on having our eyes opened by some unexpected development, to find ourselves wonderfully deceived. Nations as well as men are in the hands of God, and if, by His disposal of events, mortals are disappointed, it is undoubtedly because He consults His own, and not the counsels of men. No nation owns Him: He is the special favorite and patron of no race, or body of human beings. The earth is allotted to man. The nations should form a family, as well as individuals. This could never be, if it were in the power of one to monopolize all the resources of the earth. Perfect independence in nations should no more be expected than in individuals. Mutual dependence, as well in nations as in individual men, is a law of nature, which it can never be wisdom to endeavor to wholly overcome. How far nations or men should strive for independence is a question left for the solution of human wisdom; and, as mortals are blind and erring creatures, passionate, selfish, bigoted and conceited, they cannot be expected to always judge modestly, moderately, and correctly, on such a question. There may be some pleasure in the excited hopes of selfishness and of self-importance; but, after all, probably our happiness much depends on the true solution of this very question. Certainly a correct decision of it would save individuals much strife and mortification; and save nations angry altercations and war.

At an early period of the independent existence of the United States, Great Britain made a discovery which has since powerfully affected her foreign policy.

She found that America held her by a powerful bond. Yes, her manufactories, her fleets and commerce, were all dependent on the cotton plantations of the United States. While at war with us, her plunder from our commerce, and from that of other nations, for a while in a measure compensated for the distress occasioned by loss of American trade, and the raw material thereby drawn from this country; but, in a state of peace, British prosperity was found dependent on commerce with the United States. She manufactured for the whole world; but, unawares, she discovered that the raw material for her fabrics was the product of this country. The discovery evidently startled and distressed our venerable mother. From that day to the present she has resorted to every effort, and tried every expedient imaginable, to relieve herself from absolute dependence on America for cotton; but destiny seems to chain her as by an unalterable fiat to our control. Throughout all her expedients and resorts to emancipate herself from dependence on us for the raw material of her manufactures, she has been obliged to maintain towards us an affable, plausible, truck-and-dicker friendship. She would gladly have given the production of cotton to Hindoos, Hottentots, or Turks, at the expense of the United States; but still, as the richest of all her foreign markets for her goods was with easy, green, and unsuspecting Brother Jonathan, she ever greeted him with affected cordiality and studied politeness. She has, or rather, if we take her personified as Johnny Bull, he has smiled and stabbed, and smiled and stabbed again; but impotence has rendered his dagger harmless, as yet.

William Pitt the younger was her first great statesman that saw the secret of our superiority in the production of cotton. Though a liberal statesman, Fox could not resist the policy of Pitt, and finally embraced it. It was seen and felt that, with slavery, the United States must ever monopolize the production of that material. What should the statesmen of the British Isles do to crush this odious monopoly, that so powerfully bound British interests to the pleasure of the United States? A hasty glance of those statesmen satisfied them that the way to effect their object was to overthrow the slave-trade and slavery. The slave-trade had continued from an early period of the settlement of America, and during its continuance many millions of slaves had been imported from Africa to the West Indies, and the Spanish, French, and English colonies of America. England saw that cotton could be produced in her East Indian possessions, but not in competition with slave labor in the United States. To destroy this inequality, and to give her cheap Hindoo labor the advantage, slavery in the United States must be extinguished. To effect this it was considered sufficient to overthrow the slave-trade. The importation of slaves had never ceased, and the supply seemed never to exceed the demand. Without this supply — without this trade — it was concluded by Britain that slavery itself would soon expire in the United States.

Impressed with these views, the statesmen of Great Britain commenced a fierce war upon the slave-trade, and, as the interests of many of her people were much involved in the question, it was not abolished at once. The touching exertions and appeals of Wilberforce and Clarkson, and a host of other speakers and writers, had a powerful effect in Old and New England; but the measure was not carried until 1808. In 1808, also, the United States, less intent on material interests than on ideas of humanity, prohibited the importation of slaves. Britain was visibly and sensibly affected at this act of her unpromising son; and she could not endure to be only equal to him in efforts in the cause of freedom. The act, however, by which Great Britain prohibited her subjects from engaging in the slave-trade after 1808, was passed in 1807. The debates in Parliament at the time would disclose to any but the senses of a Jonathan the expectations of the British statesmen in regard to the abolishing of the slave-trade. It was stated in those debates that England had in her West Indian possessions upwards of four hundred thousand slaves, and it was estimated that to keep that number good an importation of ten thousand annually would be requisite. By cutting off the supply entirely, it was regarded as certain that slavery itself would in a short time cease. *The reasoning in regard to the United States, though of course not expressed, was based upon the same data.*

But, to cut off the trade so as to entirely deprive the United States of the supply sufficient to keep up her necessary slave force, it was apparent that more governments than Great Britain and the United States should renounce the trade, and enter into a league against it. The necessities of the United States would hardly resist temptation if other nations should continue to bring to her ports servants so indispensable to her. Here Britain's disinterested humanity and practical love of freedom were singularly manifested. She complimented the humanity of her son Jonathan, and especially praised all the Jonathans that had manifested a proper and becoming abhorrence of slavery, and then addressed herself to the other powers practising the hateful traffic. Denmark, Sweden, the Netherlands, France, Spain, Portugal, and other states engaged in the slave-trade were importuned, and finally with success, to give it up. None of the powers applied to were readily willing to concur with England in her work of humanity. Denmark prohibited her subjects from carrying slaves after 1804. Louis the Eighteenth promised the British minister, Castlereagh, in 1814, that France should abandon the trade; but she continued it afterwards. At the Congress of Vienna, in 1815, Castlereagh pressed the subject; but all he could obtain was a promise from Spain and Portugal to give up the slave-trade *north of the line.* It is easily perceived that it was something accomplished by England, in her work, to prohibit the slave-trade north of the equator; but this did not satisfy the humane feelings of the great champion of human rights of modern times. Spain and Portugal were, with the exception of France, the greatest dealers in slaves. As for France, Louis the Eighteenth owed his crown to British bayonets, and readily accommodated his benefactress in her work of love. But as for Spain and Portugal, their hearts had not yet been opened. They were still blinded by the passion for gain; and ministering England, like a true angel of mercy, opened their eyes by the application of handsome bonuses. To Portugal she promised about a million and a half of dollars, and to Spain she gave about two millions of dollars, as indemnification for giving up a line of business which she thus had all at once come to view as unjust and horrible. A more active humanity than that for several years manifested by our worthy and respected mother has rarely been witnessed in nations. These extraordinary exertions for abolishing the slave-trade were made immediately after her last war with the United States. But it was soon found that but little progress was made in the ruin of American slavery. The importation of slaves into South America and the West Indies, and consequently to some extent into the United States, still continued. Moreover, the anti-slavery reform, originating in England, crossed the Atlantic, and was exceedingly popular in America. Emancipation societies sprung up through the land, many of the Northern States having got rid of their slaves, and passed laws against the institution ; and some of those now reckoned as Southern States were on the point of abolishing their slavery. In America there was nothing pecuniary or selfish in the movement. By the attention the subject received, the condition of the African underwent an entire change, — a change pregnant with the most important consequences. The comfort, happiness, and morals, of the slave were provided for and secured. His treatment was more humane. His security from abuse was not only preserved by laws, but also guarded by a wholesome public feeling. American slavery at once assumed a new character, and the African became, under his American master, a new being. In all this the master's humanity was amply rewarded. In proportion as the negro was rendered comfortable and happy he became prolific. As an American-born and an American-raised negro is superior for service to one brought from the savage wilds of Dahomey, the United States had a better supply for slaves than could be afforded by the slave-trade. It is a pity that the humane movements of the earlier period of our history could not have continued undisturbed by sectional hostility; but, unfortunately, the zeal of Northern reformers outran their wisdom. Their incendiary missions among the slaves soon called for severe legislation on the part of slave states, as self-protection from the consequences of Northern fanaticism. Laws against teaching negroes to read and write were demanded as a defence against the incendiary teaching of ultra Northern reformers, who were not content with improving the condition of the servant, but must teach him rebellion and murder. It is pleasant to know that many of the severe laws, called into existence by Northern fanaticism, are regarded as only defensive enactments, and never enforced saving in extreme cases.

While England and the United States were thus warmly engaged in righting the manifold wrongs of the slave, an event occurred that shook the Union to the centre, and came near rending it in twain. In the Congress of 1818 and '19, Missouri, a portion of the Louisiana purchase, applied for admission into the Union. The House of Representatives opposed her admission with slavery, and passed a bill admitting her on condition that slavery should cease on a specified future day. The Senate refused to concur with the House, and the question went over to the next Congress. The whole North was arrayed against the admission of Missouri with slavery. They claimed that Congress had power to prohibit the existence of slavery in any new state. The South denied this, and claimed that, by the Constitution, Congress had no such power. During the recess of Congress, presses, orators, wandering lecturers, pulpits, and legislatures, were in a blaze of excitement. There was too much frenzy to allow reason or justice to have great weight in the controversy. The question involved in that dispute has been agitated till the present day; but passion on both sides has been so strongly enlisted that no satisfactory decision could be arrived at. There is undoubtedly a right side to the question, and all should strive to find it out; but the truth can never be seen through the mists of passion. Any fact, any statement, against our prejudices, or prepossessions, is at once indignantly rejected, and we only receive such impressions as harmonize with our feelings. But in matters of state, and especially in a free government like ours, where it is our duty not only to obtain our own, but likewise to concede to others their rights, we should strive to be dispassionate, and to look at things in their true light.

There are, in the popular mind, many false ideas with regard to slavery, the most of which are borrowed from England. For instance, that slavery is the creature of local law is fallacious. Slavery has been universal, and for all time. No colony or state ever established slavery by legislative enactments. Slave property, like all other property, has from time to time been regulated by local and national legislatures, but nowhere has owed its existence to such powers. It has ever been treated as a personal right. The early settlers of Massachusetts enslaved Indians in numerous instances; the noble Winthrop named Indians among his bequests; and in their public acts that colony recognized the propriety of Indian slavery. But this subjection of Indians to servitude was not authorized by any local law; it was exercised as a natural right. That colony held negro slaves on the same basis. It is true their Constitution, adopted in 1790, virtually abolished slavery, though not in express terms. It is competent for a state to prohibit a citizen's holding slaves, as it is to prohibit any traffic deemed injurious to the public good; but, without such prohibition, slavery would not have terminated quite so soon in Massachusetts. The question arose in that state after the adoption of her Constitution, and her courts pronounced the freedom of the negro as the beneficent grant of that instrument. The people of the North are so deeply impressed with the force of this truth, that they have liberally filled their statute-books with enactments against this species of property; but still, deluded by popular sounding phrases, they often utter what they little comprehend, and clamor about freedom being universal and slavery local. The fact is that the converse of this proposition is nearer the truth. There is not a state on earth where slavery is held unlawful, save by legislative or constitutional provisions.

When the Constitution of the United States was adopted, slavery was existing in all the states, and was fully recognized by that instrument. Representation and taxation were apportioned on the basis of a slave population, and provision was made for the return of fugitive slaves. At that day negroes were not regarded as of great value in the Northern and Middle States, nor of so much value in the extreme South as they have since become. The discovery by Whitney of the cotton-gin, and the subsequent marvellous increase of cotton cultivation, has given a new importance to negro labor, and the necessity of the institution of slavery stands now in a different light from that in which it stood at the period of the Revolution.

It is the unquestionable duty of government not only to look to what is right and legal, but to take into view things as they actually exist. Reformers never make allowance for obstacles. With them imagination is at the command of the will, and serves as a substitute for facts and reason in all cases. But legislators ought to be independent of popular prejudices, and should endeavor to arrive at the truth. When this impartial and candid vantage ground is attained by the legislator, he will find that American slavery is a fact, and a legal fact, and shape his measures accordingly. Negro slavery is not only a fact, but it is, so far as the negro is concerned, a magnificent one. Negro labor cannot compete with white free labor in the higher latitudes; and if negroes monopolize Southern fields, they must owe their privileges to climate alone. Slavery is not thrifty, and the people dependent on it have many disadvantages to encounter, and look with envy upon their more fortunate neighbors who can command a more profitable species of labor. But for the Southern planter there is no choice. The negro has possession of his fields, and must probably occupy them so long as the country shall be habitable. It is to be regretted that the South is controlled by so hard a necessity; that she cannot exercise a choice as to her laborers. Could the Southern planters employ free white labor, the South would soon, were it to manifest the enterprise peculiar to such Saxon energies, resemble Paradise. Could the Southern people avail themselves of free negro labor, their prospects would be more encouraging; but slavery is the only condition on which it is possible for the American people to avail themselves of negro labor. Wherever the climate and soil will admit, white free labor will exclude black servitude; but in the Southern savannas slavery or desolation must prevail. The statesman who makes no allowance for difference in race, in climate, in soil and productions, and in manners and customs, is not fit to legislate for a large empire. Our legislators in 1820 were undoubtedly in many respects contracted in their views, and judged of the whole Union as they would of a school-district. Too little allowance was made by many for the necessities of a recognized and permanent institution, and the bitterness of sectionalism usurped the place of reason.

The negro race is one of the instrumentalities with which Providence is working out the great problem of human destiny. The more reasonable of Northern abolitionists concede that this race is incapable of civilization, saving when associated with a higher race ; and that, as a general thing, the Africans in the United States are incapable of discharging the duties of citizens. None but bigoted fanatics refuse to recognize the negro's inferiority and incapacity for self-government ; although England, who was unwilling to acknowledge her legitimate children's right of self-government, is now ardent in supporting it in Africans ! The history of the African negroes is known as much as is that of any uncivilized and unlettered people ; slightly known by external observation. The interior of Africa has never been, and, on account of its extreme barbarism, cannot well be explored. In the country of the negroes it is estimated that there are some fifty millions of blacks, who, for untold centuries, have made no sensible advancement in the arts of civilized life. The negro should be tried by his native condition. Africa is his home ; the place where he was created, where he passed his infancy, and has advanced to full age. He was made for the climate, and in Africa is in his chosen theatre for action. But civilization was not an achievement designed for the negro as a race; it is clear enough that he was intended as a parasite being, and created for connection with, and subserviency to, another race. He is patient, laborious, faithful, friendly, and adhesive, and, when brought into connection with a superior people, at once springs into a new and higher existence. He has those aptitudes that render him contented and happy with a master; and every capacity with which he is blessed marks him as the subordinate and servant of a superior race. No person, who has a moderate knowledge of the world, can be deceived as to the negro's natural abilities. His lack of intellectual organs, and his peculiar organization, are significant and unquestionable facts, and should never be overlooked or slighted by the upright citizen, or the one who would treat the negro question with fairness and justice. From ignorant bigots and fanatics reason or common sense is not expected; but the intelligent and upright should accustom themselves to weigh every important fact before pronouncing on a question in which the rights of his neighbor are involved.

In the great exodus of people from the Old World to America during the sixteenth and seventeenth centuries, Africa, providentially, or accidentally, sent forth her millions. This transfer of servants from Africa to America was one of the great events of an eventful age. Like the art of printing, the mariner's compass, gunpowder, and steam, African servitude has been, in the hands of Providence, a necessary instrumentality in the great progress of human affairs which has eventuated in the birth of the freest, happiest, most prosperous, and most perfect republic that man has ever enjoyed.

If New England's boundaries enclosed our entire republic, the sentiments of New England people in regard to negro slavery would be more reasonable; but it should be recollected that this republic verges well towards the equator. The establishment of this republic all acknowledge to have been an era in modern civilization. And what one thing, steam not excepted, has done more to promote the arts of peace, and to advance in wealth, refinement, and civilization, every race upon earth, and especially our Saxon cousins in England, than the cultivation of the cotton-plant in the South? As it was destined that this Union, an instrumentality so divine, should embrace many latitudes, — perhaps the whole continent, — it was necessary that people adapted to its various physical qualities should inhabit it. The rich fields of the South were indispensable to the world; but it is clear that they could never have been occupied and improved without the conjunction, in the relationship now sustained by them, of the white and black races. The immense blessings, by the union conferred on the black race, are only equalled by the benefits conferred on the world by Southern productions; the white race in the South is less benefited by the operation. Every impartial traveller is filled with admiration at beholding the negro's improvement in every respect.* Everywhere the servants are seen, as

* There is a class of people who are ever flattering themselves by depicting the miseries of others. We have heard poor wretches, who never scarcely saw a dollar in their lives, speak with great emphasis of the poor whites in the South! The wonder is that there are any whites there at all. It is no place for them. Nature, for their presumption, annually sends her plague to sweep off thousands. And, as labor is impossible for the Caucassian in a nearly

a general thing, well clad, well fed, well used, contented, happy, mannerly, orderly, and exceedingly addicted to religious exercises. When contrasted with Africa, the African settlements in the South resemble Paradise. If the relationship between these two races, of master and servant, be ordained by Providence, it appears, from every indication afforded by the works of nature and human experience, that it is designed for only a particular climate. The negro and the cotton-plant are perhaps inseparable. They were both indigenous to Africa;

tropical latitude, why does he venture there? If he goes there he must expect to be poor, as to his race it is the fiat of the climate. Of course, there are locations which, from well-known physical causes, form exceptions. But, as to the cotton and sugar countries, it may safely be said there is no field for white labor, and the white laborer should keep away. There is but one condition on which it is possible for the white man to cultivate the cotton fields of the South, and that is by the use of negro slaves. If he has not the means of purchasing them, he had better seek other parts of the country. To a limited extent white labor is honorably and profitably employed in the extreme South; but the mass of labor is, and ever must be, performed by the blacks. Georgia, in 1735, or thereabouts, was settled by the Moravians, an exemplary class of Protestant religionists from Germany. They were highly anti-slavery in their feelings, and would not allow the slave-trade to be opened amongst them. In this they were in advance of their Puritan brethren in New England who had largely participated in that trade and its fruits; but the Moravians were exceedingly bitter against the institution. But a short time induced other sentiments. Slavery was soon found to be a necessity, — indispensable, — and, on applying to their spiritual guides in the homeland, they were told that they could without sin make use of slaves, provided they would use them well. But the example of the Moravians will have no weight with a bigoted Northern or British abolitionist; nor would the example, experience, or testimony, of the most worthy and pious of New England men who have had occasion to dwell in the South, and perceive the necessities of negro servitude for that clime.

the latter to the South. The servitude of the negro is peculiar. From the nature of his organization his services can only be valuable in a clime resembling that of his origin, and a more temperate latitude should never be burthened and cursed with his incumbrance. Virginia, Kentucky, and Missouri, have for a long while excluded, by their repulsive black servitude, energies that would have rendered those states vastly wealthy and powerful. Instead of quarrelling about abstract and impracticable ideas, the statesman should view things, and act in reference to them, as they are.

Fortunately, or unfortunately, the United States government has always possessed a large quantity of territory. The constitutional power of Congress to govern the territories as it pleases has always been claimed. It would be no more than reasonable to allow that Congress can make binding laws for the control of its territories; still, many claim that the settlers in the territories are sovereigns, and have a right to adopt their own institutions. But as to states made from these territories another question arises. The Constitution permits the admission of new states on terms of equality with the original ones and on no other terms. Therefore, when admitted, the new states may be as independent as the old ones, and adopt just such institutions, provided they be republican, as they may prefer. On the application of Missouri for admission, the North said to her that she should not come into the Union unless she should do so under a pledge to become a free state. This was a fetter not attached to any other state in the Union, and could not constitutionally have been bound to Missouri. The South were indignant, and well might have been, for the reasons here advanced.

CHAPTER XVI.

SPREAD OF ANTI-SLAVERY VIEWS IN THE NORTH. — INFLUENCE OF ENGLAND. — WHEN MADE A PARTY QUESTION THE SLAVERY ISSUES MUST NECESSARILY RENDER PARTIES SECTIONAL. — CLAIM OF ANTI-SLAVERY MEN. — ABSURDITY OF THE FEAR OF THE EXTENSION OF SLAVERY INTO NEW TERRITORIES. — CANNOT COMPETE WITH WHITE LABOR, SAVING UNDER THE PROTECTION OF A SOUTHERN SUN. — EXCLUSION OF SLAVES FROM TERRITORIES ADAPTED TO THEIR LABOR CRUELTY TO THEM. — WHITE LABOR WILL IN TIME ASSUME ITS OWN DOMAINS, INCLUDING VIRGINIA, KENTUCKY, AND MISSOURI. — SLAVERY LIMITED TO ITS LEGITIMATE THEATRE. — HYPOCRISY OF ENGLAND. — HER SELFISH PURPOSES AND CRAFTY POLICY. — ANTI-SLAVERY MISREPRESENTATIONS PUBLISHED IN AMERICA BY BRITISH GOLD. — THE ABOMINABLE WICKEDNESS OF SUCH FALSE REPRESENTATIONS. — FALSE VIEWS OF NEGROES INCULCATED. — SLAVEHOLDERS TRADUCED, ETC.

THE application for admission into the Union by Missouri aroused into action the gradually increasing anti-slavery feeling of the North. The rights or wrongs of the question, as tried by principles of constitutional law, had not been considered; but the moral wrong of slavery in the abstract had been largely discussed in the forum of conscience, and there was scarcely a man in the country not ready, guided solely by his sentiments, to act decisively in the matter. Questions of constitutional law, in connection with slavery, have since been canvassed by the people, and a somewhat sounder doctrine attained by the more intelligent and conservative portion of the community. Although there have always been multitudes opposed to the admission of any more slave states, the more intelligent, reasonable, and just portion of the Northern people have been disposed to recognize the right of the states to be admitted to act their own pleasure in the adoption of their domestic institutions.

As the anti-slavery party of the North, which imbibed its sentiments from the anti-slavery societies of England and America, has, for the last few years, received a rapid growth, and is threatening a commanding position in the councils of the nation, the wisdom and justice of its principles ought to be examined and weighed by that portion of the American people capable of dispassionate judgment. The pretensions of this party are extremely assuming, as it arrogates to itself religion, humanity, and virtue. In its political warfare it so much resembles the old crusades, that its object seems to be rather a battle for religious faith, than a contest for political rights. And then, again, its leading spirits appear too contemptuous and defiant for sincere Christians, and their demeanor and exhibitions of temper anything but saint-like. However, as the literature of Old and New England has for years breathed a hatred for slavery, which has had its effects upon millions of Americans, the anti-slavery champions, though wolves in sheep's clothing, are loved and adored "for their cause." Gullibility is an attribute, or quality, of a goodly number of the human family, and no portion is easier duped than that which professes superior sanctity, benevolence, and humanity.

That a political party based on the question of slavery could exist in this country, would seem strange to an indifferent and intelligent spectator. To be effectual, it must subvert the Constitution. Such a party is essentially hostile to our government. Many of the more intelligent and daring, and probably more honest, of the anti-slavery party, openly proclaim their object to be the overthrow of the Constitution. The pretence that a political party, based on slavery ideas, can wish to accomplish anything short of the object of those ultraists, is an absurdity. Those who proclaim disunion openly are eyed with distant but cautious reserve by the other sort of anti-slavery people. These last have a mighty work upon their hands, and, in its accomplishment, enlist a large share of the pious and good. No man was ever yet ready to see himself in the light of a dupe, nor willing, when the discovery should be made, to acknowledge himself such. Conceit is a fatal defect in the composition of man, and binds him to error more powerfully than any other passion. If men were more inclined to question the perfection of their own ideas,— were more disposed to distrust the correctness of their conclusions, and the propriety of their course of action,— knaves and hypocrites would find less encouragement for their craft, and free institutions repose on a firmer basis.

In the nature of things an anti-slavery party must be a sectional one, the tendencies of which can be nothing but strife and civil war. But let the real tendency of a party be what it may, if it make captivating professions, it will draw into its bosom the unthinking multitude, especially if led by persons of some popularity. Large masses of the Northern people have had instilled into their minds the idea that they have something to accomplish politically in regard to slavery. They think this is to be done, not in subversion of, but under, the Constitution of the United States. A more dangerous error they could not well embrace, and they must eradicate it from their hearts, or entail it, with civil war and anarchy, upon their posterity. When that Constitution was adopted, all that the people could do, with regard to slavery, was at an end. Every attempt since made by anti-slavery people has resulted against the cause of negro humanity, and been in subserviency to the great design of England to produce a dismemberment of the Union. And what do the great mass of the Northern people really and candidly claim in regard to the question? They say, first, they do not wish to disturb slavery in the states where it exists. Secondly, they do not think emancipation of the slaves of the South a practicable or advisable act, providing the power were granted; that the three millions of ignorant, stupid, and indolent negroes would be a nuisance to themselves and the country, if set at liberty. But, thirdly, they say, their eyes in frenzy rolling, "no further extension of slave territory." This is the great party war-cry of the present day, as it was of 1820.

The greatest objection to this cry is that it is senseless. That this country should be divided into two great parties on such a proposition — divided in a manner to endanger its peace and perpetuity — is absolute madness. Men of common sense must recognize the fact that the negroes increase with rapidity, and that, while in servitude at least, this increase will continue. From about half a million in 1790, their number had increased to about three millions in 1850; nearly doubling once in fifteen years. At this rate, in 1865 there will be six millions, and in 1880 twelve millions, and twenty-five millions in 1900. The fact of their increase cannot be avoided, and must bring along with it consequences that should be provided for by the statesman. The philanthropist should be humane. He must see that either now, or at some near future day, unless he be a demon, he will demand one of two things, — either the emancipation of the slaves in the states where they are, and their transportation to Africa, or the provision of new territories for their labor. No one would wish, fifty years hence, to see millions of negroes in a few Southern States doomed to wretchedness and starvation. Or, does the philanthropist think that, by confining them to a few and fast impoverishing states, the masters will soon be compelled to set their negroes free? But what, in such an event, would become of these wretched beings? When the white man can no longer make his labor profitable, and be able to take care of him, will the negro be able, if turned adrift, to take care of himself? If slavery is hateful, and it is desirable that it should cease in the states where now existing, is it a reasonable, a manly, a Christian, or a humane design to seek to confine it in a particular locality until it shall expire by the force of starvation? Suppose we admit, with the fanatic, that the white man of the South is of no account, and that his destruction, in such a catastrophe, is not to be regarded or regretted; does such an issue of slavery promise anything for the slave? The cotton and sugar plantations of the old states may become exhausted and sterile, while in the South-west will be rich and untouched tracts of soil capable of supporting millions of negroes in abundance and comfort; but the Northern philanthropist is ready to forbid its devotion to the welfare of those degraded beings. No; insane with a single idea, he thinks the increase of slave territory is an increase of slaves. This, in one sense, is so. As the comfort and happiness of the negro are increased, he increases in numbers. But who can be called a philanthropist that would abridge the negro's comforts in order to render him less prolific, and extinguish slavery by destroying the race? And yet, at what else is enlightened and philanthropic New England, under the guide of Old England, driving? What does she mean by her insane cry of no more slave territory? If she means to exclude slavery from territory adapted to white labor, she may hush her cry of alarm. White labor will in time take care of itself. The negro has no protective tariff for his labor, but a skin that will endure a tropical sun.

The Missouri question brought to light the anti-slavery feeling of the North, the extent and degree of intensity of which took the world by surprise. Its first manifestation was to strike down the constitutional rights of new states. The anti-slavery sentiment has increased greatly since 1820; but no conservative anti-slavery statesman even now disputes the right of new states to shape their institutions to suit themselves; and none but factious sectionalists and fanatics take the position, occupied by the North at the time of the Missouri controversy, that the general government should dictate in the matter. There are probably vast numbers in the North, at the present day, who stand on the ground taken in 1820; but they are not the intelligent and patriotic portion of the Northern people. Subsequent agitations have brought the Constitution to view, and its plain provisions have had weight with the honest and considerate; but as upright, patriotic, and conservative statesmen are losing their influence with the masses; as the teachings of such men as Washington, Jefferson, Madison, Adams, Benton, Clay, and Webster, among the dead, and of Buchanan, Crittenden, Everett, and Fillmore, among the living, are no longer regarded by the multitude, who prefer the excited and revolutionary doctrines of a new class of politicians who claim to be governed by a higher law than constitutions,—no one can tell how soon the sectional strife, so long cherished by British writers, and promulgated by British gold, may ripen into civil war. The position of the North in 1820 was so clearly in defiance of Southern and state rights, that a reäction, especially among the more upright and intelligent of the Northern people, soon ensued. This reäction was felt, to a great extent, amongst the people. The political leaders of those days were disposed to be guided by principles of constitutional law, and their influence was such that a radical abolitionist found for a while but little favor in the land.*

England watched the course of events in the United States with profound interest. She early saw that the

* While the political leaders, of whom mention is made, comprising such men as Clay, Webster, Calhoun, Benton, etc., were upon the stage of action, the abolition leaders were greatly depressed by the weight of their influence. Hence the feeling of relief, in short, exultation, at the decease of those eminent statesmen. We were told that the Rev. H. W. Beecher, some few years ago, in a lecture at Northfield, in this state (Vermont), set forth and inculcated the idea that it is fortunate for the country that such great men as Clay and Webster have passed away, as their weight and influence with the people had a tendency to close the popular mind to the teachings of others, and retard the march of useful reformations. The feeling of the reverend gentleman is perfectly natural. We have read of the poet who regretted the existence of such authors as Shakspeare and Milton, as, were it not for the admiration of the people for them, his own productions would be regarded. And people now will applaud in Faneuil Hall what would not have been listened to there twenty years ago.

solution of the great question of Democracy, in this country, was involved in the slavery question. From a crushing tyrant, and a relentless oppressor, she at once became the champion of negro freedom, and, Peter-the-Hermit-like, preached and intrigued for it throughout the world. Her leading anti-slavery characters have ever held intercourse with American agitators, and subscriptions in England have been freely made to forward the cause of humanity in the United States. Her sincerity has been proved to Americans by her voluntary emancipation of her slaves in the West Indies, which cost her not much less than a hundred million of dollars; and this country never saw any but motives of humanity in the glorious act! It is true, all see that Britain's oppression of her own children at home, where a powerful monarchy, and a cold-blooded and crushing aristocracy, or nobility, extinguish the last lingering hope of freedom and happiness; and that her merciless and despotic subjugation, robbery, and slavery, of scores of millions of unoffending East Indians, are not exactly consistent with her professions of regard for negro liberty; but the magnanimous American philanthropist is never disposed to analyze the motives of an act that seems to bear evidence in favor of his own merit, and to add to his own and the glory of his hobby.

The teachings of England, both by precept and example, are now beginning to be appreciated. Her policy, as demonstrated by experience, is false not only in its ostensible, but also in its secret theory. Her project of subverting American slavery by her contemplated system of Africanizing the West Indies, will never prove successful, unless, indeed, her influence in the North shall overbalance the conservative and constitutional sentiment of the Union. To bind the North to her policy it is necessary that the agitation of slavery should continue; and to keep this agitation alive, it is necessary that the sentiments of Northern people should be properly educated. She understands well enough that the great battles of the world are more controlled by ideas than by guns and bayonets. Without the employment of her writers and speakers in the unprincipled work of blackening the character of Napoleon Bonaparte, by falsely charging him with every debauchery and crime imaginable, the English people would never have sustained the British government in its years of war, and its expenditure of countless millions, and sacrifice of thousands of soldiers, to maintain legitimacy, and restore a Bourbon to his throne. The struggle was noble in the British monarchy, because the monarchical system of Europe requires mutual support in such cases, the non-observance of which would not only be fatal as an example, but infamous as a breach of faith. The British government schools her own people constantly to sentiments calculated to promote her domestic and foreign policy. Fortunately for herself, she thinks, she finds America a promising pupil, over whose destiny she can exercise control. It becomes a religious people that they should cherish peace; therefore we are taught not to meddle with the wars of the world. It is unbecoming a Christian people so to do; and England herself never goes to war! Free trade is, and for years has been, most extensively inculcated among Americans by England, and to promote free-trade doctrines in the United States, it is well known that British gold has been liberally used. The preaching here, too, must be sincere, as probably England never cripples her importations with duties! That she should instruct Northern people to detest slavery is no more than should be expected. Her tactics have not always been the most just and honorable; but they have been based on necessity, and, as in the case of slandering Napoleon, justifiable on the easy moral principle that the end sanctifies the means.

The Northern men, women, and children, who weep over the woes of the enslaved sons of Africa, little suspect how entirely delusive and unreal are the causes of their tears. They only know that they have seen the true accounts of slave tortures in veracious books, and read them in papers; and they are sure that slaves are innocent victims, and the masters monsters. Frightful cases of the cruelty of masters are freely reported. Some years ago we saw a pamphlet, or book, professing to give a thousand such; and the Key of Uncle Tom's Cabin is said to give a large assortment of that kind of evidence. Unfortunately, human nature being far from angelic, many cases of cruelty do occur. All the cruelty in the world, however, is not crowded into the slave states of America. Most diabolical cases often occur in the North, and in England, even. But the abolitionist will say that in the North such abuses are not tolerated — that there they are punished. And in this consists the cheat of abolitionism. Those anti-slavery tracts and papers that report cases of Southern cruelty to slaves, never mention the punishment inflicted by Southern laws upon the wrong-doers. An entirely false impression is produced upon the minds of the unthinking by such details of outrages, gathered from a large extent of country, reaching over a series of years, and all pressed upon the reader as evidences of the treatment of slaves by their masters. If such things were permitted by law in slave states the institution would be as barbarous as it was in the ancient governments. But everybody, of any information and common sense, knows that the Southern people are civilized, humane, and Christian. That acts of cruelty to slaves are punishable by Southern laws, is not only true, but there is also in the South an extremely proper public spirit in regard to the obligation of masters to use the objects of their trust and care with kindness and humanity. Perhaps an instance which fell under our own observation will illustrate the whole subject. In 1839, in a Southern city, a policeman heard cries of distress in a building, and, on entering, found that a slave girl had been severely whipped. The stripes upon her back were visible, in places cutting through the skin, and her shoes were filled with blood which had flowed from her wounds. The master was at once cited before the police court. There was not a person to be met with who was not filled with indignation, and the tribunal was crowded with excited and indignant slaveholders, as the court visited the inhuman wretch with the severe penalties of the law. But the money he was obliged to pay was a small affair, an honorable man would judge, compared with the contempt from the virtuous and good that his barbarity drew upon him. The newspapers reported the case, with proper comments on the offence. But, in 1842, the full details of the outrage were published, amongst others, in an anti-slavery tract, and circulated in the North, to enlighten Northern men, women, and children, on the subject of slave institutions. The case was published in the "Thousand

Cases" spoken of, to convey the idea that such things were practised generally, and tolerated in the South, and no intimation was given that such an act was regarded or treated as criminal, or that the master incurred any punishment, or rebuke, on account of his conduct. If it is necessary, for the purposes of monarchy, that the people of the North should be taught to hate those of the South, England is right in treating the latter as she did Napoleon, that is, in lying about and slandering them.

The ingenuity of the enemies of our country is manifested in many ways. Among other resorts of such persons, high-wrought fictions are invented, depicting the anguish of fraternal and parental separations. It is not supposed that the Southern people have any common understanding or practice of what is most tolerable in this matter; they are depicted as demons, who are less influenced by interest than by a native love of acts of atrocity. Neither is any allowance made for the natural character of the negro. It is not considered that such a thing as paternal, fraternal, or marital relationship is wholly unknown to the negro in his native state. In his African home, the negro, in infancy, may have filial, and enjoy the smiles of parental, affections. There is no animal that is destitute of this. But in the adult state, such a thing as parent, or brother, or a wife, is not known. The existence of such relationships amongst negroes in America is the gift of slavery, and would undoubtedly cease without it. The only civilization the negro can ever sustain must be while in connection with the whites, and, unless in very limited numbers, in subjection to them. In Hayti the negroes, since their emancipation, are degenerating into barbarism.

The marriage relation, tolerably preserved in servitude, has now become a mockery, and the promiscuous intercourse practised in Africa is prevalent.

Not satisfied with such atrocious misrepresentations as these, the amalgamating abolitionists of the North, under the pay and management of England, hold Southern men up to scorn as guilty of the grossest acts of lust and debauchery. Slavery is represented as a system of concubinage! That there are many instances, especially in the Southern cities, where the debased from all nations centre, where white and black amalgamate, is true; but the illicit intercourse, taken as to the whole black and white population, is not a thousandth time as extensive as is the same immoral practice carried on in Northern states between individuals of the purely white race. So, if there is any uncommon guilt in the people of the South, it is guilt in matters of taste — in the selection of color. This should not be considered a reproach in the eyes of an amalgamating abolitionist of New or Old England; but consistency is not a jewel when it is the exception, and not the rule, in one's principles. Slavery, since the foundation of the world, has been more or less a system of concubinage, until negro slavery came into being. If the negroes were really created for slaves, Providence provided for the preservation of their virtue, by making them, in form and feature, objects of repugnance and abhorrence. Still, in the imaginations of dreaming Northern damsels and Jonathans, negresses are painted as the lovely victims of the passions of brutal masters, forced by the lash to submit to their tyrannic lust! And that slavery in the South is a system of debauchery and crime is quite generally credited by England's easy dupes in the North.

But the Missouri struggle ended, in the Congress of 1820 and '21, by a compromise. The Missouri Compromise, so called, is too well known to everybody to need a description; it was an arrangement by which the South made concessions, and gained nothing. The admission of Missouri with slavery was her constitutional right; but, to gain it, the South had to yield the right of carrying slavery into a large portion of the Territory of the United States.

CHAPTER XVII.

JOHN QUINCY ADAMS SECRETARY OF STATE UNDER MONROE. — DESIGNATED BY MONROE FOR HIS SUCCESSOR. — PRESIDENTIAL ASPIRANTS. — CONGRESSIONAL CAUCUS NOMINATIONS. — MR. CRAWFORD'S NOMINATION. — MARTIN VAN BUREN, JACKSON, AND CALHOUN. — NO ELECTION BY THE PEOPLE. — ELECTION BY THE HOUSE. — ADAMS ELECTED BY CLAY AND HIS FRIENDS. — PARTY SPIRIT REVIVED. — FRIENDS OF CLAY AND ADAMS UNITE IN A PARTY. — THE WHIG PARTY. — JACKSONISM AND ITS SUCCESS. — ADMINISTRATION OF J. Q. ADAMS. — CHANGE OF NEW ENGLAND ON QUESTION OF TARIFF. — CHANGE IN THE SOUTH. — ELECTION OF JACKSON. — J. C. CALHOUN VICE-PRESIDENT, ETC.

During the administration of Mr. Monroe the country for the first time since the administration of Washington was free from the bitterness and strife of political parties. The second election of Mr. Monroe was without any organized opposition. The old Federal party had been completely stranded. The scattered elements of that organization existed in the country, but they were much dispersed, and in a great measure had become absorbed in the more liberal and enlightened Republicanism which sprung up during and after the war. While the measures advocated by Clay, Lowndes, Calhoun, and Crawford, were embraced by the Republican party, there was no necessity for a Federal organization, as they were generally Federal measures; that is, they were such measures as Hamilton's policy embraced, although not such as leading Federalists of a later day advocated.

For a successor Mr. Monroe had indicated, as his favorite, John Quincy Adams, by appointing him his Secretary of State. Mr. Adams was regarded as an unexceptionable Republican, or Democrat, and as such, Mr. Madison, in 1809, sent him as Minister to Russia. But the Republicans were far from being harmonious upon the subject of the successorship. There were several leading Democrats, whose names have been mentioned, who were ambitious for presidential honors. From early times it had been customary for the members of Congress, in caucuses called for the purpose, to nominate candidates for the presidency; but to select a candidate to succeed Mr. Monroe, that time-honored practice was, by a majority of the Republican members of Congress, departed from. It was seen at once that a majority of the members could not be concentrated upon any one of the aspirants, and it was therefore deemed unadvisable to resort to that machinery for a candidate. In fact, the result of the caucus which nominated Mr. Monroe to succeed Mr. Madison excited some surprise, and probably disinclined many from a further resort to such nominations. It had been the general feeling of the country that Mr. Monroe was to be the candidate; still, the industry of Mr. Crawford's friends amongst the members of Congress came near securing him the nomination.

Notwithstanding the Republicans, as a general thing, had resolved to make no congressional nomination for the election of 1824, a portion of them, and that portion a considerable minority, concluded to act otherwise. The friends of Mr. Crawford were not disposed to abide the will of the majority of the Democratic congressmen in the premises, and, consequently, had a caucus called for the nomination of a candidate. Of course, only the friends of Mr. Crawford attended, and his name was duly heralded to the country as the regularly nominated candidate of the party, in the mode in which candidates had usually been put forth in previous times. Of the two hundred and sixty-one members, Mr. C. received the votes of sixty-four, those being the only members who attended the convention; but, as no congressional nomination of the Republicans had ever been defeated, Mr. Crawford's friends made great calculations on the movement. The person who engineered this operation was Martin Van Buren, senator from the State of New York. Mr. Van Buren's subsequent history is well known, and many will say that the course taken by him in regard to Mr. Crawford's nomination was characteristic. But that gentleman's day of political expectations is past, and it would not be decorous to bring forward unnecessarily any of his acts which would be likely to revive in the mind of the reader forgotten animosities. All know that he was a successful politician; and although he may have been indebted much to his intrigues for his triumphs, he was by no means so big an ignoramus, nor so enormous a knave, as depicted by his political opponents in 1840.

Mr. Van Buren, it was said, was a Federalist during the early part of the late war with England, and supported Clinton, the peace candidate, against Mr. Madison. However, he soon was found in the Republican ranks, and was justly regarded as an able and long-headed politician. His enemies have charged him with always adapting himself with great versatility to popular principles, instead, like Washington, Hamilton, Madison, Clay, and Webster, of striving to make the public mind bend to such principles and measures as the public good should require. If these charges were correct, they only establish his shrewdness. It was the only manner in which he could win honors and gain office from the people. It is possible that Mr. Van Buren never aspired to the honors of high statesmanship, — that success in political life was all he sought. If so, he showed himself master of his art, and attained what much greater and better men could not accomplish. Let no man who desires to rise to high office in a popular government, ever dare to express sentiments distasteful to popular prejudice. The theory of Democratic governments is that the people are always right, and that the statesman who shall advocate measures not in accordance with the popular opinion, must not be trusted nor honored. Washington was elected President, it is true; but he left the office with dishonor in the minds of many. It happened to be the good fortune of Jefferson honestly to possess political principles and opinions exceedingly flattering to the feelings of the generality; and it should not be said that he espoused them for popular effect. He lived at a period when his peculiar principles were of vital necessity, and history shows him to have been a public benefactor. Madison and Monroe were considered the exponents of Jeffersonian Democracy, and, under the shelter of the Jeffersonian dynasty, administered the government with an independence not equalled by any subsequent administration.

But since those eminent statesmen occupied the presidential chair, what have been the men our people have delighted to honor with the proud title of President? We should except from slighting remarks those heroes who fought so bravely for their country, — Jackson, Harrison, and Taylor, — for, although not statesmen, nor versed in public affairs, they were patriots and good men, and the honors accorded to them were merited. But experience, wisdom, virtue, sound statesmanship, and manly independence, have not received favor from the people. Politicians have had the public ear, filled the popular eye, and enjoyed our suffrages, almost without an exception. It ill befits us, therefore, to inveigh against Mr. Van Buren for being a mere politician, until we can show ourselves capable of appreciating and rewarding political virtues of a higher order.

The candidates, with the exception of Jackson, were all able and experienced statesmen. The appearance of this gentleman in the field was, at the time, thought by the other candidates to be a piece of presumptuousness. They could scarcely believe that the general was serious. He was known to be a brave general, and had immortalized his name by his victory at New Orleans; but, as he was entirely the reverse of all the other candidates as to statesmanship, and had often previously, in declining offices, frankly acknowledged his incompetency, and had been noted for his aptitude for camp and border life, rather than employment in cabinets, it was thought hardly reasonable that he should claim, as the reward of one fortunate battle, elevation to the presidency. But, nevertheless, his appearance in the field as a competitor was immediately found to be no insignificant affair. Mr. Calhoun at once took himself out of the way, and was placed upon the Jackson ticket as candidate for Vice-President. Eastern people entertained a sectional preference for Adams, and the West and

South were contended for by the three other candidates. Mr. Van Buren's influence was recognized, and Crawford's friends trusted to him to secure New York for their candidate. He certainly made a powerful effort for this, but without success. The state cast two-thirds of her electoral votes for Mr. Adams, and sealed the fate of Mr. Crawford. The encouraging prospects of Mr. Clay were blighted by the popularity of Jackson in the Western and some of the Southern States. The canvass became animated; but it was a contention for preference among four candidates enjoying the same political principles, or, at least, belonging to the same party.

As had been expected, there was no election by the people. Jackson received ninety-nine votes, Adams eighty-eight, Crawford forty-one, and Clay thirty-seven; consequently the election by the House was limited to the three first named. The election in the House came off early in 1825, and was intensely exciting. Mr. Clay was no longer in the field, and it was seen that he and his friends would have the power of deciding the contest between the other candidates. Of course Mr. Crawford stood no chance, saving in case of some scarcely expected turn of affairs, as in event the friends of Adams or Jackson should be obliged to select him as a Hobson's choice. Mr. Clay and Mr. Crawford were friends, and Mr. Crawford's friends entertained hopes of obtaining the support of the former and of his adherents; but a recent stroke of the paralysis incapacitated the latter for the duties of the office, and Mr. Clay had no alternative but to vote for Jackson or Adams. Of his repugnance to the support of Jackson, Mr. Clay had never made any secret; and when the controversy became narrowed down to Jackson and Adams, the Kentucky statesman had no hesitation in giving his support to the latter.

The result of this election revived the bitterness of party spirit. At once the hostility between the Adams and Jackson men became fiercer and more irreconcilable than that which formerly raged between the old John Adams and Jefferson parties. The Crawford and Calhoun parties became absorbed by Jackson's; and Mr. Clay's friends supported Mr. Adams. And thus was formed the party organization, which, although at first called National Republican, afterwards took the name of Whig, and which continued a powerful, conservative, and national party until the presidential election of 1852.

Electioneering, after the election to the presidency of John Quincy Adams, took a new form, as well as a new spirit. But the Jackson campaigns are too fresh in the minds of most people to need description here. On one side were paraded, on banners, hickory brooms and other devices; on the other, in derision, coffin-handbills, gambling implements, and fighting cocks. Jackson was regarded by the masses as the true representative of the Jeffersonian Democracy, and Adams was at once placed under the ban of Federalism. The greater part of the old Federalists, it is true, supported him; but his party also received into its ranks many who had been born and bred Republicans or Democrats.

The mystery of Jacksonism was not at that day, nor is it now, really known. A party of greater vitality, energy and enthusiasm, was scarcely ever known. The hero of New Orleans was one of those men who seemed born to command. Unqualified obedience to the chief was a test of true Democracy. No matter how learned, experienced, wise, talented and prominent, he might be, no statesman, politician, office-holder or editor, in the Democratic ranks, could retain his standing a moment, if he should incur a frown from that singular man. His will was law to his party, and that party became the country. Never did Cromwell rule England with more absolute power than General Jackson governed the United States. Of course there were, and always will be, different opinions as to the merits of his administration; but no one at the present day doubts the exalted patriotism of that hero. If there were, in his administration, any errors, they were errors of the head, not of the heart.

The Adams, or Federal, or Whig party was overwhelmed by the new-born Democratic power. Every one has heard of the famous calumny, charging a bargain between Adams and Clay, and no one at this day doubts its monstrous injustice, not to say wickedness. But the credit that that improbable charge obtained was attributable to the character and spirit of the times. As the fury of the blind and idolatrous party spirit of those times abated, and men began to exercise their reason and consciences, more justice was done to the Whigs who dared to take a stand against the prevailing power of the day. At this day neither John Quincy Adams nor Henry Clay needs any vindication from the charges they were made to suffer under during the Jackson administration, and therefore the particulars of that calumny need not be brought forth from the obscurity to which their infamy consigns them.

The administration of Mr. Adams has ever been

regarded a model of dignity, economy and purity. There was scarcely any proscriptiveness in his appointments to office. In the main, his administration was based on such Republican principles as had been entertained by Madison and Monroe; and, in the presidential campaign of 1828, the contest seemed to be in regard to men, rather than touching measures, or principles. It is true, Jackson was put forth as the embodiment of Jeffersonian Democracy, and Adams was characterized as tainted with Federal blood. It was during the administration of Mr. Adams that the policy of protection reached its culminating point, as the tariff of 1828 was the last enactment for protection, intended as such, ever made by our government. During Madison's administration the West and South had favored protection, as a measure demanded by the best interests of the whole country. The ability and patriotism of the eminent Republicans who demonstrated the necessity and policy of protection were commanding; and, on reading the discussions of those days, it will be seen that the Republican statesmen kept in view sound principles of political economy, rather than party or sectional ideas. In the East all acts for protection had been opposed, as it was considered that such measures would put a restraint on commerce. Webster had voted and made speeches against the tariff of 1824; but sustained the act of 1828. The election of Adams by the aid of Mr. Clay, who was the champion of the American system, as it was called, had no doubt some effect in reconciling Mr. Adams' New England friends to the doctrine of protection; and as, under the prior tariff acts, New England had begun to invest capital in manufactures, a continuance of the protective system was deemed necessary, and the passage of the act of 1828 required, as in a measure perfecting that system. Mr. Webster at this time had but recently taken his seat in the United States Senate. The large mass of the Massachusetts delegation in the House voted against the tariff of 1828. The tariff of 1824 received less support from the extreme Southern States than did the tariff of 1816, and the act of 1828 was quite earnestly opposed by some Southern statesmen. The most of the leading Republicans had approved of the doctrine of protection, and such men as Jackson, R. M. Johnson, Thomas H. Benton, Martin Van Buren, Silas Wright, and James Buchanan, were found voting for the tariffs of 1824 and 1828.

The passage of the tariff bill of 1828 increased the Southern opposition to the Adams and Clay administration, as portions of the South at that time had begun to look upon the doctrine of protection as injurious to Southern interests. Parties had not, it is true, made the question a matter of political test. Jackson, although he had voted for the tariff of 1824, was supported for the presidency, in the campaign of 1828, by the free-trade portion of the Southern people; but subsequent events soon rendered the question of protection a party test.

Mr. Adams, as has been said, adopted the conciliatory policy. Mr. Clay, who had been a competitor for the presidency, accepted the Secretaryship of State. Another powerful rival, Mr. Crawford, was offered the office of Secretary of War; but, as he declined, a friend of his, Mr. Barbor, was placed in that department. Mr. McLean, a Jacksonian, was made Postmaster General. But the mild policy of Mr. Adams had but little effect towards conciliating the opposition which his vigorous enemies had aroused against him. No sooner had Mr. Clay manifested his preference for Mr. Adams, and, by accepting the secretaryship under him, united his party with that of the administration, than, as a necessary result, a fusion of the other two parties took place. Through large portions of the country the Jackson fever swept like a prairie fire. The hero of New Orleans was of course triumphantly elected, receiving one hundred and seventy-eight out of two hundred and sixty-one votes; Mr. Adams receiving only eighty-three. It is true the disparity between the popular votes received by the two candidates was not so great; but even there the majority for Jackson was signal.

John C. Calhoun was elected Vice-President. It will be recollected that he ran for Vice-President on the Jackson ticket of 1824, and was not, like the general, defeated. Martin Van Buren became Secretary of State, and was probably the ablest statesman, with the exception of Calhoun and Crawford, that, in the breaking up of the Republican party, adhered to the Jackson wing. Calhoun was for the time being lodged in the vice-presidency, and Crawford's health precluded his ever more disturbing the dreams of ambitious aspirants to the presidential chair. Probably Jackson used the best material he had for his cabinet, at the head of which stood Mr. Van Buren. The second place was filled by Samuel D. Ingham, who was appointed to the Treasury Department. John H. Eaton was made Secretary of War, John Branch, Secretary of the Navy, Wm. L. Barry, Postmaster General, and John McPherson Berrien, Attorney General. At a subsequent period there were changes, and such men as Taney, Woodbury, and Cass, entered the cabinet. On account of a rupture between the President and Mr. Calhoun, the cabinet was soon remodelled. Some further account of this may be necessary.

CHAPTER XVIII.

PARTY PRINCIPLES UNDERGO A CHANGE. — WHIGS ADHERE TO THE MEASURES OF MADISON AND MONROE. — JACKSON PROPOSES TO RESTORE JEFFERSONIAN PRINCIPLES. — KITCHEN CABINET. — MARTIN VAN BUREN. — NEW TACTICS. — LEADING DEMOCRATS. — WHIGS. — MEASURES OF THE WHIGS. — POLITICAL IDOLATRY. — CAUSES OF JACKSON'S SUCCESS.

THE Jacksonian Democratic and the Whig parties were in many respects new parties. Both the Federal and the Republican parties had gone through changes since their origin, and, although vast numbers of the Federalists attached themselves to the Whig party, they did not adopt any new party principles, or other than those inculcated by Madison and Monroe. The departure from Republican principles was on the part of the Jackson Democracy. It is true, the leaders of this last-named party professed the necessity of restoring the Republican principles of early Jeffersonian Democracy, as it was thought there had been a dangerous departure. Consequently, Jefferson's opposition to the United States Bank was revived, and Jackson, in his first annual message, announced his hostility to it. That message was a pretty carefully drawn paper. As to protection and internal improvement, it was so worded as to allow, without any great violence, a construction favorable or unfavorable to these measures. That these measures were as anti-Jeffersonian as the bank policy, is true, as Jefferson opposed many of the measures proposed by his rival Hamilton; but to denounce measures that he had himself supported in Congress, was a step that even the resolute Jackson might well hesitate to take. The position of the message on the navy was also characteristic, if we are to suppose that that state paper was drawn by the Secretary of State. Jefferson had opposed the establishment of a navy. President Jackson's position in regard to the naval establishment was judicious, and sufficiently restrictive to satisfy the somewhat liberalized feeling of the Democracy upon the subject.

But the most interesting feature of Jackson's administration was found in his cabinet, — Kitchen Cabinet, as it was called in its day. The pictures of Major Jack Downing are too fresh in the reader's recollection to justify an attempt at an account of it. All that need be said is, that it was a brisk establishment. We have, perhaps, no reliable disclosures of the secrets of that cabinet, as possibly Downing's account will hardly pass for history. We can only draw our surmises from results or events. The presence of Mr. Van Buren in that domestic establishment was an undisputed fact. His connection with events, or influence in their production, cannot in all cases be demonstrated, because the secrets of the council-chamber have never been revealed. Mr. Benton was not privy to the doings of the *penetralia* or innermost recesses of the cabinet, and therefore his labored exculpation, in his Thirty Years in the United States Senate, of Mr. Van Buren from intrigues against Mr. Calhoun, is not to be regarded as decisive in the matter. Perhaps, on the other hand, the universal opinion at the time should not be considered as conclusive. One thing is very certain; if Mr. Van Buren espoused the cause of Jackson, shaped the policy of his administration, and engineered the plots and conspiracies of the day, with a view of attaining the presidency, no one can sneer at his efforts, or laugh at him for the result. Those usually laugh who win.

Mr. Van Buren brought into Jackson's cabinet a fiercer party spirit than ever had been entertained in any previous President's cabinet. The tactics of the Albany regency were transferred to the national administration. The proscriptiveness of the Democracy of New York, which had been excessive, was, with the elevation of Van Buren to a place in the President's cabinet, adopted in regard to office-holders under the general government. Removals became general. Under Washington and the elder Adams there had been but few,—some nine or ten under each,—and none at all on account of party spirit. Jefferson, under the extraordinary excitement of his times, made but thirty-nine; Madison but five; Monroe but nine; and John Quincy Adams but two; but thousands of removals were made by Jackson, and the practice of the present day, of making the change of administration a signal for rotation of office-holders, had its origin with his administration.

The Democrats, during and subsequent to the war with England, had been preëminent for able statesmen; but the more radical Democratic party that sprang into existence under Jackson found itself confronted with a powerful array of talent. The bad fame of Federalism was at that time at its height amongst the masses of the American people; and because the Federalists, as

17

a general thing, espoused the new organization, the Democratic leaders were quite successful in rendering the National Republicans, as they were called, unpopular, by charging them with Federalism. And with the Democracy there was no lack of ability. Martin Van Buren's talents can be recognized when it is recollected that he encountered the ablest men in both parties, and triumphed over them. His ambition was to attain the presidency; and to reach that goal he cleared his path of every obstruction, and was crowned with honors that Crawford, Calhoun, Benton, Webster, Clay, and other able cotemporaries, sighed for in vain. Benton, Van Buren, and Webster, were all born in the same year (1782), and were not far from the ages of Calhoun and Clay. There were among other able congressmen who adhered to the Democracy of Jackson, Henry Hubbard, who had formerly been a Federalist, James K. Polk, Cave Johnson, Richard M. Johnson, J. Y. Mason, George McDuffie, C. C. Cambreling, Tristram Burgess, Andrew Stevenson, Levi Woodbury, Silas Wright, Mahlon Dickerson, John Tyler, Robert Y. Hayne, John Forsyth, Felix Grundy, William R. King, James Buchanan (in boyhood said to have been slightly tinctured with Federalism), Isaac Hill, and David Crockett. The most noted, whose names readily occur, are mentioned; there having been others, perhaps equally able, who are omitted. The Whigs, however, were led by Clay and Webster, with as fine an array of talent and genius in their ranks as is often found in a political party. Mr. Adams was in the House in the Twenty-second Congress, and remained ever true to the principles of the administrations of Madison and Monroe. He continued in Congress during his life. The leading

Nationals, or Whigs, who were in Congress during Jackson's administration, need not be named, as they are in the recollection of most readers. Everett and Choate were there, with other able men from Massachusetts, such as Bates, Davis, Appleton and Briggs. George Evans, John Bell, Thomas Corwin, Thomas Ewing, S. F. Vinton, Theodore Frelinghuysen, Samuel Prentiss, Millard Fillmore, and many more might be named who led in the National Republican ranks in Congress. Mr. Benton, in his Thirty Years in the United States Senate, is not very minute as to his views and course on the prominent measures of his day prior to the Twenty-second Congress, but contents himself with an ample display of his championship of the Democratic measures of that and the subsequent period of his senatorial life.

The National Republicans, as the Clay and Adams party were at first termed, or Whigs, as they were afterwards called, and as we will hereafter call them, greatly annoyed and embarrassed the Democrats, as we will hereafter style the other party, by making political issues, and putting forth principles and measures as party tests. The United States Bank, Internal Improvements, the Tariff, &c., were at once unfurled upon the Whig banners, and the advocacy of these measures was claimed as the distinctive characteristics of the Whig party. This was regarded as unfair by Jackson and his friends, as the most of them were or had been favorable to, and had sustained, these measures. It was supposed by the Whigs that the administration, were it to change front on such long-mooted, and, as was thought, finally settled systems of policy, would bring upon itself certain destruction. It was supposed that the people were competent to weigh and correctly decide questions of national policy, and that a departure by the administration from what the clearest-minded statesmen had demonstrated, and the experience of the past had established, to be for the best interests of the country, would bring down upon it popular disapprobation. It was, therefore, with great reluctance that many leading Democrats accepted the issues tendered by the Whigs, which established, as it were, a new system of electioneering. When the trying moment came, — when the instant for acting in defiance of settled convictions was at hand, — some disposed to be Democrats, and follow the fortunes of Jackson, found their sense of duty and honor too strong, and became the victims of their consciences. But correct principles do not always secure the triumph of a party. The success of party frequently has its basis in anything but truth. The greater the error, the greater the enthusiasm. The Whigs placed their whole hopes on the right and justice of their cause, while their antagonists sought theirs in the passions of the multitude. The Democracy, under the lead of Jackson, triumphed over the Bank, the Tariff and Internal Improvements; but no sensible reader supposes that in this the triumph was in the reason of the people. To suppose that the mass of the American voters had deliberately examined and pronounced upon the great questions so carefully weighed and settled by such Democrats as Clay, Calhoun, Lowndes, Crawford and Cheeves, and had intelligently reversed the decisions of these men, would be ridiculous. Politics, like religion, is with the masses a matter of faith.

We all remember the enthusiasm that pervaded the

Democracy of those days — styled Jacksonian Democracy. In what the real spirit of that party consisted, it would perhaps be hard to tell. Reason never acts with such impulse. The candid reader must admit that the passions were more involved than the intellect. The Whigs of those days denounced the blind and devoted attachment of millions to their chief, as "man-worship." The Whigs, of course, were more or less prejudiced; but, after all, it is not disputed that, in the passionate devotion manifested by multitudes to General Jackson, there was something resembling idolatry. The object of idolatry may be worthy or unworthy, may be right or wrong; but, whatever its qualities, its perfections or imperfections, its virtues or vices, it is never regarded by its worshippers in the light of reason. Idolatry is not an intellectual attribute; it is a passion that overwhelms and extinguishes the intellect. And idolatry pervades all nations, all people. He is a rare man who has no touch of it in his nature. Priestcraft and kingcraft, that have endured since man has existed, are founded on it. Old systems, old *régimes* decay, but only to make places for new ones. The form undergoes a change, but the principle remains always the same. It matters little whether the priest be a Christian, a Druid, or a minister of Jupiter, if he be but idolized. There is no understanding, no reason, no operation of the intellect in the matter. The love of Mahomet is pure and devoted. The enthusiastic worship of Brahma has endured for ages. Joe Smith has left as ardent worshippers as any earth-born god of ancient or modern days. Cæsar, Alexander, and Napoleon, were all men of transcendent abilities, and each was endowed with a peculiar faculty of exerting power over the affections of men. Their empires were in the hearts of men. Washington was cast in a different mould. He possessed none of that power of fascination peculiar to the great captains mentioned, and which was in an eminent degree enjoyed by Jackson. The confidence reposed in Washington was of slow growth, and the love he inspired was the passion warmed into existence by the clear rays of the intellect. From the outset he was beset with conspiracies, cabals and traitors, and at times the Continental Congress was itself largely poisoned against him. But, step by step, as he conducted our little forces through the most trying perils of the Revolution, did his firmness, his judgment, his prudence and his undying vigilance, wring from the intelligent and judicious the verdict due to his merits. His moderation and caution; his circumspection, that seemed almost timidity; his long-continued retreats and refusals to risk engagements; his patience and coolness, that never betrayed him into a rash or hazardous battle; his self-sacrificing firmness in resisting the popular clamor for action, and in persisting in risking nothing that might endanger a cause that he knew was safe, have demonstrated his greatness and prudence, and caused the intelligent to think that he must have been raised up by Providence specially for the crisis. But Washington's most ardent admirers and most devoted worshippers are, and always have been, among the cultivated and intellectual. In the army he was by no means the stony image of a Wellington, for his soldiers could not repay his superhuman devotion to their comfort and rights with indifference; but to win applause and love from the populace, the hero must be a popular hero; he must show himself great in attributes that are peculiar to all men. The masses have but little sympathy with moral or intellectual heroes. The most profound intellects of modern times may have made lasting impressions on their age, but have inspired anything but enthusiasm amongst the people. Probably millions of their contemporaries were acquainted with the names of Newton and La Place, who could not tell for what either was noted; and the most transcendent intellects are not the ones that usually receive the admiration of the multitude. There seems to be in the heart of man an innate feeling of reverence and love for military achievements, to which General Jackson's exploits ministered in a high degree. The war with England had been vastly popular with the larger portion of the people, and nothing could have made a deeper impression upon their hearts than his truly heroic triumph over the British at New Orleans. Furthermore, the people of the United States have, from the foundation of the government, been divided into two parties—the Conservative, and the Liberal or Democratic;—and up to the administration of Jackson, an overwhelming majority had belonged to the latter party. In founding the Democratic party, Jefferson had advanced principles and measures which were evidently inspired by hostility to Hamilton and the Federalists; but, for all this, the rapid increase of the Democracy was mainly owing to its being based on the hatred and bitter prejudices lingering in the hearts of the people against England. It was, in its origin, as much the creature of the passions as of the reason, and consequently its occasional changes of measures, principles and policy, by its leading men, have been attended with no particular detriment to its popularity. The Federal party, of course, was only in degree its superior in regard to its mode of existence. Parties are parties; some good, some bad, and all more or less the creatures of the passions. The Federal party, at the period of the last war with England, was not the Federal party of the days of John Adams' administration; and the National Republican and Whig parties were not identical with either. It is true that the members of the old Federal party, as a general thing, adhered to the last named parties; but what is meant is that the anti-Democratic parties were no more uniform in their principles than the Democracy itself.

CHAPTER XIX.

MR. VAN BUREN'S SUPPOSED ASPIRATIONS. — QUARREL BETWEEN CALHOUN AND JACKSON, HOW PRODUCED, AND OBJECT. — CABINET REMODELLED. — VAN BUREN APPOINTED MINISTER TO ENGLAND, AND APPOINTMENT NOT CONFIRMED BY SENATE. — JACKSON'S ADMINISTRATION. — SOUTH CAROLINA RESISTS THE TARIFF. — POSITION OF THAT STATE ON THE QUESTION OF SECESSION. — DEBATE IN THE U. S. SENATE, AND WEBSTER'S REPLY TO COL. HAYNE. — DANIEL WEBSTER AND HIS CHARACTER. — HIS DEMOLITION OF THE NULLIFICATION AND HIGHER-LAW DOCTRINE, ETC.

If the opinion of the times is any test, we shall see that Mr. Van Buren was the master-spirit of Jackson's administration; that he was the controlling genius of the Democracy of those days. Considering Mr. Van Buren's standing and abilities, and his controlling influence with the Democracy of the controlling State of New York, it was nothing strange that he should have been placed at the head of Jackson's cabinet. No one better than that gentleman understood the advantages of his position, and but few knew better how to use them. His eye was at once fixed with a steadfast gaze upon the presidential chair. His favorite, Crawford, was no longer in the field. Clay and Webster were of the opposition. Mr. Adams made no further pretensions. There was but one rival, and that rather a formidable one. The Vice-President, John C. Calhoun, it was well known, had a right, on account of his eminent abilities and faithful services, to indulge in presidential expectations. He was an eminent statesman, and of commanding influence in the Democratic party. Unless Mr. Calhoun's claims could be averted, there would be no prospect for Mr. Van Buren, and the disposal of this rival was the most serious labor on the hands of the last-named gentleman.

It was at the time, by Whigs at least, supposed that the quarrel between Jackson and Calhoun (which fulminated early in 1831) was brought about by Van Buren. Many expedients, it was said, had been resorted to in vain for the purpose. The ears of Jackson had been filled with stories of Calhoun's falsehood and political ambition ; of his machinations to oust the general at the next presidential election, and so forth ; but at all this, and much more of the sort, Jackson was indifferent — unmoved. But, at last, the President's ire was aroused to the highest pitch, and Calhoun's fall from the Democracy was one of the strange political events of those eventful times. It appears that, during Mr. Monroe's administration, Jackson had, without any authority, entered the Spanish province of Florida, taken possession of Pensacola, and acted in rather an arbitrary, but nevertheless quite a salutary manner, in a neighbor's dominions. The Indians from that quarter had been accustomed to sally forth to murder our citizens ; and emissaries of Britain were there to provoke, in accordance with her ancient practice, such savage depredations upon our borders. Impelled by necessity, which many thought sufficient law for the occasion, General Jackson entered Florida, broke up the haunt, reduced the savages to terms, and executed two of those British agents. The affair was not only taken up in

Congress, but, as afterwards turned out, was also considered in the cabinet at the time. Some of the ablest members of that cabinet thought the act of the general should be censured. It was the feeling of no one that he should be anything more than censured, or punished nominally, as by a temporary suspension, or something of that kind; but, as he had acted clearly without authority in entering the province of a neutral power, many thought that some notice should be taken of it. Mr. Calhoun, it seems, so thought. But, finally, the matter was passed over, and, as Spain was of not much consequence, no great attention was paid to the transaction. Such cabinet consultations, however, are considered confidential, and are generally kept secret; but after the lapse of years, and after Calhoun's election to the vice-presidency on General Jackson's ticket (Mr. Calhoun having, in 1824, taken himself out of the way as a candidate, and given his support to the general), the precious secret came to light. It was obtained from Mr. Crawford, who had been at the time a member of the cabinet, and so published in a correspondence as to meet the president's eye. The spark had reached the magazine at last, and the explosion was terrific. Mr. Calhoun did not deny that he had favored some such action; but, at the same time, he thought it no disparagement to Jackson. He claimed that he had proposed no such censure or punishment as an enemy of that personage, but as a step which the government could not, under the circumstances, omit with safety or decency.

The rupture between Jackson and Calhoun led to the necessity of remodelling the cabinet. To smooth the way for this, some members resigned, and, among others, Mr. Van Buren. This gentleman, as will be recollected, was appointed Minister to England; and it will also be recollected that his appointment was not confirmed when brought before the Senate. This fact will show the party bitterness of the times, and the enmity that Mr. Van Buren had excited against himself. There were prominent men in the Senate who thought that he was too ambitious for the presidency, and who seemed to think that the refusal of that body to confirm his appointment would cast a blight upon his fast budding popularity. But the favorite of the hero of New Orleans was not to be put down in this manner. He was obliged to return from England; but his rise to the presidency was rather favored than injured by the action of the Senate.

It will not be necessary here to speak of all the exciting measures and transactions of Jackson's administration, as the questions as to the policy of many of them are already slumbering in the tomb of the past. Even the currency question, so long, so powerfully, and so fiercely agitated by the ablest statesmen of the age, is now scarcely heard of. The removal of deposites; the Senate's resolution of censure; the President's protest; the expunging resolution; were all ephemeral transactions, and have now no value as political events. The question in regard to the proceeds of the sales of the public lands has lost much of its former interest; and the Indian removals, the West India trade, and many other topics, of lively interest in those days, have but little bearing upon the politics of the present times. There are some measures which were discussed during Jackson's administration, however, that have come down to us as party issues, and still are the subjects of vigorous contention. Among these the most prominent is the tariff.

The tariff of 1828 had been unsatisfactory to the leading politicians of South Carolina. The enmity in that state to the doctrine of protective tariffs had been growing for some time, and was quite decidedly fixed by the act of that year. Travellers from the South had found that Northern cities were growing faster than some Southern ones; that the principal Eastern emporiums were flourishing better than Charleston, of South Carolina; and the conclusion was very rashly jumped at that this was all the result of the tariffs. Charleston and other Southern cities, it was said, had retrograded, and were not even so prosperous as they had been in the colonial state. There was some plausibility, though but little justice, in the South Carolina theory in regard to the matter. They saw that the principal exports of the country were from the South, and were of products not benefited by protection; and that the North were alone enjoying all the benefits of the tariff system. The tariff, they urged, was in effect a tax on exports, and the whole revenue of the government a charge upon the South. And, further, it was, they thought, the interest of the South to maintain free trade with England who bought their cotton, hemp and tobacco, as a prohibition of British goods would have a tendency to diminish the British demand for these products. This last position was seriously entertained by many Southern statesmen. The politicians of South Carolina yielded themselves up without reserve to the conviction that they were the victims of partial legislation. They had no doubt of the fact, and really felt that the selfish and ungenerous North and West were throwing upon their shoulders unjust burdens, and making themselves rich out of Southern industry. That the sons of Carolina should feel unutterable indignation at the thought that they were the objects of a systematic oppression by a selfish and unyielding majority, was nothing strange; and that, goaded to despair by such a feeling, they should, Green-Mountain-Boys-like, rather than submit to such an outrage, take up arms and "make war on human nature at large," would appear nothing marvellous to a brave man. However, that they were influenced by a sad delusion is apparent enough. They too readily embraced the belief that they were the subjects of partial and unconstitutional legislation. The mass of the South Carolina people easily yielded their faith to the opinions of leaders who had formed their conclusions too rashly. Being themselves naturally a liberal and generous hearted people, they were the last in the world that would tamely submit to what their sentiments of justice and honor taught them to consider mean, base, and oppressive.

We are apt to think that all legislation which thwarts our interests or passions is unconstitutional. Alien and sedition laws, annexation laws, embargo laws, non-intercourse laws, fugitive slave laws, Wilmot proviso laws, territorial intervention laws, bank laws, temperance laws, and multitudes of other laws, have from time to time been denounced, as well as tariff laws, as unconstitutional. This plea is a natural resort, under our system of government, when we find the majority against us. But it has, as a general thing, since the foundation of our government, been customary to defer, on all questions as to the constitutionality of the acts of Congress, to the decisions of the Supreme Court of the United States.

Even Virginia, the leader in the states-rights doctrine, the promulgator of the celebrated resolutions of 1798, — resolutions inspired by the famous alien and sedition laws, — never dreamed of questioning the conclusiveness of the decisions of the Supreme Court of the United States on all such questions; and although she looked upon these alien and sedition laws as entirely unconstitutional and most abhorrent, still, Callender was arrested for their violation, and imprisoned in her capital, and her citizens never thought of resorting to any higher law than provided by the Constitution of the country. Perhaps the excitement in Virginia was not so fierce, in regard to those sedition laws, as it was in Massachusetts, at a later date, against the embargo acts. The frenzy in the latter state was so extreme as to cause some of her citizens to think that their legislature could afford them relief from the laws of the United States. But, during the noblest part of her history, Massachusetts has taught nothing but obedience to the acts of the national legislature. It was the misfortune of South Carolina to fall into the error embraced, at an earlier period, by some of the more ardent, and less considerate sons of the Bay State; and a convention, not unlike what the Hartford Convention was usually thought to have been, was contemplated by the irritated citizens of the Palmetto State. The statesmen of South Carolina took the position that the union of the states is but a compact, the Constitution being its grant and limitation of powers. They claimed that the passage of an act unauthorized by the Constitution is an absolute nullity, and not binding upon anybody; that it is for each state to determine for itself the constitutionality or unconstitutionality of the acts of Congress. The Constitution, according to their theory, is but a congeries of concessions, or conceded powers, to the general government, made by the states; all powers inherent in the states, and not surrendered at the time of the formation of the Union, remaining still in them respectively; and that, as a matter of course, each state reserved the right of judging for itself as to the constitutionality of any laws that this government might enact. It would be no compact, they contended, if the state acceding to the Union were to be bound by the acts and decisions of that Union, with no power of judging as to its own rights. And, further, they claimed the right of secession, or withdrawal, from the Union.

The first appearance of these Carolina doctrines in Congress was at the time of the celebrated debate by Webster and Hayne, in 1830. Mr. Webster had watched the symptoms of disaffection in the South, and seen the spread of those dangerous principles with a great deal of apprehension. At this time he was not a violent party man, — in fact, he never was. Our country has not produced a more substantial, upright, patriotic, and independent statesman, than Daniel Webster. That he was not always popular, and was, during the most of his political life, in the party of the minority, should be regarded as evidence that he preferred his country's to his own welfare. His stand on public measures, and his support of men and parties, were not fixed by the decrees of fate, but were matters of his own choice. He could have continued the supporter of Jackson, and been made President; but where, had such been the case, would have been those luminous and unparalleled discourses on constitutional law, and on the domestic and foreign policy of our government, for all which our country is indebted to his opposition to the administration of that great, but not politically perfect, man? Mr. Webster's course in regard to public measures was never shaped by the consultations of caucuses, nor by the intrigues of party plotters. As questions of public policy arose, he at once applied his mind to their investigation, and without hesitation, and with the boldness and power peculiar to his nature, announced his convictions in regard to them. His intellectual faculties were conceded to be unparalleled in the age in which he lived; and, of all the transcendent powers and affections of his mind and heart, his perception and devotion to principles were the most commanding. With an intellect highly philosophic in its cast, he possessed those high moral qualities which rendered his love of truth and principle a controlling passion. It was scarcely possible for a mind constituted like Mr. Webster's to act otherwise than in accordance with his convictions of right; and consequently he was naturally averse to compromise. His congressional experience, at the time of his debate with Col. Hayne, had been considerable; it will be recollected that he was then (1830) forty-eight years of age. He had been elected to Congress (from Portsmouth, N. H.) when he was about thirty years old (1812), and was again returned from the same place in 1814. In 1816 he removed to Boston, and from that city was sent to Congress in 1822, and was continued in the House until his election to the Senate in 1827.

We see that Daniel Webster was not a native of Massachusetts. He was a son of New Hampshire, the Granite State, as it is called; a granite boulder that the frosts of penury had rent from his native mountains, and, after having been for some time drifted at the mercy of the elements, at last lodged upon the grateful bosom of the Old Bay State. To continue the figure, it may truly be said that he became the "rock of her defence." When she was attacked, — when her history was assailed, — when poisoned arrows were aimed at her heart by an envenomed foe, — Daniel Webster was her rampart — her Gibraltar. Mr. Webster had not been born to wealth, nor advanced in youth by the appliances and influences of power. His father was an humble farmer, and Daniel was brought into existence in an obscure rural section of the country, — a section only known for its ungrateful soil, its rugged hills, and the poverty of its inhabitants. In this respect Henry Clay was more favored than his younger contemporary. Almost at the outset of Mr. Clay's life he was thrown into the society of men of standing, learning, and wealth ; and Mr. Clay's lack of the knowledge of books was perhaps more than compensated by his endowment with the peculiar ability of obtaining that knowledge at second-hand, by readily drawing it from book-learned men. Furthermore, there is a difference between the people of the South and the North in regard to their encouragement of talent. In the South, it has been often observed, the first dawnings of talent are hailed with admiration ; and the young man of promise and worth is advanced, and receives every aid and support that his merits will warrant. A fair field and a fair trial are given him, with every sympathy in his favor. But in the North, talent and worth must fight their way into favor ; and then, unless the individual shall sacrifice his manhood and independence by doing homage to the bigoted notions or prevailing prejudices of the hour, the talents and virtues of a Webster would not save him from neglect and contempt. Fortunately, Mr. Webster removed to Boston at a period when her able, great and good men had influence with the people of Massachusetts. His abilities were recognized and appreciated, and the Old Bay State had cause to rejoice in her acquisition. The career of Webster is too well known to justify even a slight repetition. In the House, in the Senate, and in the highest courts of the land, he at once took the first rank. As a legislator he regarded his position as a trust to be exercised for the benefit of the whole country. Narrow or sectional feelings could find no entrance, much less abiding-place, in his heart. Throughout his life he was characterized for an enthusiastic love of country. Patriotism was his absorbing passion. His father had been a Revolutionary soldier, and Webster's infancy immediately succeeded the great drama in which that father had been an actor. Hence the earliest impressions of his uncommon mind must have been favorable for the promotion of lasting sentiments of patriotism. The Constitution of the United States was formed and promulgated to the country when Daniel was about eight years of age. It was a topic that commanded intense interest among the hardy yeomanry of the country; and the sentiments of loyalty with which that instrument was treated by his parents and neighbors inspired young Webster himself with a veneration for it that became, in after life, a marked and enduring feature of his character. The adoption of the Constitution by the people of the United States formed an epoch in the country's history. It was something new, interesting and important, and was at once published everywhere. It was doubtless printed in many forms, and on many fabrics. As a significant anecdote, it is said that Mr. Webster never forgot that in those days he used to peruse the great charter of American liberties printed upon his pocket-handkerchief.

Therefore, when Colonel Hayne, in the United States Senate, advanced the new-born South Carolina doctrines, and in that high tribunal openly advocated nullification and disunion, it was by no means strange that the vast "deeps" of Mr. Webster's soul should have been stirred. The Senate to Mr. Webster was a sacred place. He looked upon all the institutions of his country with veneration, and never entered the humblest court of justice without a feeling of awe for the sanctity of the tribunal. But the Senate of the United States was invested in his eyes with peculiar sacredness. Much of this feeling is manifested in his celebrated reply to Colonel Hayne. But that great speech of Mr. Webster is well known to every reader of the English language, or should be. The higher law set up by the nullifiers received a signal overthrow, and the Constitution an interpretation that has never since been questioned by any sensible man, North or South. The nullifiers were at the time too far committed to their course of nullification to retreat; but no doubt that thousands, in other parts of the South, to whom the Carolina theory had looked plausible, were, by the great argument of Mr. Webster, at once and forever saved from the gulf of nullification.

Colonel Hayne was a learned, talented and eloquent orator. He was no doubt firmly impressed with the correctness and justice of his views. There is something plausible to the superficial inquirer in the doctrine that a state should not be bound by what to her may clearly appear to be an unconstitutional law. And, more especially, when the national legislature shall make an enactment that appears to cleave down the natural rights of a portion of the people, — that tramples upon and enslaves them, — it seems hard to insist that such people shall be subject to no relief but the national tribunal, that is supposed to sympathize with the majority which controls the national legislature. Fallacious and disorganizing as such higher-law doctrines may be, the country has not always been free from them. At their first appearance in the Senate, they were rebuked by Mr. Webster. That such principles should be rebuked by a Massachusetts man inspired great indignation in the heart of Colonel Hayne. He did not limit himself solely to a defence of his doctrines, but turned upon Massachusetts, and represented her as ever having been the champion of higher laws, and as possessing the least possible reverence for such acts of the general government as displease her prejudices. The controversy, as initiated by the South Carolina politicians, was made to take a sectional character, and it opened by fierce onslaughts by members of one section of the country upon the history, character and institutions of another. Colonel Hayne could, without difficulty, find imperfections in Massachusetts humanity, and Webster could, if he had been disposed, have made quite a railing speech in regard to Carolina's antecedents. But Webster's triumph was in the loftiness of his sentiments, his magnanimity, and the more than sun-light clearness with which he demonstrated the position that the only alternative was obedience to the laws of the United States, or revolution. The Senate he regarded as no arena for the indulgence in sectional aspersions; and, instead of expending his force in discovering and exposing, in glowing colors, the errors and mistakes of a sister state, he dwelt on the past glories of both Carolina and Massachusetts, and shrank with horror from the contemplation of the time when the bonds of union shall be rent asunder. His vindication of Massachusetts was so noble,—he so obscured the follies of her insane fanatics by enlarging upon that earlier period of her history when she was ruled by statesmen and patriots,—he made "the past, at least," of the old Bay State so brilliant and glorious, that all the errors of a later day became invisible.

CHAPTER XX.

EFFECT OF JACKSON'S ELECTION ON THE PROTECTIVE SYSTEM. — CLAY AMBITIOUS FOR THE PRESIDENCY. — HE HAD FORCED THE TARIFF SYSTEM AS AN ISSUE ON JACKSON. — WEBSTER'S AMBITION. — JACKSON DID NOT NEGLECT HIS OPPONENTS. — WHIG NATIONAL CONVENTION, DEC. 1831. — PARTY PLATFORM. — CLAY CANDIDATE. — CAMPAIGN OF 1832. — UNITED STATES BANK QUESTION. — JACKSON REËLECTED. — VAN BUREN VICE-PRESIDENT, ETC.

The first election of General Jackson left the American system of Mr. Clay in rather an equivocal position. Mr. Clay and his party had offered themselves as its peculiar friends, and were defeated; but neither Jackson nor the greater part of his supporters had pretended to be hostile to protection. It was not till the next presidential campaign (that of 1832) that the national election was made a test as to the protective policy. That it was imprudent to risk so important a measure by carrying it before the people, there can be no doubt. But Mr. Clay had unbounded confidence in the discrimination and judgment of the people, and concluded that by making his elevation depend on the fate of a popular measure, the measure would receive no detriment, and his success be beyond a doubt. Mr. Clay had a noble ambition to become President. He looked upon the station as one that should be the reward for high merit and patriotic services. He would win it. He did not desire to worm himself into that, or any other office, by tortuous intrigues. He regarded the honor as the gift of the people; and to the American people he addressed himself for its acquisition. He devoted himself to such measures as he deemed for the best interests of the country, and trusted that, as the people had their own welfare at heart, they would of course cherish and promote the statesman best able and most inclined to advance those interests. The American system was substantially Mr. Clay's; that is, he had more assiduously advocated it than any other American. It was, perhaps, no more than just that he should endeavor to identify his hopes with the fate of a measure of his own construction, especially as he, as well as many other eminent statesmen, considered that the true interests of the country were involved in the fate of that measure. Mr. Clay was peculiarly situated. He was surrounded by competitors for the glorious station to which he aspired with an ambition as pure as ever fired a patriot's heart. Why should he not raise his eyes to that exalted position? Would the proud honor be any the less grateful to him on account of his recollections of his humble origin — of the days of his orphanage and destitution? But to gain that elevated seat, — the presidency of the United States, — Mr. Clay could not, without a radical change of his nature, resort to any but the most honorable means. No one sooner than he saw the nascent popularity of General Jackson. In 1825, when, as a senator from Kentucky, he sustained Mr. Adams (in the House) for the presidency, he acted in defiance of the instructions of his state, because he conceived that his duty required him so to do. Jackson and Clay did not differ at that time in politics, and the latter had not a few intimations, if not direct offers, of advancement, if he would consent to throw his influence for the general. But his nobler impulses forbade. His spirit was too proud to suffer him to glide into so high an office by clinging to the skirts of one whom he regarded as, in every essential qualification for such office, very much his inferior. The result was that those who were willing to sail under Jackson's colors triumphed in their ambitious schemes, while those who presumed to question the correctness of his administration were doomed to disappointment and humbler stations. Mr. Webster, likewise, had a lofty ambition for the presidency; but his was not an ambition which, like that attributed to Van Buren, would drive him into intrigues; nor was it one, like Clay's, that would impel him to exertions calculated to lead the people to his standard. Mr. Webster was the best constituted by nature, the best fitted by education and training, and the best adapted by his moral and mental qualifications, for the presidency of this Union, of any man, with the exception of Washington, that has ever yet filled the presidential chair. The neglect of the country to place him in that office was the country's loss. But, although the first of American statesmen, Mr. Webster was never a politician. He ever acted on the principle that the officer, and not the office, should be sought.

In the struggle for ascendency, General Jackson was by no means guilty of negligence, or want of vigilance. He had been a military captain, and understood something of fortification. At the outset, he commenced with the precaution of keeping none but true friends on guard; and all his office-holders became, under the discipline they received from the heads of departments, faithful minute-men. Calhoun was sacrificed, leaving, of his own political organization, but one eminent statesman, and that one content, and probably pledged, to await the proper time for successorship. An organ, also, was established at head-quarters, to promulgate the faith, and fulminate anathemas upon the unfaithful. That organ was the Washington Globe, edited by Francis Blair. Although a popular man, and strongly entrenched in the hearts of his countrymen, General Jackson found that attention to his party was necessary. He saw that a powerful array of talent was uniting against his administration, and that some vigilance was indispensably requisite.

The Whigs, or National Republicans, as then called, held their convention at Baltimore as early as December, 1831, to nominate candidates for President and Vice-President, for the November election of 1832. The delegates at that convention adopted a party platform, among other measures, putting forth the Bank, Tariff and Internal Improvements. Some of these measures had incurred the opposition of the President already, and the election which came off in '32 was considered decisive as to the fate of the whole of them, so far as the popular voice could be indicated by an election. At that convention Henry Clay was nominated for President, and John Sargent, of Pennsylvania, for Vice-President.

Early in 1832 the campaign opened with much vigor. The long term of Congress was in session, and was somewhat made use of for electioneering purposes. It was important that the members of Congress should by their action be made to signify their position in regard to important questions; and if, by fair and honorable tactics, leading statesmen should be driven to an exposition of their principles, the state could not be said to receive any injury, even if it was not benefited by the operation. Party leaders have always claimed the right of thus forcing issues upon their adversaries, and this Clay did in that Congress with wonderful effect. The United States Bank had long been, like Hamlet's ghost, a questionable monster; and Jackson, in his patriotic resolve, at the commencement of his career, to restore the pure principles of Jefferson's administration, had signified his hostility to it, and expressed his opposition to its receiving a new charter. The first United States Bank received its charter under Washington's administration, in 1791. Washington's cabinet was divided upon the question of its policy and constitutionality — Hamilton being in favor of, and Jefferson opposed to, the institution. The first charter expired in 1811, during the administration of Mr. Madison; and the prevalence of the original Republican sentiments at that time prevented its renewal. The war with England ensued, from which the country emerged much crippled in its finances, and embarrassed in its exchanges. Republicanism became universal, and a new set of statesmen were in the halls of the national legislature. The question was discussed in regard to its merits as a measure for improving the currency, and without regard to party tenets; and the result was the granting of a new charter, during the last year of Mr. Madison's term (1816), which was to run twenty years. This charter would expire, of course, in 1836. The passage of an act granting a renewal of that charter was not necessary before 1834 or 1835; but the Whigs saw fit to bring forward the subject early in 1832. It was well known that there were many Democrats in Congress who would support an act for the recharter of the Bank, and the Whigs thought it advisable to commit them to the measure, and then force Jackson to an acquiescence, or array against him that part of the Democracy which was in its favor. Accordingly, early in July, a new charter for the United States Bank passed both houses, and promptly received President Jackson's veto. The United States Bank had really grown up to be something of a monster, so far as its power was concerned, and its life was not to be yielded up without a struggle. When its various branches in different parts of the country are considered; and when we recollect the numbers of wealthy and influential men, directly and indirectly interested in its existence; when the vast amount of its capital, the enhanced value of its stock, the profits of its dividends, the great numbers of its officers and attachés, and its intimate connection with the business of the country, are all brought to mind, we shall not be surprised at the great excitement occasioned by the President's veto of the new charter.

The utility of the Bank as an instrument for the collection of the revenue was manifest; and, as a regulator of the currency, and a medium of exchanges, it was thought highly necessary, if not absolutely indispensable. The power of Congress to establish a Bank had been canvassed by political theorists from the foundation of the government; and long prior to Jackson's election to the presidency, not only had the United States Supreme Court virtually settled the question of its constitutionality, but the ablest Democratic statesmen had yielded all scruple in regard to that question. Some statesmen had located the power to establish a Bank in that section of the Constitution which authorizes Congress to regulate the currency. But almost every statesman had come to the conclusion that a Bank was necessary as a means of carrying into effect the general provisions of the Constitution by which the government is established. That the most powerful, and most rapidly growing government on earth had not power to establish a Bank for its own convenience, as an instrument for the transaction of its extensive and varied fiscal operations, such as the collecting and disbursing, annually, about a hundred millions of dollars, — and these operations, not limited to this continent, but requiring the transmission and disbursement of funds throughout all parts of the habitable globe, — seemed to every reflecting man, to every reasonable person who could consider the question with unprejudiced mind, as absolutely absurd and ridiculous. The constitutional power of Congress to establish a Bank cannot admit of much question; but the expediency of such an establishment, though a branch of the constitutional, is in reality, the only question in the matter. Though in many respects highly valuable and useful, it was urged that the United States Bank system was fraught with evils. The enemies of that system brought against the Bank every charge imaginable. Horrible frauds were charged upon it. It was alleged that it had exercised favoritism; that it had, by expansions and contractions, encouraged speculations in produce and other property; that its officers had themselves made use of the institution for cotton and other speculations; and, worse than all, it was alleged that the whole establishment was a busy and powerful electioneering concern. How much truth there was in these charges it is unimportant now to inquire; but, nevertheless, it seems as though our government ought to have wisdom enough to establish a moneyed institution, based upon the government funds or securities, that would be free from the objections charged upon the monster beheaded by Jackson. The specie, sometimes amounting to many millions, locked up in the government vaults, ought to be represented in the business channels of the country. The loss of just such a medium as the government might gratuitously and without inconvenience give to the country, is a pure sacrifice upon the altar of party prejudice and folly. In a country like this, — where the undeveloped wealth is millions and millions of times greater than the developed, and where capital bears no proportion to the country's resources, — it is certainly suicidal to adopt and persist in a system which takes from business a part of its limited capital. The government might supply, to a proper extent, a circulating paper currency, which would not only facilitate exchanges, but likewise to some extent equalize the rate of interest, useful everywhere, and shedding untold blessings upon the border states.

But the veto of the Bank charter so early in 1832 brought the whole question fully into the campaign of that year. Everything that well could have been said upon the subject of currency was urged by Clay and Webster, and by thousands of others, statesmen and editors, in all parts of the country. The veto detached many leading and influential men, in various sections of the land, from the support of Jackson. The storm of abuse that burst upon him was terrific. He was denounced as a tyrant. At the capitol, and at the most business points throughout the country, the scolders seemed to be largely in the ascendency. Judging from the declamation, and the tone of the press, one would suppose an entire revolution in public sentiment had taken place. But during this dark hour it was said that the old hero — as the President was usually called — remained unmoved, and expressed unshaken confidence that the people would sustain him. And in this he was not mistaken. His knowledge of human nature was superior, as it turned out, to that of any of his competitors. The storm of indignation raised by bank capitalists, speculators, merchants, and manufacturers, redounded upon the heads of his opponents. The people only saw a fierce conflict between their beloved hero and a moneyed aristocracy. They saw him assailed by the champions of privilege, the advocates of banks and other corporations, and the old general became dearer to them than ever. That his enemies were loud in praise of a tariff was enough to excite the jealousy and hostility of the populace against that measure. The second election of General Jackson was more triumphant than the first. His administration was endorsed by the people, and his opponents rebuked in a terrible manner. Out of two hundred and eighty-six votes, Jackson received two hundred and nineteen; Henry Clay forty-nine; John Floyd eleven; and William Wirt seven. The votes for Floyd, a Virginia ex-governor, were cast by South Carolina; and the seven cast for Mr. Wirt were cast by Vermont, which was at the time uncommonly exercised by the masonic question. Mr. Van Buren was elected Vice-President by one hundred and eighty-nine out of two hundred and eighty-six votes. Pennsylvania cast her votes for Jackson, but repudiated Van Buren. The rejection of Mr. Van Buren's appointment as Minister to England, if prompted by political considerations, proved not to be productive of very valuable results to the leaders of the movement.

CHAPTER XXI.

SOUTH CAROLINA NULLIFICATION ORDINANCE. — THE HIGHER-LAW FANATICISM OF SOUTH CAROLINA CONSIDERED. — THE RESOLUTION OF A PEOPLE TO RESIST A LAW OF THE LAND AN EVIDENCE OF THE WANT OF A CHRISTIAN SPIRIT. — THE APPROVAL OF THE INDIVIDUAL NOT NECESSARY TO RENDER A LAW BINDING ON HIS CONSCIENCE. — EXEMPTION FROM THE FORCE OF THE LAWS OF SOCIETY BY APPEAL TO HIGHER LAWS A BADGE OF PAGANISM. — THE AMERICAN DOCTRINE, ETC., ETC.

THE vote of South Carolina, at the election of 1832, was cast for William Floyd. Her politics were greatly perturbed. The modification of the tariff by the act of 1832 had not been satisfactory. The result of the presidential election, although it had virtually settled the tariff question favorably for the South, did not arrest the course of the nullifiers, but immediately after that election, to wit, on the twenty-fourth day of November, appeared the celebrated ordinance of nullification. When everything is considered, perhaps it will be thought that there was nothing remarkably strange in the course taken by the disaffected Carolinians. The philosophic reader will see in their performances but a repetition of one of the most common phases of human nature. It should be constantly borne in mind that for several years the people of that spirited state had labored under the belief that they were the victims of unconstitutional legislation — that they were plundered to enrich other sections of the country. Such thoughts would not be comfortable to the coolest-tempered people in the world ; and having been for a long time entertained by the Carolinians, the result could hardly be considered surprising. People in such a situation should not be expected to construe the Constitution with the impartiality of a disinterested spectator. Their case is daily seen everywhere. The opposite litigants in a lawsuit are equally confident of their respective constructions of a statute, as passion ever affords a medium for vision that never illuminates but one side of the question. Such an exciting agitation could not for a long time continue without leading to ultraism — without engendering fanaticism. When a people imagine themselves the subjects of oppression, and this conviction is continued for any length of time, it would be strange indeed if their feelings and measures should be precisely adjusted to the necessities of their redress of grievances. This would not be natural. Reason, it is true, is the highest of human faculties; but it would accomplish but little without the aid of passion. Like a pent-up river, the longer the passions are obstructed, the more they accumulate, until at last no barrier will restrain them. One-idea people, as they are called, are fearful folks. Whether that one idea be a wrong of their own, or of a fellow-being, makes but slight difference; for, if we adopt a neighbor's quarrel, we in effect make it our own. But Carolina was aroused for her own rights, and little did her sons stop to calculate their strength, or to consider the consequences. What though the whole Union, with an efficient army and navy, stood arrayed against them? What though the President thought them in the wrong, and was resolved to execute the act of Congress which was so odious and hateful? What though every statesman and jurist in the land had held such acts, as the one in question, constitional? What though Congress, and all the heads of the departments, were of the opinion that the people of South Carolina were carried away by a fanatical hatred of a law that was not only constitutional, but perhaps useful and necessary for the whole country? What though the duty of the Carolinians, if dissatisfied with an act of Congress, was plainly pointed out in the Constitution? Fanaticism was never awed or moved by such considerations. The tariff was thought unconstitutional — oppressive — a blow at the liberties of the South. Constitutional remedies could not be thought of. Every heart was inspired with a higher law. The disaffected with one voice resolved that the odious act should not be executed. They could not conceive it possible for them to be in an error; their reason told them that the law was a nullity; the promptings of their consciences, which they could not disobey, taught them that obedience would be degradation, and morally infamous. There are no people on earth that are without a God, or destitute of consciences. The people of South Carolina, although nullifiers and slave-holders, are not, probably, formed much differently from those of the North. They are of the same race, possessing the same moral, intellectual, and physical faculties that distinguish their Anglo-American brothers in other parts of the country. Travellers give excellent accounts of their characters, representing the Carolinians as a high-minded, generous, virtuous, and, in every respect, an estimable people. Particular and minute accounts are given by some travellers, showing them possessed of really lovely traits of character, and truly eminent for the Christian graces. And this is no doubt so. The more we look into the character of our Southern friends, the more, no doubt, we shall be charmed with their good qualities. But this charitable view is, nevertheless, only found behind the record. We should not be allowed, *prima facie*, to accord to South Carolina so good a character. We could not suppose that a people which had arrayed themselves against a law of Congress, taken redress into their own hands, and refused to submit to the jurisdiction of the Supreme Court of the United States, were Christians; that is, true followers of Christ, and governed by his precepts and example. The Carolinians pronounced a law of the general government unrighteous and oppressive, and claimed that it was not binding upon their consciences! They scouted at the idea of resisting that law from pecuniary considerations; they were impelled to resistance by conscience, which could not be bound by an unjust enactment. Here was their fatal error — their departure from Christian duty. Their Saviour, who was no less, in effect, than the Deity himself, held the laws of bloody Tiberius binding upon his conscience; and these were the laws of a black-hearted despot. Then whence the authority for the American doctrine, that an unjust or unrighteous law is not binding on the citizen's conscience? Is it not strange that people, enjoying the most equal and just government that ever existed on earth, should assume that the acts of the legislature are no further binding upon their consciences than in accordance with their conceptions of right or wrong? A grosser delusion than the theory that each individual must test the obligatory force of a law by the dictates of his own conscience, never existed in this republic. Conscience, if exalted to such an imperial position, would rule the land with many conflicting laws. What this sovereign would establish as right in one heart, it would proscribe as infamous in another. Judging by experience and observation, we should suppose conscience to be, not an intellectual faculty, but a moral sentiment, ever dependent for its guidance upon the intellect. And the fallibility of the human intellect ought not to be doubted, and was not, by the framers of our government. The fact was recognized that men would differ, in their ideas of right and wrong, about many things; and if all government, saving the immemorial and ordinary one of military despotism, had been postponed until all minds should become impressed with the same ideas, and the same sentiments should reign in all hearts, it is quite clear that our republic would never have been established.

The Constitution was a series of concessions and compromises. The government was instituted on the principle that full, complete and entire obedience, in all time to come, to the enactments of Congress, should, as a compromise, be sacredly observed. The legislative power, it was expected, might frequently act contrary to the ideas of considerable portions of the people; but the solemn pledge and oath of every citizen demand a faithful regard and observance of all legislative enactments. As no man can positively say that his mental powers are perfect; as no one can say that he is infallible; as weakness, imperfection and error, are acknowledged by Christians to be the attributes of every soul; as, if universal consent were required as necessary to make a law obligatory on all, no government nor laws could ever be made; it should be considered nothing humiliating, dangerous nor wrong, for the most eminent and godly men to submit their consciences to the arbitrament of the highest authority the state can provide. Supposing that, prior to the legislative act, a radical difference of opinion had existed? And supposing that, after the enactment, the dubious citizen cannot bring his mind to concur with the opinion of the legislators, shall he therefore assume that the law has no binding force upon his conscience? That, because he has not the same light that illuminates the legislators, he is under no obligation to regard their acts? Such, in effect, is the doctrine of those who profess to owe allegiance to a law higher than the state. That such views in a Protestant country should obtain any currency would be strange. Romanism has ever been charged with raising, and assuming to raise, its head above the temporal power; and the presumption of the priesthood, in holding allegiance to a power superior to the state, has ever been violently denounced by the opponents of that sect. And it really seems a powerful objection to that religion, if its priests really do claim to owe allegiance to a head that claims the right of testing legislative acts by a higher law, before they shall become binding upon the consciences of its followers. Such doctrines can only be tolerated by the benighted subjects of a priesthood. They are the same that for ages have bound the inhabitants of the earth in blind idolatry, and nourished the despotisms which have ground the masses of mankind into the dust. In the East, from ages remote, the civil magistrate has been subordinate to the priests of Brahma, Juggernaut, or some other all-powerful god. In Greece and Rome the priest of Jupiter was more regarded than the decrees of senates. In the modern states of Europe the Pope's ancient temporal power has been divided amongst the prevailing monarchies. Formerly European kings reigned subject to the supervision and control of the man of God, whose higher law could dethrone and crown them at pleasure; but in modern days kingcraft has swallowed up priestcraft, and it is only by virtue of the divinity which modern monarchs have ravished from the See of Rome that kings claim and are believed to reign by "divine right." But America, the world supposes, has never imported to her shores any of the craft of kings and priests that has enslaved mankind since the creation. Our government was formed on the theory that it was to be purely a government of men. Such a thing as a divine interpreter of the will of the Deity was not thought of. The people recognized, in the formation of their institutions, no power but that which emanated from, and centred in, themselves. They contemplated no government that should ever recognize or be in subjection to an order of men claiming allegiance to higher powers, or charged with duties incompatible with an observance of the laws of the state. In the construction of this government, no state was more prominent than South Carolina, and her patriots and statesmen ranked with the first in America. Their vigilance, their caution, and their wisdom, are embodied in our Constitution. It is the legacy of the great and good men of their day, and is the proudest monument that could be erected to their memory; and we never look at or think of that glorious instrument without bringing to mind those immortal men by whom it was formed. Should it endure ten thousand years, it could not outlive their memory and glory. As its destruction would be the overthrow of the most durable monument that can keep in remembrance and love the great statesmen that formed it, its preservation should be passionately desired by every American who has any regard for the glory of his ancestors. The government left to us by those ancestors is no despotism. It is based upon the principle of self-government, and substitutes the will of the people, lawfully expressed, for the rule of a hereditary aristocracy, and a priesthood. Every guard against unjust laws is provided that it was possible to provide. Laws must be passed by a majority of the direct representatives; then by a majority of the Senate; and, finally, be approved by the President, and by him signed, before they become obligatory. Thinking that, even with all these deliberate steps in the enactment of laws, some unconstitutional ones might occasionally be made, another department of government was established, with full power to revise and pass upon all legislative acts. A judiciary, composed of learned, independent and disinterested judges, was provided, before which any law of Congress may be brought, by proper steps, for adjudication. And here all resorts against a law of the land must end. Good or bad, just or unjust, constitutional or unconstitutional, in the eyes of a citizen, after an act has been passed through all the regular forms, and adjudicated by the Supreme Court of the United States to be in accordance with the Constitution, it is, and must remain, until that adjudication be reversed, an obligatory law. There is no duty to a higher law that will absolve the citizen's conscience from its observance. If his wisdom and feelings distrust the correctness of the law, it is proper for him to agitate its repeal, or try it by all constitutional remedies and tests; but to undertake to oppose or thwart its execution, renders him a traitor; and to deny its obligatory force on his conscience, and refuse to execute it, is to incur the guilt of perjury.

South Carolina refused to resort to the United States Supreme Court for redress. In this she was governed by passion. She seemed to distrust that tribunal. She supposed that, as the Northern, Middle and Western States were all favorable to the system of protection, a majority of the judges would be opposed to her. However, her leaders were high-minded men; and, although they distrusted the impartiality of the national tribunal, they had the decency to observe towards it a respectful bearing, and made no efforts to bring it into contempt, break it down, and destroy its authority with the people.

CHAPTER XXII.

SOUTH CAROLINA ORDINANCE TOO LATE. — THE FATE OF THE TARIFFS SETTLED BY THE ELECTION. — JACKSON'S COURSE IN REGARD TO SOUTH CAROLINA. — SUSTAINED BY WEBSTER. — COURSE OF CALHOUN. — COMPROMISE ACT. — REVOLUTION OF MEASURES DURING JACKSON'S ADMINISTRATION. — HIS ADMINISTRATION FURTHER CONSIDERED. — THIS COUNTRY NO FOREIGN OR DOMESTIC POLICY. — TRUE POLICY FOR US. — EXCESS OF IMPORTS AND EFFECT. — COMMERCE WITHOUT MANUFACTURES WILL EXHAUST THE COUNTRY. — WITHOUT THE LABOR EMPLOYED ON THE RAW MATERIAL OBTAINED FROM THE UNITED STATES, BRITISH COMMERCE WOULD BE COMPARATIVELY SMALL. — FOLLY OF EXPORTING OUR RAW MATERIAL TO BUILD UP A RIVAL, WHEN IT MIGHT GIVE AMERICA THE MONOPOLY OF THE COMMERCE OF THE WORLD. — BRITISH SYSTEM. — HER AMBITION TO PRODUCE THE RAW MATERIAL. — THE INSANE IDEA OF THE SOUTH THAT ENGLAND IS TO BE HER ONLY MARKET FOR COTTON SUICIDAL TO THE COUNTRY, ETC.

THE people of South Carolina, in convention at Columbia, on the twenty-fourth of November issued their ordinance of nullification, declaring all the acts of Congress, then in force, laying duties on foreign importations, unconstitutional, null and void, and of no binding effect on the citizens of that state. The ordinance further ordered that it should not be lawful for the authorities of that state, nor of the United States in that state, to enforce the provisions of those revenue acts. It also further ordained, among other things, that there should be no appeal from the state to the United States court, on any question involving the legality of these acts, and provided that if the United

States government should attempt to coërce the state into submission, it would secede from the Union, and form itself into an independent government. This ordinance was by its terms to take effect on the first day of the ensuing February.

But the ordinance of Carolina came too late. There was a moment when, perhaps, this step would have occasioned demonstrations, to some extent, in other Southern States, as the protective system had many enemies in that section of the country. Two things had occurred to injure this movement of Carolina; namely, the speech of Mr. Webster in reply to Colonel Hayne, in 1830, which had demonstrated that forcible resistance to a law of the United States is treason; and the then recent presidential election, which was considered a popular verdict against the American system. The ominous cloud raised by the first breath of nullification had been dispelled. The powerful speech of Mr. Webster found a ready response in the American heart everywhere, and was as cordially received by an enlightened and patriotic minority in South Carolina as anywhere else. The union sentiment was all-pervading and powerful; and, after that able performance of Mr. Webster, in which he riddled to atoms the web of higher-law nullification sophistry, went forth to the country, no one saw any worse event of the South Carolina movement than a disgraceful retreat, or a tremendous flogging of the nullifiers.

Many doubted General Jackson's political wisdom, and thought his administration, in many respects, a blunder; but no one questioned his high-toned patriotism. To him the conduct of South Carolina looked exceedingly childish. That the people of that state could successfully resist the general government, or subvert the laws of the land, scarcely occurred to the President. He had no doubt but he could execute the trust reposed in him by the American people ; and he had no idea of attempting to escape from the duties of that trust. The menacing attitude of Carolina looked to him like a farce. All remember his kind, conciliating, but able, firm and dignified, proclamation to the people of that state. This was issued December the tenth. It took the same ground, and made use of the same arguments, advanced by Webster, in his celebrated Hayne speech. And he gave the people of South Carolina to understand distinctly that the laws of the United States government should be executed. The excitement among the nullifiers, however, was not mitigated by the President's proclamation, but rather aggravated. The state began to put herself into a hostile attitude ; to organize a military force, supply herself with the munitions of war, &c. But the end of that controversy is familiar to all. The recent election had called for a reduction of the tariff, and, with that reduction, as by a parachute, South Carolina was let down from the precipice over which she was hanging. The leading nullifiers, however, had some little occasion for serious reflection before the issue of their troubles. President Jackson's character was well known, and it was found that he was not disposed to trifle with those who had put at defiance a law which duty and honor called upon him to execute. He began to take careful and systematic steps in the business, and, if it had been necessary for blood to flow, the example which he would have made of the leaders of so daring a resistance to the government would have been a warning to nullifiers for ages. In President Jackson's movements in the premises, he received, and, it is said, solicited, the aid of Mr. Webster. The Force Bill recommended by the President, was sustained by Mr. Webster in the Senate. Mr. Calhoun threw into the controversy all his powers. His famous nullification resolutions were introduced about the middle of February, and his speech upon them was the ablest he ever made. Mr. Webster replied to him in full, and, with overwhelming force, demolished the whole citadel of nullification, so that not a respectable fragment remains to adorn the antiquarian's cabinet.

But with the ruin of the South Carolina doctrine of states' rights and higher laws, came another ruin, whose wrecks, relics, and fragments, are abundantly numerous. These ruins were cotemporary, but not necessarily connected with and dependent on each other. With the ruin of nullification expired the protective system which had existed from 1816. Mr. Clay was the parent and protector of that system, and was at this time seriously alarmed for its safety. A presidential election had just taken place, bringing with it the election of a new Congress, and the principles of free trade had triumphed. The present Congress was friendly to his system ; but he saw that the next one would be its enemy. Mr. Verplank had introduced a bill entirely destroying the protective system ; but although it was not apprehended that this bill would meet with success at that session, the success of it at the next seemed certain. Mr. Clay was justly alarmed. Under the protective acts of 1816, 1824, and 1828, millions of dollars had been invested in manufacturing establishments, which, by the sudden repeal of those acts, would be a total sacrifice; and the voice of the American people, as indicated by the late election, demanded the repeal. In this emergency Mr. Clay brought forward his compromise. He offered it as an amendment to Mr. Verplank's bill. The measure provided for a gradual reduction of the rate of duties for ten years, at the expiration of which time (1842) there would remain only a horizontal revenue duty of twenty per cent. By this compromise, the change from the protective to the revenue system would be gradual, and those having capital invested in manufacturing establishments be able to take care of themselves. Mr. Calhoun and his friends embraced the overture as satisfactory. It readily passed, and put an end to the famous South Carolina difficulty.

Without dwelling upon those familiar acts of Jackson's administration, such as the veto of internal improvement bills, the veto of the bill to charter the United States Bank, the removal of the deposits from the old bank, and placing them in the state banks, it may in brief be said that, during his administration, the leading principles of our national policy underwent an entire retrograde revolution. The elevation of Jackson was effected in opposition to the views and feelings of the greatest statesmen of the Democratic party; in consequence of which, as already seen, that party was dismembered, and old and well tried Madisonian Democrats united themselves with the new-born party, which finally went by the name of Whig. The Democratic statesmen, who refused to follow the fortunes of Jackson's political camp, adhered to the principles and measures of Madison and Monroe; and the President, to impress his Democracy upon the people, and to show himself sounder than any of his opponents, professed, as parties since his days have done, to restore the principles of Jefferson in their purity. Experience was valued as nothing. The name of Jefferson was at that day potent with the people. He was recognized as the founder of Democracy, and hailed as one of the first of the statesmen and patriots of the Revolution. His ability was not to be doubted. He was well read, and profound, — was well acquainted with constitutions and the governments of nations. But, at the outset of our government, Mr. Jefferson made many suggestions, as to the measures of domestic policy, which time and experience showed to be impracticable, or not profitable. In fact he lived to acknowledge his mistakes in regard to many measures; but no one, on account of this, thought any the less of his wisdom and patriotism. No one, without trial, could have foreseen exactly what policy in every respect was to be best suited to a young country just starting into existence like this. However, nearly forty years' experience had, it was thought, demonstrated the prudence if not necessity of certain measures; and when Jackson proposed to ignore this experience, and disclaim the wisdom which unwearied research, discussion and observation, had taught such men as Madison, Monroe, J. Q. Adams, Henry Clay, Calhoun, Crawford, Loundes, Cheeves, and many more, all Jeffersonian Democrats, it was not strange that the most intelligent statesmen of the country should oppose him. But there was no remedy for the mistake of his elevation and rule: he was not a man that could come into power under the lead of experienced and able statesmen, and subject himself to their advice and guidance. He must command, or have no part in the councils of the nation. It is true, he was dependent on subordinates for light and direction in many things ; but these subordinates never presumed to offer him advice and counsel: they had the address to discover, as by intuition, the opinion and judgment of their chief on important measures, and simply limited themselves to an humble approbation of the same. The courage, the independence of mind, the resolution, and the decision of character of General Jackson, were as well known as his name. But for all this, when measures dictated by the abstruse principles of political economy were to be adopted, he could not be otherwise than dependent on others ; and of the correctness of the opinions of such others as he might repose confidence in, how could he possibly judge? The best statesmen of the day were in the opposition. He would not have placed inferior men in his cabinet, had he not been compelled by necessity to do so. That he would have been proud to have Clay or Webster in his cabinet, no one can doubt. But the politicians on whom he was forced to recline were emphatically adventurers. They were ambitious of advancement, and were laboring for a dynasty for themselves. Well tried and approved Democratic principles, embraced by their distinguished opponents, were to be put down, and new ones established, or, after the retirement of Jackson, they would have no claim themselves upon the country for elevation. It therefore became an imperative necessity for them to establish a new system of national policy; and this, as we have seen, was done.

President Jackson commenced his administration when the country was under the full tide of experiment in the principles of Madison, Monroe and Adams. Our foreign and domestic policy was that established under these presidents. The country was at the height of its prosperity as Jackson entered the presidential chair, and his term of administration seemed just long enough to work an entire revolution of the measures of his predecessors. The consequences of his acts were predicted; and if they fell as a legacy to his successor, it may be said, in the figure of the poet, that they were visitations to "plague the inventor." The grounds on which all his changes of policy were made were theoretical. There was at the time no occasion for complaint that the country was not prosperous and happy, as the prosperity of that day has not been exceeded. This the President acknowledged. The country had at previous periods passed through revulsions, panics, and all sorts of monetary distresses. The causes of such reverses and calamities had been examined into carefully, and a course of policy adopted, as was thought, that would avert the future recurrence of such convulsions in the business of the country. But the muniments provided against these revulsions by the safest statesmen, considering their experience as well as ability, that our country has produced, were all swept away by the administration of Jackson; and the insecurity for which our business and monetary systems were noted in early times has continued to the present day. The fact is, we are a country without any policy at all, either foreign or domestic; we are at the mercy of the world, and are only kept from bankruptcy by an uncommon run of good fortune. With natural advantages only equal to other countries, we should long ago have been in the abyss of destitution and poverty. But to acquire our new lands, the millions of men and gold from Europe are constantly pouring in upon us, and, as if to compensate us for our want of wisdom and foresight, some good-natured deity has thrown into our lap rich treasures of the precious metal. With these providential advantages, we can nearly keep clear from debt to foreign nations, but not quite. The day is at hand when our prosperity will depend more on our principles of economy than it has heretofore, and when nothing but attention to those principles will save us from the wretchedness of worse than colonial serfdom.

The resolution and fierceness with which General Jackson placed his foot upon that monster, the United States Bank, has been recited and sung for years. But the currency question is not one that can well be considered by itself. The interests of agriculture, manufactures and commerce, are so blended with the question of currency, that the latter cannot well be detached from the others and viewed separately. The currency is not properly speaking an interest; it is an instrument. Prosperity is less dependent on it than on the substantial interests of the country. Without this instrument of course there could be no business. It is to the community and the world what the blood is to the human body. It is a medium for the transmission of nutriment to all parts of the system, and indispensable to all growth or increase.

If the farmer would stretch out his mind from the limits of his farm to the bounds of his country, and look upon that country as a great family, to be provided for, governed, and regulated, on such principles as each prudent family is controlled, he would at once become a political economist and statesman, and find no difficulty in determining what measures are indispensable for the prosperity of the nation. Good common sense would be all that is requisite for a solution of the great questions that have so much agitated parties for years, if a person could only break through the mists that theorists and politicians have thrown over these subjects.

As with the family, the nation that consumes or imports more than it produces is on the road to bankruptcy. A fortunate concurrence of circumstances may for a while keep its tottering head from beating the earth; but, in the end, such a country must fall. I say tottering head, because our country is meant. These continually recurring monetary revulsions are but the too palpable effects of its crippled and debilitated faculties, showing that it is only with the utmost difficulty and pain that it can stagger along. This is the country, the improvident country, that has ever imported more than it has exported. The amount of the excess of imports over the exports is familiar to all who take the trouble to inspect the reports of the departments. A glance at the figures will show what reason would have required us to expect. Passion and party frenzy may blind a man to obvious facts, or render him indifferent to things dimly seen through the mists of prejudice; but every sensible and unbiassed mind will at once confess that a system which constantly exhausts, and never replenishes, our national resources, must be ruinous. Without going back further than to the administration of Monroe, we see that the excess of our imports over exports — taking no notice of foreign goods exported included in the account — was, during his second term, upwards of $16,000,000. During J. Q. Adams's term, upwards of $17,500,000; during General Jackson's first term, about $35,000,000; and, during the second term, upwards of $129,000,000. There has been scarcely a year since that the imports have not greatly exceeded our exports, and the aggregate of the excess of our imports from Jackson's to Buchanan's administration, must amount to several hundred millions of dollars. The excess of our importations during the last term of President Polk was upwards of $114,000,000, and the excess from 1847 to 1857 is in round numbers upwards of $250,000,000! *

The only substantial check ever attempted for these

* An inspection of the tables annually presented by the Secretary of the Treasury will show the following astonishing facts. The specie imported during ten years, from 1847, immediately after the tariff of 1846, to 1857, including those two years (fiscal years),

was	$84,208,989
Export of specie and bullion during same period,	343,062,217
Excess of exports over imports, ...	$258,853,228
The total amount of imports of goods and specie during the same period was, ...	$2,566,350,318
Exports, specie included, ...	2,512,129,741
Leaving a balance of indebtedness, . . .	$54,220,577

Or thus:

Imports, exclusive of specie from 1847 to 1857, .	$2,482,141,329
Exports, exclusive of specie, " " " " .	2,169,067,524
Balance of trade against this country, . .	$313,073,805

What does this show but a clear loss to this country, in consequence of its want of policy, of upwards of *three hundred millions of dollars*? What a commentary on our national system! We have cast the specie exports since the California mines commenced their products, to show into whose pockets their treasures find their way. The reader need not be told that this is all wrong; that our commercial system should have been such as to have saved the products of our gold mines, undue importations were the tariff enactments of 1828, and 1842, and although they both produced marked effects, their continuance was too brief to mar the symmetry of our studied system of folly and stupidity. Modern secretaries have struggled to obscure the returns of our custom-houses, and to break the effect of their prophetic balances. The exportation of gold has been charged in the accounts of our exports, to render our foreign trade apparently more equal; and, in the imports of specie, the money brought by immigrants is alluded to as an item of importance, supposed to be large, but not to be stated! The fact is, our position is a ruinous one, and every candid man must see that our policy must be changed, or our Californias, and other accidental resources, will not save us much longer from the gulf of ruin.

and, instead of paying, to have received by foreign trade a balance of one or two hundred millions annually.

EXPORTS FROM THE UNITED STATES TO FOREIGN PORTS.

Year ending June 30.	Domestic produce.	Foreign produce.	Specie and bullion.	Total exports.
1845...	$ 98,455,330	$ 7,584,781	$8,606,495	$114,646,606
1846...	101,718,042	7,865,206	3,905,268	113,488,516
1847...	150,574,844	6,166,754	1,907,024	158,648,622
1848...	130,203,709	7,986,806	15,841,616	154,032,131
1849...	131,710,081	8,641,091	5,404,648	145,755,820
1850...	134,900,233	9,475,493	7,522,994	151,898,720
1851...	178,620,138	10,295,121	29,472,752	218,388,011
1852...	154,931,147	12,037,043	42,674,135	209,642,325
1853...	189,869,162	13,096,213	27,486,875	230,452,250
1854...	215,157,504	21,661,137	41,422,423	278,241,064
1855...	192,751,135	26,158,368	56,247,343	275,156,846
1856...	266,438,051	14,781,372	45,745,485	326,964,908
1857...	278,906,713	14,917,047	69,136,922	362,960,682
1858...	241,351,033	20,660,241	52,633,147	324,644,421

Since General Jackson's administration, our country has gone back to its earlier condition. Before the last war with England, Massachusetts asked but for free trade, as restrictions upon importations, it was thought, would diminish the business of her merchants and skippers. For a while, under the tariffs of 1816 and 1824, she invested largely in manufactures; but the inconstancy of government in rendering protection to this interest has checked its extension, and the main interest of that state is again seen upon the ocean. But recently two of her leading statesmen, of her dominant party, proclaimed for free trade. For a few years past the commercial interests of the country have prospered and become extended with great rapidity. California and Australia have been treasures to the merchants as well as to the miners; and the extravagant consumption by our people of foreign, in preference to domestic, goods, has caused the mercantile interest to flourish. But where, in the end, will this commerce land us?

IMPORTS INTO THE UNITED STATES FROM FOREIGN PORTS.

Year ending June 30.	Dutiable.	Free goods.	Specie and bullion.	Total imports.
1845...	$95,106,724	$18,077,598	$4,070,242	$117,254,564
1846...	96,924,058	20,990,007	3,777,732	121,691,797
1847...	104,773,002	17,651,347	24,121,289	146,545,638
1848...	132,282,325	16,356,379	6,360,224	154,998,928
1849...	125,479,774	15,726,425	6,651,240	147,857,439
1850...	155,427,936	18,081,590	4,628,792	178,138,318
1851...	191,118,345	19,652,995	5,453,592	216,224,932
1852...	183,252,508	24,187,890	5,505,044	212,945,442
1853...	236,595,113	27,182,152	4,201,382	267,978,647
1854...	271,276,560	26,327,637	6,958,184	304,562,381
1855...	221,378,184	36,430,524	3,659,812	261,468,520
1856...	257,684,236	52,748,074	4,207,632	314,639,942
1857...	294,160,835	54,267,507	12,461,799	360,890,141
1858...	202,293,875	61,044,779	19,274,496	282,613,150

Where are we to get our money to pay these constantly accruing balances against us?

Our free-trade friends say that the importations should be in excess, as the excess indicates the profits. Truly, Jonathan is kind to take all his profits in nick-nacks, paying for his ships, labor, and expenses, out of his home purse!

The truth is, the correct policy for this country was overthrown by the powerful arm of General Jackson; and our leading statesmen, who plainly see the deplorable condition into which we are sinking, admonished by the fate of Clay and Webster, have not the moral courage to espouse the correct principles, and urge them upon the country. The people will by degrees become enlightened upon the subject, and in this, as upon the question of internal improvements, get in advance of their cowardly leaders, and lead them to the right path. It was a promising indication to see a Democratic Congress, by a constitutional majority, pass improvement bills over the veto of Mr. Pierce; and the day is not far distant when tariff bills will be enacted either with or without the President's consent. This will be brought about by sound judgment as a prudent precaution, or by the saddest experiences, which never apply their teaching in vain.*

* As evidence of the great change going on amongst the Democrats in regard to the doctrine of Protection, we may mention the significant and highly encouraging fact that, during the political campaigns of 1858, many leading Democrats, in different parts of the country, emphatically announced themselves in favor of Protection. Leading Democrats in Massachusetts, Pennsylvania, and other states, did so. Mr. Hallet was decided upon the question; and from the Boston Post, the leading organ of the administration, in New England, we extract

It has ever been a great fault of the people of this country to be governed more by party spirit than by ideas of state policy. Every countryman should think of his national family, as well as of his domestic circle. The substantial and permanent interests of the country are not so varied as to be beyond the comprehension of any person of ordinary information and judgment, if he would exclude from them the mists of speculating

the following, by the Post copied from the Pennsylvanian, a leading Democratic paper:

"HENRY CLAY ON THE TARIFF. — To those old line Whigs who sincerely regard the opinions of Henry Clay, the following on the subject of a tariff are commended at this time. In 1844, when Henry Clay was the Whig nominee for President, he delivered a speech before a meeting of his political friends in Raleigh, North Carolina, which speech we find in the Clay Bugle of July 25th, 1844, a Whig campaign paper, published at Harrisburg, by J. Knabb, Esq. In this speech Mr. Clay makes use of the following emphatic language:

"'Let the amount which is requisite for an economical administration of the government, when we are not engaged in war, be raised exclusively on foreign imports; and, in adjusting a tariff for that purpose, let such discriminations be made as will foster and encourage our own domestic industry. ALL PARTIES OUGHT TO BE SATISFIED WITH A TARIFF FOR REVENUE AND DISCRIMINATIONS FOR PROTECTION.'

"So said Henry Clay in 1844; so said the Democracy from the earliest stages of the tariff issue, and so say they now, in every public meeting that passes resolutions concerning the tariff. They have been honest and consistent in their course, while the Black Republicans have been dishonest in every act with reference to this important issue. Will the friends of Henry Clay join with that party which is opposing every principle which he laid down in his Raleigh speech? Can they strike hands over an issue which their great leader would not accept where he present? Henry Clay said, 'all parties ought to be satisfied with a tariff for revenue and discriminations for protection.' The Black Republicans are not satisfied with this, and theorists, and look at them in the light of common sense.

As with the family, if the nation would become rich it must sell more than it buys. This is the fundamental principle on which the whole system of political economy must be based. Unless the policy adopted shall attain this end, it will be an erroneous one. The truth of this position will be acknowledged by every

hence are opposed to the principles of Henry Clay. Yet this faction asks the support of old line Whigs? Such an appeal is an insult to the intelligence of the sincere admirers of Henry Clay."

The rate at which this country is going to ruin is now pretty plainly apparent to every intelligent man, and is made conspicuous by our annual trade returns. It seems that we import of cotton fabrics about one half the amount we manufacture. We have about $75,000,000 invested in cotton manufacture, which consume, of the raw material, upwards of 650,000 bales per annum, worth upwards of $30,000,000. The value of the articles wrought from that raw material is nearly $60,000,000; of which some 6 or 8,000,000 — a coarser fabric — is exported. A country like this, with sole command of raw material, with abundance of manufacturing skill and enterprise, and with every necessary facility for manufacturing, import four times as much value of cotton fabrics as it exports!

It is evident enough that this country can never prosper until it establishes a correct policy. Political parties have been a great injury to us, and that injury, unless the people shall profit by the lessons of the past, and change their course for the future, will continue. We must cease our sectional jealousies, and all endeavor to promote the best interests of the country. The Northern man must not think it his mission to overturn, by civil war and disunion, what God has himself established; but we must feel grateful to the enterprising and courageous Saxon who will brave a tropic sun to supply us with the material which in a short time may make New England the counting-room of the trade of the world. And the Southern man must recollect that the God that formed this country for a great nation, or empire, never intended that any one part of it should one. To realize this policy is the aim of every nation on earth saving the United States. There is not a nation in Europe that does not struggle, and generally with success, to keep the balance of trade in its favor. Even France, since the accession to power of Louis Napoleon, although encountering many obstacles, and forced to a less favorable system than she would desire, has, as a general thing, especially during peace, exported

enjoy all of its advantages. Manufactures must have their place, commerce its centre, and agriculture its field. The Southerner must recollect that his is an agricultural section, and that his true policy consists in securing a good, safe and permanent market for his produce. To endeavor to seek that out of the sphere, and at the expense, of his own country, cannot be safe. He must learn to feel grateful in the reflection that the people of the North, acting with the rest of the Union, are able to open that good and permanent market; and he must cease to be annoyed with the evidences of thrift which Northern industry everywhere evinces, and submit to the conditions on which Providence has permitted him to develop the wealth of the South. How admirably, how cunningly this Union is formed! Pennsylvania, its back-bone, is of iron; facing the East, upon her right hand, the South—upon the left, the North. The grain-growing regions in the far West so situated as to conveniently supply the great manufacturing cities of the North, the iron manufacturers of Pennsylvania, and the cotton and sugar planters of the South, with direct communication with all parts of the world at every point of the compass. That is, saying nothing of the Hudson and the prospects of a ship canal to Lake Erie, there is the great channel of communication by the Lakes and St. Lawrence, by the Mississippi river, and by the Columbia river, which will shortly be connected by railroad with the head-waters of the Mississippi. By a glance at the physical constitution of this country, it is easy to see that no ambition can profit it that is not an ambition for the whole country. No one part can possibly be built up, on a sound and enduring basis, without building up the whole; and he who would, by his policy, retard and cripple the energies of a part, aims a blow at the whole.

more than she has imported. Her balances have been comparatively healthy.

The American people will learn before long that the only reliable and steady market for breadstuffs is to be found at home. Occasional wars abroad, or a famine, may create a temporary demand for grain; but it is a wretched nation that cannot, as a general thing, furnish its own bread. The Yankee, who would feed an Englishman with his bread, will be obliged to butter it well with duties. A little reflection will satisfy us that we must look for a sale of the produce of our farms to our domestic markets. It is the calculation of every nation to be independent in the necessaries of life, and to secure this end is the policy of every nation shaped. America is rich beyond measure in agricultural resources; but their development and the realization of the wealth they may afford, will be at a period far remote, unless other interests on which they are directly dependent are regarded. Commerce, as one thing, is necessary; but how can commerce be sustained without a healthy foreign trade? A trade that impoverishes the country must soon consume the life-springs of commerce, and all industry will be paralyzed. Then what shall, or should, our merchant vessels be carrying over the oceans of the earth? There is but one reliable basis for such a commerce as will enrich the country. On this is placed the commerce of England, who is becoming the richest nation in the world. Her wealth is in the skill and energy of her mechanics and manufacturers, and she finds the producing power of the brain and muscle of her industrious citizens a mine that never fails in its yield of gold. And unless the United States shall build up its manufacturing interests, what shall we expect? The statesmen of the South have for years prided themselves on possessing the principal exports of the country. The production of immense quantities of cotton is certainly creditable to our Southern neighbors; but its shipment to Europe is a disgrace and shame to America. The cotton crop of this country is the basis of British power and prosperity, and has been for years. In encouraging her export of her raw material to be manufactured by a foreign nation, the South commits an act of folly for which she is not pardonable, and will, sooner or later, reap a suitable reward. The exclusive possession of that raw material has for years rendered England her jealous and deadly enemy, and every moment this power is seeking her overthrow and destruction. The ruin of the domestic institutions of the South has ever been considered by England as the sure means of overcoming Southern competition in the production of cotton. When the slaves of the South are freed, England, in some of her colonies, may raise cotton as cheap as she. As slavery in the West Indies ceases, Britain finds the production of sugar in her East India possessions profitable. She cannot compete with slavery; but with the West Indies and the Southern States cultivated by free blacks she can to profit produce her sugar and cotton in her Eastern possessions; and to bring about this state of things is her constant study and employment. Should she fail in her schemes against Southern slavery, she may not in obtaining the command of the raw material for her immense manufactures. She is striving for this constantly, and already produces in the Indies quite a respectable proportion (about a fourth) of her raw cotton imports. That England will ever remain dependent on the United

States for a raw material of such vast importance, no sane man should expect. The produce of India must already sensibly affect the Southern crop; and how long will it be before it shall have a controlling power over it? Will it be five, or ten, or twenty years from this? How long ago was it that the cotton crop of the South did not exceed the present Indian crop? And when the demand for American cotton is so much decreased as to gradually reduce its production, how is the South to help herself? She will then find it too late to encourage a home market by having her raw material manufactured here, and putting the American manufacture in competition with the English. England will, by that time, not only have the manufacture, and the trade with the whole world, but she will likewise have the supply of the raw material in her own hands. The golden opportunity for putting the cotton interest beyond the reach of fortune is passing by. England has had no raw material until within a short period. Had our land been supplied with manufacturing establishments, and the raw material kept at home, and here manufactured, the supply of cottons for the whole world would have been in our hands, and no power on earth could take it from us. Under a liberal system, ere this time our manufactures would have been as extensive as those of England. Neither China, the Indies, nor any nation or people on the globe, would prefer to be supplied by England in preference to America. But the South set out in 1828 with the idea that England was the only purchaser for the bulk of her crop that earth would ever produce, and thought her interest consisted in securing a constant sale of her cotton in that market. And that stupid idea has been since hugged with John-Bull-like pertinacity. The Southern planters have made a gross mistake. They have turned with utter forgetfulness and indifference from their poverty-stricken, painstaking, industrious and ingenious brothers, whom a hard destiny has cast upon the sterile rocks of New England. Those rich and lordly planters have passed us by until idleness has filled our heads with mischief which wholesome employment would have averted. Had the cotton crop of the South been annually worked up in Northern mills, the sin of slavery would never have been dreamed of, and the Union would have been bound in bonds that all the nations of earth could not sunder.

CHAPTER XXIII.

MISTAKEN POLICY OF THE UNITED STATES. — OUR SUPERIOR ADVANTAGES FOR SUPPLYING THE TRADE OF THE WORLD. — HAVING THE RAW MATERIAL, WE COULD ABSOLUTELY COMMAND THAT TRADE. — EXPENSE OF ENGLAND FOR COTTON. — THE EMPLOYMENT IT GIVES HER PEOPLE. — HOW SHE PAYS US FOR IT. — TO WHAT SHE IS INDEBTED FOR HER COMMERCIAL SUPERIORITY. — THE FOLLY OF AMERICA. — BRITISH PROFITS ON OUR RAW COTTON. — HER EXPORTS. — HER PREACHING AND PRACTICE IN REGARD TO FREE TRADE. — OUR SECTIONAL QUARRELS RUINOUS. — INTEREST OF ALL SECTIONS THE SAME. — UNLESS THE SOUTH SOON SECURE A MARKET FOR HER COTTON IN THE NORTH, BY HELPING TO BUILD UP MANUFACTORIES THAT MAY CONSUME HER CROPS, SHE MAY FIND IT TOO LATE. — ENGLAND AN ENEMY OF THE SOUTH. — SHE ENCOURAGES SECESSION OR DISUNION, THAT WOULD EITHER RENDER THAT SECTION A COLONY OF ENGLAND, OR OVERTHROW SLAVE-LABOR. — PROBABLE EFFECT OF A DISMEMBERMENT, ETC.

THERE have been marvellous ideas of progress in this country; but the progress has been in the acquisition of territory, instead of the achievements of mechanical industry. Were we to use our territory as well as England does hers, we could comfortably dispense with two-thirds of what we now have, and relinquish our insane longings for more. Our population is as great as that of the British Isles; but Great Britain is but a trifle larger in extent than New England. The basis of her prosperity is her manufacturing industry. Without the constant results of her manufacturing energies, all vitality would depart from her commerce, and her beautiful merchant ships would decay in her harbors. Whatever her industry can produce is protected by formidable duties; but the raw material necessary to keep her machines in motion is admitted to her ports substantially free. Her own people are relied upon for the production of every species of the raw material that it is in their power to raise. Her policy does not benefit the manufacturer alone, but gives also to the farmer a profit in every article manufactured. The millions of people engaged in her work-shops, stores, warehouses and merchant service, are fed by the farmer, who finds a ready and sure market for his breads, and all the raw material he is able to produce. The raw material for her cotton fabrics is a sore charge upon her. She is obliged to pay the United States about $100,000,000 per annum for this article, which is the imperial lord of the commerce of the age. Nature has placed the elements of national superiority and power in our hands, and, Esau-like, we truck them off to England for messes of pottage. To pay us for this staple, she sends us back, in cottons from her mills, about $30,000,000; in woollens about the same amount; and about the like amount in iron and iron manufactures. These three articles, all of which should be produced and manufactured in our own country, nearly pay us for our cotton exports; and, for the privilege of selling to Britain our peculiar advantages and resources, which, if judiciously used, would make us at once the greatest power on earth, we consent to sacrifice our iron mines and forges, our wool-growing and manufacturing interests, and to take from England nearly a third in value of our cotton crops in cotton manufactures!

But England, according to the theory of our free-trade statesmen, must drive an unprofitable trade with all the world. She exports more by millions than she imports; she has not that excess of imports which is charged to the account of profits! And this must seem strange; for her exports are of articles she ought to have a profit on. Her exports of cotton — that is, the various kinds of fabrics made from the raw material purchased of this country — must, even after supplying the demands of the British Isles, amount to between 150 and 200 millions of dollars. The value of all her manufactured goods, annually exported, of every kind, cannot be of less value than 400,000,000 dollars. Of these goods, her vast possessions, say the Cape, the Mauritius, St. Helena, and the Ascension Isles, Australia, British North America, West Indies, Ceylon, and the East Indies, must take over one-third, and the United States nearly one-quarter. Our country is, as a consumer of British fabrics, about equal to all her colonies, and more profitable to her, a thousand times over, as her outlay for influencing our elections, and instructing our people in the sciences of free-trade and free-labor, is but a trifle compared with her expense of governing and keeping in subjection her distant and rebellious possessions. England has not yet obtained currency for her free-trade preachings on the continent, and but a trifle more of her manufactures are purchased by the whole of Europe than by the United States. This country is the only one in the world that disregards all the laws of trade, and acts without any policy. It has no future destiny in view, and is as destitute of prudential considerations as the prodigal who wasted his substance in riotous living. The shrewd politicians of America see many objections to the doctrine of protection. It is thought to enhance the price of goods, and benefit manufacturers at the expense of consumers! The United States is content that trade shall regulate itself, and considers it folly for the country, as such, to attempt to exercise any control over our material interests. The result is that we are more useful to England, under the system of policy that she adopts and rigidly enforces, than all of her colonies put together.*

* To show not only the tendency, but also the practical working, of Southern policy, in regard to free-trade, and opposition to domestic manufactures, let us state a few more facts in regard to the cotton trade. The United States export upwards of 1,000,000,000 pounds of cotton annually. From 1851 to 1855 the average annual export was 1,025,654,156 pounds; but England took about two-thirds of these exports. Other countries in Europe for some years past have been fostering cotton manufactures with great success. But both England and the continental nations receive quite a proportion of their raw material from other sources than the United States. They are dependent on us for about *three-fourths* of their cotton; full one-fourth of all the cotton consumed in the manufactories of England and the continent is obtained from other parts of the world. The British East India Company commenced their efforts for the promotion of the growth of cotton in India, in 1788. The increase of the crop has been steady. In 1814 the exportation was upwards of 4,000,000 pounds, and it now averages some 165,000,000 pounds per annum. England herself, in her importations of cotton from the East Indies, from 1851 to 1855, averaged upwards of 122,000,000 pounds annually. During the same period she averaged in her importations from Brazil upwards of 22,000,000 pounds, and from Egypt upwards of 28,000,000 pounds. The average importations of cotton by England during those five years was 838,335,984 pounds per annum; of which the average annual amount received from the United States was 661,529,220 pounds. France, now quite a consumer of cotton, as well as England, is looking for independence of the United States in its production. Slavery is unanimously reprobated by the crowned heads of Europe; but philanthropy warrants the practice of what is called the *apprentice* system! The trader's vessel appears off the coast of Africa, where reigning negro kings supply traders with slaves; but, instead of buying the bodies and souls, as the abolitionists would say, they only buy the use of the servants for a certain number of years. The

Providence has never made a country better adapted to the manufacturing interest than the United States, and

contract is made, and the negro goes to his steady home for the term. When taken he is a barbarian, and when his term expires he will be not much less so ; and, as a compensation for not being an outright chattel slave, he has two signal privileges : one, a tolerable passage across the Atlantic, free from the asperities of the slave-passage, and the other, an entire freedom in old age, when unable longer to toil, to go where he pleases. Further, as this system seeks nothing but labor for a limited period, without property in the servant's issue, none but males are transported, so that the harrowing scenes of family separations can never occur. England and France have but one intent in the movement. It is their determination to render themselves independent of us ; and there is no problem that so thoroughly puzzles the minds of the British and French statesmen as the question of European interference in matters pertaining to this continent. But should Europe eventually obtain its supply of cotton independently, or comparatively so, of the United States, it will have occasion for congratulating itself on having made a very narrow escape. This especially will be the case with England. Her foreign wars, and vast commercial and manufacturing interests, have been for years supported by and entirely dependent on us. Had our country continued under the wise system instituted by such statesmen as Calhoun, Crawford, Lowndes and Clay, and which was pursued from 1816 to 1828, by this time we should have monopolized the principal manufacturing business of the world. Having the raw material, which others could not get, how could the world avoid being dependent on us? And the spindles and forges are the sinews of commerce. The policy then instituted would soon have reduced the British Isles to their natural importance, and have exalted this country to unparalleled wealth and power. With a monopoly of the raw material, and the manufactures also, no power could ever have competed with us, and our ascendency would have been permanent ; but, neglecting manufactures, and rendering ourselves dependent on England, instead of making her feel her dependence on us, our enemies, in spite of us, are daily building up, under our eyes, quite reliable resources for cotton, and will, sooner or later, be in a great measure independent of us.

they are equally well adapted to the agricultural and commercial interests. This country is located, constructed, and every way planned, for the seat of a great empire ; and it seems a pity that its high promise may not be realized while in its republican state. But to see it throwing away the advantages nature has given it, and shaping its national policy on ideas of local interest, is prophetic of the result of the present form of government. What revolutions, convulsions, and scenes of anarchy and blood, America is to pass through before she becomes what she seems evidently designed for, — a great, wealthy and commanding nation, — is only known to higher intelligences. We are loth to believe that it is fated that her glorious mission is not to be achieved under republican institutions. Although of nations, as of individuals, it may be truly said, "There is a destiny that shapes their ends ;" still that destiny, we are anxious to believe, is more or less subject to the purposes of human wisdom. It sometimes seems, it is true, as though it was never the intention of Providence that the fate of nations should be under the control of popular wisdom. The career of a nation appears as much the subject of the laws of nature, and as much influenced and affected by circumstances, as the stream that flows from our hill-sides, and empties into the ocean. Whether governed by the voice of one, or of all its people, is the same. The subjects of permanent despotisms are such by the operation of natural laws, over which they have no control. It is not denied that physical force sometimes temporarily rules a people ; but generally the government of the world is by ideas. Ideas are as various as the localities of the earth, and as the organizations of men. Reason is the boasted prerogative of man; but, unfortunately, reason appears to have a higher duty than the government of men; this duty is assigned to the baser and grosser passions. Reason is useful for purposes of philosophy, and speculation into the nature of things, but not much used in the conduct of human affairs.

It does not need great wisdom to see that no nation can flourish by favoring the exportation of the raw material for manufactures, instead of encouraging its use at home. And for a country like this — that is capable of commanding the trade of the world, and, by the encouragement of manufactures, of blending together the interests of all sections, thus laying the foundations for lasting prosperity — to pay no attention to its situation and advantages, and to adopt a course that creates no bond of union between its different parts, but leaves them estranged and jealous of each other, is evidence that we are devoid of a national character, a national policy, and a national spirit.

Under the sectional rule of local interests the harmony of our Union has long been disturbed. The alienation produced by supposed conflicting interests is still onward, and is ministered to constantly by all the enemies of our country, domestic and foreign. The South have seen fit to treat her interests as incompatible with those of the North and West, and has been firmly committed to the doctrine that manufacturing, without which agriculture cannot flourish, can only be favored by government at her expense. In this foolish and ruinous idea the South, we are happy to witness, has not been a unit. Such states as Kentucky, North Carolina, Tennessee and Louisiana, have been governed by more liberal views, and handsome minorities in the other

Southern States have recognized sounder principles. But the mass of the South have seen proper to repudiate and make war upon the only policy under which the rest of the country can prosper, and without which, it is humbly submitted, the South herself will sooner or later perish. Let us see.

The views and feelings of the ultra leaders in the Southern Rights party are often announced. We have heard of them in Congress, in Southern conventions, and read them in Southern papers. The leaders look upon the North as their enemy, and expect the day when an attack upon their rights shall drive them from the Union. They say that the North is certain, at no far distant day, to invade their constitutional rights, and that already they have refused to carry out, in good faith, the constitutional compromises. The North, they say, are making war upon them in every conceivable manner, misrepresenting their institutions, and abusing them personally. This, it is true, is the feeling of large masses of Southern people; and, actuated by this feeling, and not being indifferent to their fate, they are naturally led to form plans for future emergencies. But how vain and dangerous are all their speculations of which we have as yet had any indications! England! England! In all their visions this royal mistress of the ocean is their first and last hope. Should Cuba and Mexico be acquired, and, together with the Southern States, forced to the step by the intolerance of Northern fanaticism, formed into a powerful republic or empire,—England, it is thought, will be the only country from which floods of wealth are to flow into her lap. That England would favor such an empire, and be its natural ally, no one doubts. The London Times — the British government organ — predicts the immediate absorption, by the United States, of Mexico, and favors the idea, saying, that no opposition would be made by foreign nations. But there are objections to this scheme which should condemn it at once. The rupture of the Union for the formation of a new empire could not take place without violence. The new empire or republic would be born amidst the blaze of war; and at its birth would be without armies, munitions of war, or a navy. In such a movement the South of course sees no possible chance of success, saving by the aid of the Holy Alliance. This dreadful alternative will ever be sufficient to stay every step in the direction of secession. Men of sound judgment will never be likely to embark in such an undertaking without a proper consideration of all the probable consequences. And it can escape the discernment of no one that the birth and independence of such a Southern confederacy or government, under the auspices of European monarchs, must end in rendering the Southern people the vassals and serfs of European lords. It is conceded that, in a struggle between the relics of our republic in the North and the new confederacy in the South, European powers would see that they would be interested in preventing the subjugation of the latter by the former. The same policy that impelled France and England to resist the encroachments of Russia upon Turkey would cause the same powers to maintain the new government that should spring up in the South. But how would such a conflict end? If, by pouring into the South her immense armies, Europe, after a struggle of years, should be successful in overthrowing freedom in the North, would the South emerge from the storm in any but a ruined condition?

And if the North should preserve their institutions, and, after a bloody and protracted contest, treat with all the combined powers for the independence of the new empire, in what condition would the Holy Alliance be likely to leave our Southern friends? Do the ultra Southern nullifiers and disunionists who can only base their hopes on such foreign alliances, ever look to the consequences of their mad projects; or are they moved solely by a blind, impetuous fanaticism? It is hoped that the views of this part of the Southern people do not spread, as the only hope for freedom, prosperity and happiness, both of the people of the South and North, is in union. He who looks beyond the Union for redress of grievances stares destruction in the face.

CHAPTER XXIV.

POWER OF IDEAS. — COMMERCIAL SUPERIORITY OF ENGLAND, HOW ATTAINED AND PRESERVED. — ADVANTAGES OF AMERICA SEEN BY ENGLAND. — HER POLICY IN REGARD TO THE UNITED STATES. — DISUNION THE ONLY POSSIBLE MEANS OF PREVENTING THIS COUNTRY FROM EVENTUALLY ENJOYING THE TRADE NOW ENJOYED BY ENGLAND. — HER SCHEMES. — HER SLAVERY QUESTION. — HER SACRIFICES IN THE WEST INDIES. — HER LABORS INJURIOUS TO THE NEGRO. — ALISON ON EMANCIPATION IN THE WEST INDIES. — MISSIONARY MOVEMENT IN THE WEST INDIES. — CIVILIZATION OF NEGROES ARRESTED BY EMANCIPATION. — EFFECT OF WEST INDIAN EMANCIPATION ON THE UNITED STATES. — SIMULTANEOUS EFFORTS OF BRITISH ABOLITIONISTS IN THE UNITED STATES. — RESULT NOT THE SAME AS IN THE WEST INDIES, AND THE REASONS. — INCENDIARY PUBLICATIONS AND PETITIONS IN 1835 AND 1836. — ANTI-SLAVERY OPERATIONS OF THOSE DAYS INSTIGATED ABROAD. — COURSE OF SOUTHERN MEN IN THOSE DAYS. — REMARKS OF MR. CLAY ON THE OBJECTS OF THE ABOLITIONISTS. — NEW ENGLAND DUPED BY OLD ENGLAND.

In recent ages, in particular, great political changes have been effected, less by the sword, for the avowed purpose of plunder, than by the power of ideas. Political ideas have frequently wrought revolutions; but religious ones have borne the greatest sway. The spread of Mahometanism shows what a motive power in the human breast are religious ideas. The enthusiasm and desperate courage of the Mahometan, however, is not perhaps peculiar. The crusader, under another creed, was not less fierce and enthusiastic than his Saracen antagonist. The crusades were great movements, caused by the steam-like power of religious ideas. The empire of Charlemagne, as well as that of Constantine, was won by a war inspired and sustained by them; and, in fact, the principal revolutions and popular commotions of modern times have been occasioned by religious fanaticism. The recent war between Russia and Turkey, as between these powers, was a religious one. The education of the serf's mind is in the hands of the Czar, and the serf is by that hand rendered as obedient as the engine to the hand of the engineer. But few monarchs, in modern days, attempt to hold a people by the power of the sword alone. A conquest may open the windows of a nation for the light of the conqueror's religion; but the conquest is not regarded safe until this enters. But conquests now-a-days rather succeed than precede the missionary. That is, the ambitious monarch prefers, by propagating revolutionary ideas, to first excite a division among his enemies, as his yoke is thus more easily forced upon them. An idea is a far more effective weapon with which to overthrow an enemy than a bullet. Let the idea once be fairly lodged in that enemy's mind,—let the honest countryman once receive into his mental organization the peculiar religious bias,—and through it his adversary will control him with more effect and certainty than he could by the appliance of any physical force ever invented. Considerations of patriotism are at once lost sight of in the presence of the peculiar religious ism, for which everything will be freely sacrificed. Dynasties are built on creeds, and the regulation of the balances of power, so much talked about in modern times, is but, in fact, the proper adjustment by alliances of the powers of the earth with regard to conflicting religions.

The governments of Europe wield their respective people entirely through their mental organizations, and, having the schools, pulpits and presses, in their own hands, no horseman with a rein directs his steed with more ease and certainty than the monarch controls his subject. Ideas are not dug from the earth, do not grow upon trees, nor are they rained down from heaven. They are a communicated power, usually received from without, and rarely from within. The mind, like the soil, cherishes whatever is committed to it, and is as generous and lavish of its riches upon an evil as upon a good plant.

In the earlier ages, when a people became too numerous in a particular nomadic family, portions, from time to time, would separate themselves from the parent stock, going forth, under new leaders, to conquer new homes, and repeat the process of multiplying tribes. Europe was in this manner settled from Asia; but America was not in this way settled from Europe. Before the discovery of America, nomadic life had become pretty much obliterated from Europe, its numerous tribes having become blended into nations. These nations owed their birth and consolidation to the power of religious ideas; and to the same power was America indebted for her settlement. Emigration took a new form. About the time of the discovery of America, ideas began to burst forth from the tombs in which they had been buried for centuries. The treasures of ancient thought were dug up from manuscripts saved from the wrecks of antiquity, to be buried again under a rigorous censorship more stifling than mediæval darkness. As ideas in conflict with the divine right of the ruling monarch rendered the subject an enemy of the state, and guilty of treason, governments were cautious to suppress their introduction and circulation. Despite the vigilance of kings and emperors, thoughts subversive of the ruling dynasties gradually crept in amongst the people ; and hence the emigrations to the wilds of America.

It is as true now as it was centuries ago that, "as a man thinketh, so is he." The idea is the sovereign lord and master of the man, and to this each looks as his higher and supreme law. Life itself is less cherished than a creed. The martyr burning at the stake expires in a paroxysm of joy at the thought that his faith is triumphant over the power of man. In the ardor of the affection with which a faith is cherished, there is no difference between those who follow the true, and those who follow the false god. There is certainly no less enthusiasm in the Mahometan than in the Christian ; and the atheist is as religiously devoted to his idea as either of them. As man's ideas are, is his allegiance determined. The words of the serpent transformed Eve from a servant of God to a servant of Satan. Dynasties and thrones, as well as republics, are only sustained by ideas. If republics are less stable than monarchies, it is because the perpetuation of conservative opinions is not so likely to occur in the hands of a mob as in those of a despot. The British crown has frequently been the foot-ball of shifting religious ideas. Religionists will sacrifice liberty in preference to making a surrender of their peculiar notions ; and hence the great check to the establishment of free institutions in England, and Europe generally. Neither Scotland nor Ireland would have been subjected so long to the British crown, but for the conflict of religious notions among the people of those isles; nor, without such conflict of ideas among their people, would the Canadas till this day have remained subject to British rule.

It is the object of England, as it was with ancient Athens, to maintain her naval supremacy over the whole world. But as England, for this, has not within her bosom the natural resources for such ascendency, she is forced to maintain it, if at all, by policy. In this, also, she resembles her Grecian model. The ancient mistress of the seas was vigilant, shrewd and daring. No power of old was more artful and prompt to ferment troubles amongst its neighbors, and take advantage of them, than the subtle Athenians. It is plain enough that if England is to remain the commercial centre of the world, and continue to maintain that balance of power which a naval superiority commands, she must accomplish it by far-seeing counsels, and by a bold, firm and daring course. The extension of those powers possessing superior resources must be firmly and decisively checked and restrained; and, for this purpose, all those who may share her jealousies should be allied to her policy. France, ruled by the great Napoleon, would have been a powerful competitor for the palm, and, by the triumph of peaceful arts alone, might have shorn England of much of her power and glory. The effort of England to put down that great man was a struggle, not only for ascendency, but for self-preservation. But the policy of England demanded Napoleon's overthrow. To stop short of this would have been a surrender of the vast power and consequence which the artificial system of that little isle has acquired in the world. The greatness and power of Britain are extorted from other nations by a deep-laid policy, backed by a strong arm, and are not the results of vast national dominions, people and resources. Her colonial dominions are large; but they are only held by a commercial tenure. They are no part of England proper, and drop from her when the commerce of the world glides from her hands. That commerce is now forced. The raw material for her principal fabrics has to be bought at an enormous expense, and shipped across the Atlantic, giving to each article of British cotton manufacture consumed in America a journey, in the raw and manufactured state, of upwards of six thousand miles. The United States, in the nature of things, must be a competitor of Britain in manufactures, and must soon, unless checked in their career of greatness, take the trade of the world into their own hands. This century will give us a hundred millions of people. The increase of population will materially affect the policy of our statesmen. All classes will encourage home industry, and the South, that distrusted the home market for her staple when we numbered only ten or twelve millions of people, will thwart our national prosperity no longer.

England studies and understands the tendency of our career better than we do ourselves. She sees that we hold in our hands the commerce of the world. She sees the approaching absorption of Cuba, Mexico and Central America, giving us an unlimited and perpetual control of the cotton staple; and then her vision is greeted by manufactures sufficient to supply the whole earth. Her vision does not stop here. She judges the future by the past, and sees our population expanded to hundreds of millions, with magnificent railways stretching from the Atlantic to the Pacific Ocean; and, as her eyes glance at the harbors, at the termini of these railways on the Pacific coast, she is startled, and, for a moment, alarmed. These harbors she sees filled with the fleets of the world, with steamers plying between them and the Indies, pouring the commerce of the East upon these Pacific thoroughfares. As this all passes before her aching eyes, she looks again, and in vain peers about the world for her own magnificent commerce and possessions. She discovers that the island of Great Britain has ceased to be the centre of commerce; that Russia has really at last slipped into the seat of Constantine; and that the United States have succeeded her Britannic Majesty in India — the Indian possessions being peacefully resigned by those who have no further use for them. England is as clear as day in these visions, and knows them to be real, and to be realizable, provided the Union shall last half a century longer. The cry which Rome uttered in regard to Carthage, she uses towards the United States. The only thing which can possibly preserve the ascendency of British commerce is the dissolution of the American Union. Her arts are all concentrated for the accomplishment of this. Her *modus operandi* has been alluded to. Let us look a little further into her doleful wailings for the wrongs of American slaves.

The powerful efforts made by the British government early in the present century, and, in fact, continued to the present day, to suppress the slave-trade, have been far from successful. The exportation of negroes from Africa has not been discontinued; but the sufferings of the middle-passage have been increased ten-fold; showing that an attempt to thwart by legislation the decrees of Providence is of but little avail. The exportation of slaves to America is comparatively a recent matter, and is a happy vent to the slave-traffic, compared with the negro-trade that has been carried on for thousands of years with the rest of the world. But England has not endeavored to stop the sales of slaves to the traders who convey them over the Great Desert, nor with the drovers who move them down the Nile. She has been more in dread of the sufferings which Sambo would be likely to experience in the hands of a savage Yankee, than moved by fear of what he would suffer in the power of the Oriental races. A Turk or an Arab is regarded as a mild and Christian master compared with a Jonathan; and no sigh is ever heard for the mutilated wretches who are borne from Africa into the East. There are, in their equatorial hive in Africa, some fifty millions of negroes; and there their tribes have been for ages. Enterprise is the gift of mental organization. The negro has it not. He has the physical faculties for labor, but not the intellect that will excite him to it. He seems designed for a servile and subordinate position, as without compulsion he cannot be induced to labor. The motives that impel the people of other races to effort have no effect upon the negro. Consequently, he is by nature a barbarian. Under a civilized master he becomes civilized, and experience teaches that his highest *status* is brought out in servitude.

The error of England in making herself so officious in endeavoring to put a stop to the slave-trade and negro slavery is, as a humanitarian movement, now clearly seen by everybody. Her policy, so far as her material interests, and the happiness and prosperity of the negro are concerned, has been a mistaken one. This is, on the whole view of the subject, fully and frankly asserted by Mr. Alison, in the volume of his History of Europe (Vol. 7) just published. "Like all other great movements of the human race," says Mr. Alison, speaking of the slave-trade, "brought about by the irresistible laws of nature acting by physical necessities or moral influence, this vast transportation of mankind, however violent in its origin, or painful in its completion, was calculated to produce, and will ultimately confer, great benefits upon the species. It promised to effect what all the changes of time, and all the efforts of philanthropy, from the beginning of the world, had failed in accomplishing — the ultimate civilization of the African race." Then, speaking of the legislation for the suppression of the slave-trade, Mr. Alison quotes the report of Mr. Bruxton, an advocate of emancipation, which says, "Twenty years ago the African institution reported to the Duke of Wellington that the number of slaves who annually crossed the Atlantic was 70,000. There is evidence before the parliamentary committee to show that about one-third was for the British Islands, and one-third for St. Domingo ; so that, if the slave-trade of other countries had been stationary, they ought only to have imported 25,000 ; *whereas, now* (1838) *the number landed in Cuba and Brazil alone is* 150,000 *annually;* being more than double the whole draft of Africa when the slave-trade controversy began ! Twice as many human beings are now its victims as when Wilberforce and Clarkson commenced their noble career ; and each individual of this increased number, in addition to the horrors which were endured in former times, has to suffer from being cribbed up in a narrow space, and on board of a vessel where accommodation is sacrificed to speed. Painful as this is, it becomes still more distressing if it shall appear that our present system has not failed by mischance, or want of energy, or want of expenditure; but that the system itself is erroneous, and must necessarily end in disappointment." And, adds Mr. Alison, "Thus the effect of the emancipation of the negroes has been to ruin our own planters, stop the civilization of our own negroes, and double the slave-trade in extent, and quadruple it in horror throughout the globe." Mr. Alison's chapter on slavery ought to be carefully perused by that portion of the New England people who have formed their opinion on the subject without examination. As a historian, Mr. Alison, although a British writer, with prejudices in favor of British interests, could not, without the grossest misrepresentation, and the most glaring falsehood, have drawn any different picture from that presented us.

But the British government had other motives than those of humanity. The monopoly of the cotton product by the United States can never, she has thought, be overthrown, save by striking it through the American system of negro servitude. The sacrifices of England to put an end to the slave-trade have been alluded to. It was during the administration of President Jackson that England (1834) passed her first act for emancipating the slaves of her West India possessions. The emancipation of her slaves was not contemplated by England when she commenced her warfare on the slave-trade; but that measure was hastened on by the agitations of the slavery question in England, and by the state of things brought about in her slave islands by these agitations. After a deep sympathy had been aroused in England for the slaves, ministers and missionaries commenced their labors in the British West Indies. As might and ought to have been expected, those missionary labors were ruinous to the peace and happiness of the slave, and soon superinduced a state of things that demanded legislative aid, or rendered emancipation absolutely necessary. Alison, speaking of the effects of those abolition labors, says: "Riots of a very alarming character took place in several districts, some arising from the indignation of the planters at the missionaries, others from the highly excited feelings of the negroes in consequence of their preachings. Shrewsbury, a missionary in Barbadoes, was a victim to violence of the first kind, and only saved his life by flying from the colony; and the imprudent zeal of another, named Smith, in Demarara, produced an insurrection among the blacks of so threatening a character that martial law was proclaimed in the colony, and continued in force for five months." Of the insurrection in Jamaica, in December, 1831, the historian says: "The blacks proceeded to break into houses and take arms, or bring out weapons of their own which they had secreted, and, assembling in large bodies, marched in every direction over the island, inciting the slaves to join them, and burning and destroying every plantation or building which came within their reach. The houses and settlements of the free people of color, however humble, shared in the devastation equally with the larger plantations of the European. The unchained African marked, as he had done in St. Domingo in 1789, his first step towards freedom by murder, conflagration, and every crime at which humanity recoils. The whole island was illuminated at night by the light of burning edifices;

the sky darkened by day with the vast clouds of smoke which issued from the conflagrations." The condition of the islands had become such, under the influence of abolition emissaries, that emancipation was at last, although the planter obtained but about one-half the real value of his slaves, a welcome measure. But the effect upon the prosperity of the islands, as well as on the condition of the negro, has been exceedingly detrimental. This is shown by Mr. Alison's account of West India slavery, and that author is forced to the observations: "Generally speaking, the incipient civilization of the negro has been arrested by his emancipation; with the cessation of forced labor, the habits and tastes which spring from and compensate it, have disappeared, and savage habits and pleasures have assumed their ascendency over the sable race. The attempts to instruct and civilize them have for the most part proved a failure; the *dolce far niente,* equally dear to the unlettered savage as to the effeminate European, has resumed its sway; and the emancipated Africans, dispersed in the woods, or in cabins erected amidst ruined plantations, are fast relapsing into the state in which their ancestors were when they were torn from their native seats by the rapacity of Christian avarice."

But the emancipation of her slaves by Great Britain was an indispensable step in her crusade against American slavery. The abolition of slavery by England was a great fact, and has had immense power upon the minds of Americans. There has been no occasion to examine into the propriety, expediency, or humanity of the act; everybody, until of late, has considered the sacrifice of money involved in the measure as sufficient evidence that it could have been prompted only by principles of justice. Without examination, without reflection, and without question, the step taken by England in emancipating her slaves, has been placed to her credit, and for that act her praises have been preached and sung in all parts of the United States.

The course pursued by England towards her slave colonies was, under the lead of British emissaries, attempted by the free upon the slave states in this country. It was thought that the insurrections of St. Domingo and Jamaica could be repeated in the South, and immediately on the passage by Parliament of her first act of emancipation, the subject of emancipation in the United States was opened with uncommon violence. American abolition societies were formed under the lead and auspices of British societies, and, by the aid of foreign gold, the United States was deluged with anti-slavery publications. In 1834 the number of abolitionists in this country was small; but, with the aid they received from abroad, they were enabled to create a profound sensation by their labors, and to one who was unsuspecting of their foreign alliances and subsidies, their exertions and expenditures were thought astonishing. British abolitionists were in correspondence with our Congressmen and other prominent public men, and abolition emissaries from that country came across the Atlantic to teach the true principles of liberty. It was during the administration of Jackson, and about the time of the British emancipation movement, that a noted George Thompson, for instance, made his appearance amongst us. But England soon found that this country was not prepared for the active measures she would enforce upon us. The United States, that power was again taught, was not exactly the West

India Islands. All of sufficient age well recollect the attempt to repeat in the South the West India missionary movement. Under the auspices of the British instructors Northern abolitionists commenced their labors in the slave states, and began to awaken the apprehensions of slaveholders. But the Southern masters were not dependent for protection on a legislature three thousand miles off, in which they had no voice ; and, as they were disinclined to submit to the fate experienced by the slaveholders in St. Domingo, they dealt rather summarily with the Yankee crusaders; and hence the stringent laws in the South against giving instruction to slaves. Several emissaries of Northern and British abolition societies were in those days caught in the humane and philanthropic mission of exciting slaves to rebellion and murder; but the harsh justice dealt out to them by Judge Lynch, who happened to hold his court in the South, at once put an end to the system which had accomplished so much in the British West Indies. In those days the aggression was from the North; Southern aggression was not then so popular a phrase. Such assaults upon their institutions exasperated the Southern people, and taught them what they were to expect from their Northern neighbors, and did much to bring into existence the ultra Southern pro-slavery party, which is impatient to dissolve all connection with the North. But perhaps those attempts upon Southern institutions, of which mention has been made, were too rudely checked. Some Northern missionaries were tried by lynch-law — perhaps executed. Southern barbarity was then gravely enlarged upon, and the blood of God's servants was made the seed of the Northern abolition church. But, as the overthrow of slavery could not be effected by the missionary movement, the tract system was next tried. The mails were loaded with incendiary publications for distribution among the slaves — publications intended and calculated to arouse their passions, and excite them to insurrection. The attempt was one directly upon the institutions of the South, in the original slave states. It was an effort to subvert Southern institutions, acting from the North, but emanating from England. It has ever been the pretence of Northern men that they have no desire to meddle with slavery in the states where it exists by local law, and that the prevention of its further spread is all that concerns their bleeding hearts. But, at the period of which we are speaking, a powerful effort was made to incite the slaves of the South to insurrection, that they might murder their masters, and, under the protection of England and Northern sentiment, establish their freedom, and perhaps wrest the South from the Union. Every resistance of the South to such aggressions from the North was sounded through New and Old England as evidence of the cruel, abandoned, and fiendish disposition and character of Southern men. The mails, as we have said, were loaded with prints and pictures designed to arouse the vengeance of the slave. These pictures were smuggled amongst the slaves in many ways. The wrappers of packages of goods, such as tobacco and other articles consumed by negroes, were, upon their inner sides, covered with pictures representing the slaves in chains and rags, with lordly masters holding scourges in their hands; and many other designs of like character were impressed upon articles of dress, and pieces of paper smuggled into goods consumed by the blacks, and thus sent amongst them. For those that could read, incendiary publications, directly advising them to assert their liberties, were poured upon them in great abundance. Considering the limited number of the political abolitionists in the North in those days, we should be surprised at the lavish expenditures to produce insurrections in the South, did we not know that a foreign power was at the bottom of the movement. These efforts produced a powerful commotion at the time. Congress was exercised with the subject. Mr. Calhoun, we think it was, proposed a bill making it penal for a postmaster to transmit or deliver from the mail, prints, pictures, and publications, of the kind referred to ; and, if recollection serves right, we think there was, during those days, much complaint in the North about Southern lawlessness in exercising or requiring their post masters to exercise a surveillance over the matter passing through the mail. That was one of the grave charges against the South.

During the administration of Jackson, also, and at about the same time of which we have been speaking, the nation was thunderstruck at the simultaneous appearance, from all parts of the land, — from Ohio, Pennsylvania, New York, New England, and almost every free state, — of petitions for the abolition of slavery in the District of Columbia. And, as these petitions were all signed by a conscientious and highly Christian people, the petitioners could not forego the solemn duty of denouncing slavery as a damning sin, and a scandalous reproach to the nation. That Southern senators and members of Congress should manifest impatience at such representations of their institutions, was only another instance and evidence of the abandoned and sunken moral condition of that section of the country. The North knew that slavery was a monstrous sin. If the Southern people doubted it, so much the more benighted must they have been. Mr. Calhoun objected to the reception of the petitions on the ground of privilege; he thought that the member's constituents should be protected from insult as well as the member himself. But, although scarcely a member of either house was in favor of the object of these petitions, many were in favor of their reception, out of regard to the sacredness of the right of petition. The appearance of these petitions occasioned much discussion and excitement in Congress, and the covert object of their movers was seen by the leading men of the day. The attack upon the South was systematic and vigorous. Up to that day, at least, the South had been passive under the encroachments of the North. The acquisition of Texas and other gigantic strides of the slave power, as we term it, have taken place since that time. But Southern men saw the object of those who were at the bottom of the petition movement, and exercised a conservative forbearance in the matter. The remarks of Mr. King, of Georgia, in 1836, upon the motion of Mr. Calhoun not to receive one of these abolition memorials, were conceived in a clear insight into the aims of the Northern agitators. "We may seek occasion (says Mr. King) to rave about our rights, appeal to the guarantees of the Constitution, denounce the abolitionists, &c. &c., and Arthur Tappan and his pious fraternity would very coolly remark, 'Well, that is precisely what I wanted; I wanted agitation in the South; I wished to provoke the "autocratic slaveholder" to make extravagant demands on the North, which the North could not consistently surrender to them. I wished them, under the pretext of securing their own rights, to encroach upon the rights of all the American people. In short, I wish to change the issue.' " And, although he regarded such petitions as insulting, and a gross outrage upon the South, Mr. King advised their reception as the most effectual way of defeating the real object of their originators.

That the object of the abolition movements of those days was not humanity, but to produce a sectional hatred between the North and South, was clearly discernible by every rational observer. The means of the truly Christian reformer are gentle and peaceable, and originate in love ; but diabolical hatred has ever been the prominent characteristic of the abolitionist. His language and acts have ever marked him as one in league with the enemies of our country. This has been seen, felt, and regretted, by the intelligent and patriotic portions of both North and South. Hatred begets hatred. There could be no surer way to alienate the South from the North than for the latter to array itself against the former. The tendencies of these Abolition crusades were at an early day pointed out by our first statesmen ; by none with more force and feeling than by Henry Clay. Speaking of the means made use of by the abolitionists, he said (1836) : " Another, and much more lamentable one, is that which this class is endeavoring to employ, of arraying one portion against another of the Union. With that view, in all their leading prints and publications, the alleged horrors of slavery are depicted in most glowing and exaggerated colors, to excite imaginations and stimulate the rage of the people of the free states against the people of the slave states. The slaveholder is held up and represented as the most atrocious of human beings. Advertisements of fugitive slaves, and of slaves to be sold, are carefully collected and blazoned forth, to infuse a spirit of detestation and hatred against one entire and the largest section of the Union. . . . Why are the slave states wantonly and cruelly assailed? Why does the abolition press teem with publications tending to excite hatred and animosity on the part of the free states against the slave states? . . . Why is Congress petitioned? What would be thought of the formation of societies in the slave states, the issuing of violent and inflammatory tracts, and the deputation of missionaries, pouring out impassioned denunciations against institutions under the exclusive control of the free states? Is their purpose to appeal to our understandings and actuate our humanity? And do they expect to accomplish that purpose by holding us up to scorn, and contempt, and detestation of the people of the free states, and the whole civilized world? . . . Sir, I am not in the habit of speaking lightly of the possibility of dissolving this happy Union. The Senate knows that I have deprecated allusions, on ordinary occasions, to that direful event. The country will testify that, if there be anything in the history of my public career worthy of recollection, it is the truth and sincerity of my ardent devotion to its lasting preservation. But we should be false in our allegiance to it, if we did not discriminate between the imaginary and real dangers by which it may be assailed. Abolition should no longer be regarded as an imaginary danger. The abolitionists, let me suppose, succeed in their present aim of uniting the inhabitants of the free states as one man against the inhabitants of the slave states. Union on the one side will beget union on the other.

And this process of reciprocal consolidation will be attended with all the violent prejudices, embittered passions, and implacable animosities which ever degraded or deformed human nature. A virtual dissolution of the Union will have taken place, while the forms of its existence remain. The most valuable element of union, mutual kindness, the feelings of sympathy, the fraternal bonds, which now happily unite us, will have been extinguished forever. One section will stand in menacing, hostile array against another; the collision of opinion will be quickly followed by the clash of arms."

The part taken by England in educating the masses of the North for disunion is not visible to everybody, because, as in the case of the Henry mission, her operations are secret. Her long-continued jealousy of our growing power and influence we have seen and felt; but that she would secretly intrigue and labor for our overthrow we cannot credit, because she is a marvellously benevolent nation, and is opposed to slavery!

CHAPTER XXV.

CAMPAIGN OF 1835, 1836. — CURRENCY QUESTION. — RETROGRADE REVOLUTION OF THE DEMOCRACY. — THE NEW SYSTEM BROUGHT ABOUT BY VAN BUREN TO INSURE HIS SUCCESSION. — VAN BUREN ELECTED. — SPEECHES OF WEBSTER. — COMMERCIAL REVULSION OF 1837, AND CAUSES. — BENTON'S THIRTY YEARS' VIEW. — VAN BUREN'S SUB-TREASURY SCHEME. — TRAITS OF THE ADMINISTRATION. — SPEECHES OF CLAY AND WEBSTER ON THE SUB-TREASURY. — JOHN C. CALHOUN AND HIS RECONCILIATION WITH THE DEMOCRATIC PARTY, ETC.

THE campaign of 1836 is too recent to need a lengthy notice. The veto of the United States Bank charter; the removal of the government funds to the state banks; the resolution of the Senate censuring the President for that removal; the President's protest to the Senate against that resolution; and the expunging act of the Senate, were the subjects of warm political debates during those days. Henry Clay and Daniel Webster were the acknowledged leaders of the Whigs, and the grounds on which these statesmen opposed the administration were accepted by the party generally, and adopted as in accordance with Whig principles. The expositions of Clay and Webster, in regard to currency and political economy, were considered rational and sound; and, although in the minority, the Whigs embraced a large share of the talent and business experience of the land. Under ordinary circumstances their efforts would infallibly have insured success; but the popularity of the hero of New Orleans was an extraordinary obstacle in their way. To the millions who were incapable of investigating and deciding on the principles of political economy, the name of the patriotic soldier was more potent than that of the civilian. Posterity will decide correctly upon the administration of Jackson. Although he may have made some wretched blunders during his presidential term, his administration was not, as his biassed opponents were disposed to claim, altogether a failure. But the candid reviewer of the administration of the General must acknowledge that his affected attempt to carry the principles of government back to the policy of Jefferson, was a sad mistake. It effected, as already shown, a revolution in the domestic policy of the country. It was a leap backwards over the combined wisdom and experience of a quarter of a century. And what renders that retrograde step particularly censurable is, that it was not taken as a means to secure the triumph of President Jackson, — which was secure enough without such a resort, — but was taken to secure the success of his successor. Unless a new policy should be adopted, — a policy glossed with the glory of the hero, and exclusively supported by the chieftain's favorite, — that favorite would fare poorly, it was thought, in his struggle for the presidency in competition with many abler and more popular statesmen than himself. The scheme was successful. Jackson reigned long enough to see the monster crushed, and the American system of protection overturned. The campaign of 1836 opened with Van Buren, the sole exponent of the measures of Jackson's administration, upon the track. He was pledged to follow in his predecessor's footsteps. The undertaking was a daring one, as represented by the caricaturists of that day. General Harrison was the Whig candidate. Although Mr. Van Buren was successful, it was seen that the faith of the nation had become somewhat shaken in the new principles espoused by the Democracy. The vote in opposition to Van Buren was large enough to startle the administration party, and did somewhat surprise them, in view of their decline from the immense majorities of General Jackson. General Harrison received seventy-five electoral votes; twenty-six (namely, of Georgia and Tennessee) were cast for Hugh L. White; fourteen (of Massachusetts) for Mr. Webster, and South Carolina voted for Mr. Mangum: whereas Van Buren received but one hundred and seventy. The doctrines and principles of the Whigs had, even at that period, made a powerful impression on the minds of the American people. The speeches of Clay and Webster were quite generally read, and those of Mr. Webster, put forth in the United States Senate, and on the stump, during the Jackson and Van Buren administrations, are the most masterly expositions of the principles of political economy to be found in our language. For research, for originality, for depth of thought, and for thorough analysis of the principles of the Constitution, of currency and of trade, Mr. Webster's speeches were immeasurably superior to Mr. Clay's. Mr. Clay was undoubtedly, in many respects, the most pleasing orator; but the speeches of Webster became at once not only oracles in matters of political science, but also treasures of literature.

No party ever had a brighter array of upright, intelligent, and popular statesman than rallied in the Whig ranks throughout all parts of the Union; nor has a party ever been so noted for the number and high character of its public journals. The eight years in the minority, prior to 1836, had not been without promising results. Probably the world never before witnessed such a struggle; it was a struggle between reason and prejudice; an encounter of moral forces, without the interposition of physical power. The struggle was not in vain. The principles then espoused by the Whigs, so far as they have triumphed in the councils of the nation, have shed blessings upon the country; and, so far as they were right, will sooner or later become all-prevailing. Party organizations are not stable creations; but political principles are enduring.

The error of the Van Buren dynasty (for, although the new system of Democratic policy was ostensibly carved out by Jackson, it was thought in reality to be the handiwork of Van Buren) was soon revealed by its disastrous fruits. The overthrow of the national currency, and the expansion of credit consequent on the deposit of the government funds in the state banks, enhanced the prices of foreign commodities, and aided, with the reduction of duties by the compromise tariff, immense importations of foreign goods. The fatal consequences that must inevitably flow from such a state of things a sane people would have foreseen. During the last four years of Jackson's administration, the excess of importations over exportations was $130,000,000. This was in a great measure the result of the compromise measure of 1832. Under that measure each year saw a reduction of duties on foreign goods. But, as the destruction of the national bank occasioned the creation of a large number of state banks; and as the state banks, encouraged thereto by the deposit of government moneys, and the recommendation of the Secretary of the Treasury, loaned out their bills with great liberality, the insidious workings of the compromise tariff act were for a long time unperceived. General Jackson left the presidential chair congratulating himself on the prosperous and happy condition of the country. But scarcely had Mr. Van Buren been inaugurated (March, 1837) before the premonitory symptoms of the most terrible monetary revulsion this country has ever experienced were felt. In fact, the first act of his administration was to call a special session of Congress, for the purpose of rendering some relief to the country. Such wide-spread bankruptcy was never witnessed. As the fruits — not the cause — of the rotten system of currency established by the policy of the administration, much wild speculation had been indulged in, which greatly added to the devastation and ruin brought upon the land by the continued drain upon our precious metals, to pay the balances which our foreign trade continually created against us. Our trade, foreign and domestic, was subject to no regulator — no regulation. The currency bore no relation to the intrinsic value of property, nor to the amount of specie in the country; and as soon as the day of adjustment and settlement with the creditor at whose mercy our trade placed us, arrived, we found that both our money and our property were but fictions.

But Mr. Van Buren met the storm with stoic coolness. He was still the exponent — many thought him the inventor — of Jacksonian Democracy. Both houses of Congress were still true to the faith. The Whigs urged, as means of relief, the reëstablishment of the measures overthrown by Jackson; but Mr. Van Buren was not diverted from the system he had for some years been maturing. From occasional expressions made use of by General Jackson, in his messages, it had for a long time been apparent that he or his cabinet contemplated some new method of collecting and managing the public revenues. The scheme thus meditated was by Mr. Van Buren put forth in his Sub-Treasury Bill, or Independent Treasury, as it was called. It was the main measure of his administration. It appears that he had investigated extensively the treasury systems of the little states of Europe, and framed his sub-treasury after their model. The system was based upon the idea that it was not the duty or business of the general government to furnish the country with the ordinary currency with which the business of the world is carried on; that its duty is limited to the regulation of the basis of that currency — to wit, of the gold and silver. The new theory of Democracy was that Congress had no power to act beyond the letter of the Constitution which provides that government shall have the exclusive power of coining money; and the provision that Congress shall regulate commerce was not considered as having a bearing upon the subject. As commerce could not exist with nothing but a specie currency, and as the safe and correct adjustment of the mixed or paper currency is of perhaps more vital importance to the American people, and more essential to their prosperity and happiness, than the proper regulation of simply one of its main or principal elements, the Whigs, and many of the Democratic statesmen, insisted that the general government should charge itself with the duty of exercising a control over the natural and ordinary currency of the country. The argument is somewhat potent. The reason why the state legislature may not as well enjoy the privilege of coining specie, as of creating paper money, is not apparent, as legislative abuse in the latter is more likely to occur than in the former kind of money. It is well to give the coinage of hard money to the general government, and still better to give it the charge of the real currency of the land.

The innovation of the new dynasty was evidently in opposition to the better judgment of the leading members of the administration. Both houses of Congress were strongly Democratic ; but they repudiated, at its first presentation, the independent treasury scheme of Mr. Van Buren. The history of those days is familiar to the reader. It will be recollected that the rejection of the United States Bank charter was by veto, and in opposition to the majority of a strongly Democratic Congress. The workings of the state bank system will occur to the mind of the reader. The fact that an overflowing treasury, from receipts of millions from sales of public lands, was giving those state depositories of public moneys still further power of expansion, will not be forgotten. The forward-cast shadow of the subtreasury scheme seen during Jackson's administration, to wit, the specie circular, as it was called, will be borne in mind. The astonishment with which that circular, which was an order to revenue officers and others, that pay for lands should be only received in specie, burst upon the country, can never pass out of the mind of one who lived in those days. The propriety of such a measure was tried in Congress by Mr. Benton, and almost unanimously rejected, although that Congress was strongly Democratic. Still, eleven days after adjournment, the President, on his own authority, and against the advice of his cabinet, caused that circular to be issued. It was a preparatory step to the sub-treasury measure, but was taken too late. The previous course of the administration had favored a state of things that rendered the adoption of the sub-treasury policy revolutionary and ruinous. The revulsion came, and fell upon the administration of Mr. Van Buren. The banks all suspended, the business of the country was ruined, credit destroyed, and millions of people who had been wealthy, or in comfortable circumstances, rendered bankrupt. The country for a long time staggered and reeled under the malady, like a person prostrated from loss of blood. It was a touching spectacle. The country was young, full of energy, courage and hope, and frequently brought to play all of her powers to arise and shake off her troubles; but, as with the ambitious and impatient invalid, her faculties would not obey her will. Specie payments by the banks were only renewed for new suspensions; manufactories were closed; exchanges destroyed; money disappeared; and the value of property depreciated beyond precedent.

Mr. Van Buren had nothing but his sub-treasury to offer. He repudiated the idea that it was the concern of government to render aid or protection to the business interests of the country. It was asserted that the people had been improvident and rash in speculations, and that it was sufficient for the government to look out for its own revenues, without embarrassing itself with the unthrifty affairs of the people. The administration was afflicted with the misfortunes of the land; the treasury was empty; the suspension of the banks closed upon the nation's money, and the officials of the administration were without funds for ordinary expenses. Revenue came in slowly and in small quantities, leaving government to its ordinary shifts in such cases of issuing treasury notes, and obtaining loans. The sub-treasury project of Mr. Van Buren was adhered to, and finally passed, under his administration. By this a divorce was proclaimed between the government and the people. The improvidence of the people was no longer to torment the government. The revenues, by the sub-treasury system, were to be collected in hard money, and kept in the hands of the agents of the government, subject to the order of the Secretary of the Treasury. That this is a simple and safe method of managing the state's finances, no one will dispute. It is the miser's system. It is a cautious, careful, safe, and entirely reliable system; without mystery, without the intricacy of scientific principles, and without the complications of the abstruse principles of finance. It is well intended to carry out the theory on which it is based — that is, that government has no concern with the business interests of the country. Despotism is the simplest of all governments, and republics the most complicated. The sub-treasury system is as old as despotism, and as simple. In proportion as people have emancipated themselves from despotic authority, and established free institutions, the ruling power has been administered with special reference, not to its own ease and security, but to that of the people. England is the freest government in the Old World, and consequently her system is intricate and complicated; although not so much so as that of the still more free United States.

The stability of the English currency is due to the controlling wisdom of the British government, which has never yet, like an ancient despot, divorced itself from the people, or declared itself without any duty in regard to the regulation of commerce and currency. America can prosper, and has prospered, under the sub-treasury system. It prospered under the confederation, when we could hardly be said to have any government at all. We get a sound specie basis from Congress, and the states, fortunately, usually afford a fair paper currency. But, without the control of the general government, the currency, especially as the laws of trade are disregarded, and all authority of government over them is repudiated, must ever be unstable, and subject to revulsions.

The sub-treasury measure, of course, was ably discussed in and out of Congress. The principles of currency, and of the duties of our government in regard to it, were ably and unanswerably set forth in the speeches of Mr. Clay and Mr. Webster. The speeches of Mr. Webster upon the sub-treasury project are the most instructive expositions of the principles of currency to be found. They contain a mine of information, and the doctrines embodied in them will some day burst forth, from the dust that now covers them, with volcanic power. It cannot be that such men as Madison, Hamilton, Adams, Jay, Washington, Monroe, Crawford, Lowndes, Clay and Webster, were the victims of delusion in regard to these matters. It cannot be that the Democratic Congresses through which Jackson and Van Buren were unable to force their scheme, were the corrupt, bank-bought knaves that the friends of Jackson and Van Buren charged them to be.

It is matter of history that the sub-treasury project, at its outset, found but little favor in Democratic Congresses, or among Democratic cabinets. It was an emanation from the brain of Mr. Van Buren. It at all times had one friend; that was Thomas H. Benton. He favored the sub-treasury, and its forerunner the specie circular. Colonel Benton, in his Thirty Years' View, has put forth a curious history of these measures, and has labored, in some instances with shallow perceptions, to vindicate them. For instance, he represents that the great revulsion of 1837, commencing with bank suspensions, was the work of Nick Biddle and the Whigs, got up on purpose to embarrass the administration! For this purpose, he gravely gives accounts of speeches, meetings, letters, etc., which no more indicate such a purpose than they foreshadow a gunpowder plot. But what renders laughable all this lengthy effort in his work to prove that these revulsions were not the results of a really mismanaged currency, but the stratagems of political opponents, is the fact that Mr. Benton, in his same Thirty Years' View, boasts that he himself had, the preceding year, foreseen that such a crash was inevitable! Yes; he tells us that upon one occasion he took the President aside to caution him; but, as Mr. Van Buren treated his suggestions lightly, simply asking him if "he was not exalted in the head upon that subject?" he was disgusted, and concluded that he would let his friend proceed in his happy ignorance. The colonel, however, says that he afterwards regretted that he did not overlook Mr. Van Buren's levity, and expose to him the true state of affairs. He tells us, that, from his connection with committees in the Senate, he had better means of information than the President, and has no doubt but Mr. Van Buren would have done justice to his statement of facts, had he felt like making it to him. Now, as the colonel knew that there was a real occasion for such a revulsion, from his acquaintance with the financial affairs of the country, his attempt to charge it upon the Whigs, as an affair got up by them to afflict Mr. Van Buren, must be thought rather a queer piece of business. But, as Colonel Benton was an upright man, and had the real interests of the country at heart, his visions and vanities may, at this day, be passed by without much comment.

The election of Mr. Van Buren led to the restoration of Mr. Calhoun to the Democratic ranks. The position of Mr. Calhoun for some ten or twelve years had been unnatural and false before the people. That gentleman was at heart a thorough Democrat, and the great inconsistencies of his political life resulted from the position he was forced into by the unjust and cruel quarrel which had been provoked between him and Jackson. He was Vice-President during President Jackson's first term, and had been powerfully instrumental of the general's election, and was the most prominent man in the party for his successor. Mr. Calhoun was an able statesman, and truly devoted to the interests of General Jackson ; but, as before has been shown, the general's wrath was excited against him, and a bitter personal quarrel ensued between those leading Democrats. Although Mr. Van Buren enjoyed the benefit of that rupture, was substituted for Mr. Calhoun as Vice-President, during Jackson's second term, and became the general's successor in the presidential office, still Mr. Calhoun was disposed to overlook and forgive all, for the sake of again finding repose and a home in the bosom of the party that he really loved, and from which he had thus been an exile. To favor his return to the favor and support of the Democratic party, General Jackson, at the solicitation of Mr. Van Buren as was supposed, issued his certificate, acquitting the latter from all complicity in the quarrel which had rendered Mr. Calhoun an enemy of his administration. The support of measures by Mr. Calhoun, under the administration of Mr. Van Buren, which he had opposed under that of Jackson, subjected his political life to the charge of inconsistency, which he could not satisfactorily defend, and which his enemies, not liberal enough to sympathize with him under the unjust and cruel usage he had received from General Jackson, would not overlook or excuse. Anything like liberality, in our view of Mr. Calhoun's course, would disarm criticism of much of its edge, for the heart of that statesman abounded in the noblest qualities. He was open and undisguised in his opinions and feelings, and scorned all attempts at carrying a measure by intrigue and circumvention. His nature was free from guile, and his breast was uniformly animated by the sentiments of truth and honor. His defence against the powerful and scathing attacks of Mr. Clay, after his espousal of the measures of Mr. Van Buren's administration, can never be read by a political enemy without inspiring feelings of respect for the true nobleness of his nature, against which Mr. Clay's generous heart was far from being proof. The ingenuousness of Mr. Calhoun's disposition was ever apparent, and the fact that he always possessed the respect and esteem of his opponents, is unanswerable evidence of his uprightness and integrity. If the machinations of Mr. Van Buren were the cause of the exile of Mr. Calhoun from the ranks of the Democracy, the former knows now the full extent of the injury he has inflicted upon the latter ; as experience alone, it is said, can make one realize the discomfort, pain, and sufferings, of being thus a wanderer from the bosom of his party.

CHAPTER XXVI.

CAMPAIGN OF 1840. — HARRISON AND AVAILABILITY. — TYLER VICE-PRESIDENT. — DEATH OF HARRISON, AND TYLER'S PRESIDENCY. — RESIGNATION OF THE CABINET. — SUB-TREASURY, UNITED STATES BANK, AND TARIFF OF 1842. — WEBSTER, SECRETARY OF STATE, RETAINS HIS SEAT TILL 1842. — TREATY OF WASHINGTON, ETC., ETC.

THE presidential campaign of 1840 was a noted one. William Henry Harrison, whose character and history are well known, was elected over Martin Van Buren by an overwhelming majority. The election of General Harrison was, however, a gross mistake, and led to the ruin of the Whig party. Had Clay or Webster been nominated, either would have been elected, and Whig principles would have been so firmly established as to secure their permanent ascendency. But, as the prospects of the Whig party, for the last few years, had begun to look promising, many naturally rallied under its standard who had more regard for place than for political principles. Such are ever the advocates of availability. The principle of availability was adopted in the nomination of the hero of North Bend.

The nomination of the hero of Tippecanoe was an act of injustice to such statesmen as Clay and Webster. They were, it may be said, the founders of the Whig party. From its first dawnings they had been its champions, and had been faithful to its principles and fortunes in its darkest days of adversity. To the eloquence and devotion of those eminent statesmen was the Whig party finally indebted for its triumph in 1840; and, as its prospects brightened, it was unfair and unmanly to thrust them aside for some leader whose election would be less a test of the popularity of political principles than of the nominee. A party that thus conducts offers but little encouragement to its talented members for devotion to its cause. It cannot be called a party of principle. It is a party, it is true; but a party whose main and controlling object is too apparent to entitle it to the confidence of an honest people. If the principles of a party are vital and dear to it, its able, tried, and faithful champions should be placed at its head, and there kept. With the triumph of those principles which their champions have enforced upon a doubting and distrusting people, the champions themselves should triumph; and a party taking any other rule for its guidance, or resorting to other means of success than an unshaken reliance in its principles, deserves to be overthrown. General Harrison was an estimable man, and received votes that, perhaps, would have been cast neither for Clay, Webster, nor Van Buren, and was elected as the opponent of the Democratic party. But the Jackson Van Buren dynasty had become unpopular. The unsoundness of the Van Buren policy had been demonstrated, and the people — the honest masses — had passed sentence of condemnation upon the sage of Lindenwold. His overthrow was by a popular whirlwind. There was nothing in the previous exploits of General Harrison to charm people from a sense of propriety, but enough in the blunders of Van Buren to drive a nation distracted. Clay and Webster everywhere advocated the election of Harrison, and were received by the masses of the people, with unbounded enthusiasm, as the exponents of correct political principles; and either of these gentlemen might have been run against Martin Van Buren with entire safety. But the Whig party had become too anxious for success, for the mere sake of success.

There is a certain limit within which a party, in making its nominations, may have regard to availability; but when this principle is made to slight the fundamental principles of the party, and sacrifice those who have been its honest and faithful exponents, it can bring nothing but destruction in its train. In nominating General Harrison, the feverish Whigs imitated their Democratic opponents in nominating General Jackson. The election of Jackson was a sacrifice of the ablest statesmen in the Democratic party, and hence the overthrow of that party, in 1840, and its subsequent precarious existence. When Jackson was first offered for the presidency, the Democracy was so powerfully in the ascendant that their opponents, the Federalists, scarcely pretended to make any opposition at the presidential elections. The Federal party, as it was then called, was almost entirely exterminated. By keeping their statesmen at the head of their party, the Democrats might have preserved their ascendency, unimpaired, for years; but the new dynasty carved out by Van Buren, with the sword of Jackson, brought upon that party the calamity of 1840,—yes, and the disgrace of 1848! Unwisely, the Whigs, in 1840, followed an example that was destructive to them, and in twelve years their name was only known in history!

The election of General Harrison was providentially unfortunate to the Whigs. His death, taking place soon after his inauguration, threw the administration into the hands of the Vice-President, John Tyler, who soon found himself at war with the Whig party. In the nomination of the Vice-President, also, availability had been studied, and the result was that, in about a month from the inauguration of President Harrison, a Democratic President was at the head of government. The Democracy of Mr. Tyler, however, was not so radical as that of Mr. Van Buren. In many things his administration was favorable to Whig policy; but on the currency measures he entertained views hostile to those of the Whig party. His vetoes of United States Bank and Fiscal Agent bills made disturbance enough. The Whigs denounced him. The cabinet constructed by General Harrison, with the exception of Webster, all resigned, and the administration thenceforth was a mongrel concern.

On the election of General Harrison, he called Mr. Webster to the head of his cabinet, in the formation of which he took his advice; and Mr. Webster did not immediately resign his place in Mr. Tyler's cabinet, although, perhaps, he would have done so if he had been more devoted to the fortunes of the party than to the interests of the country. His position was not like that of the other members of the cabinet. He was, of course, disappointed at the course taken by the President, in relation to the currency measures, and did, after about two years' service in the office of Secretary of State, resign his place; but the event showed that an immediate resignation would have been a sacrifice of the highest interests of the country. The country was at the time on the verge of war with England. The controversy in regard to the North-East Boundary had existed from the establishment of Independence, and, at the time in question, was threatening an issue in war. All remember the fearful excitement existing in Maine, and upon the Canadian frontier, where the inhabitants of the two countries were menacing each other with arms. To add to the excitement and danger of the moment, the controversies growing out of the Canadian rebellion were then pending, and McLeod, a soldier engaged in the Caroline affair, was at the time imprisoned in the state of New York: England, also, in her philanthropic zeal to stop the slave-trade, as usual, had taken the liberty of overhauling some of our merchant vessels upon the coast of Africa, for which this country was disposed to have redress. The manner in which Mr. Webster effected an adjustment of all these difficulties, by the celebrated treaty of Washington, is well known. The settlement of the boundary question was itself a proud achievement in diplomacy. Mr. Webster's papers on the subjects of the Caroline; McLeod's imprisonment; the right of search or visit; the Mexican difficulty; the practice of impressment, etc., are the most masterly expositions of the laws of nations, upon the topics involved in those subjects, to be found in any language. The principles laid down in those papers are now looked upon, by statesmen of all parties, as authorities, and as such are quoted upon all suitable occasions.

Although the Whigs, during the administration of Mr. Tyler, were unable to establish a United States Bank, they were successful in passing a protective tariff, which has since been much talked of as the tariff of 1842; and they repealed the sub-treasury act. The tariff act of 1842 was immediately felt. Under Mr. Van

Buren's administration the excessive importations continued until the country was prevented from the purchase of foreign goods by almost universal bankruptcy.

The propriety of the resignation of Mr. Tyler's cabinet, on his refusal to sanction the enactment of a bank charter, was much doubted by some of the ablest members of the Whig party. By that resignation there was no prospect of effecting anything, saving what might be accomplished for the service of the Whig party, and it is not correct for persons in official stations to determine on their course of action wholly with regard to party effect. Those members of the cabinet were men of the highest standing for ability and worth, and acted, no doubt, from honorable impulses; but still it seems as though the interests of the country lost more than they gained by the course pursued.

CHAPTER XXVII.

CAMPAIGN OF 1844. — HENRY CLAY AND JAMES K. POLK. — ANNEXATION OF TEXAS. — POLK'S ELECTION. — FREESOIL CANDIDATES. — INTEREST OF ENGLAND IN POLK'S ELECTION. — TARIFF OF 1842 REPEALED. — TARIFF OF 1846. — MEXICAN WAR THE GREAT MEASURE OF POLK'S ADMINISTRATION. — CREDIT GAINED BY WHIG GENERALS RECONCILED THE WHIG PARTY TO THE WAR. — GENERAL TAYLOR POPULAR WITH THE DEMOCRACY. — AVAILABILITY AGAIN TRIED. — POLITICAL PRINCIPLES BY WHIGS BUT LITTLE MOOTED. — THE ABOLITION SPIRIT AROUSED. — VAN BUREN THE ABOLITION CANDIDATE IN 1848. — CASS DEMOCRATIC CANDIDATE. — THE FREESOILERS PUZZLED, BUT VAN BUREN GETS A LARGE VOTE. — TAYLOR ELECTED. — MILLARD FILLMORE VICE-PRESIDENT. — TAYLOR'S DEATH. — FILLMORE PRESIDENT. — W. H. SEWARD. — HIS ONLY HOPES FOR REACHING THE PRESIDENCY THROUGH THE TRIUMPH OF SECTIONALISM. — INCREASE OF FREESOILISM, ETC.

Henry Clay was the Whig candidate in 1844, and was defeated by James K. Polk. The campaign was a severe one, and the contest close. Mr. Clay received a very large minority of the popular vote, and was not defeated by fair means. His support was almost entirely native American, as one of the measures he proposed to the people during the canvass was an alteration of our naturalization laws, requiring foreigners to reside in this country twenty-one years before being permitted to enjoy the privilege of voting. The multiplication of Democratic voters in the city of New York during that campaign, by fraudulent naturalizations, was said to have been beyond precedent. It was supposed that without such naturalizations Mr. Clay would have been elected. Mr. Clay was also opposed to the annexation of Texas, and so announced himself; in consequence of which he lost much support in all parts of the country. The annexation of Texas was a favorite measure with many portions of the South, and was desired by large classes in the North. In a commercial point of view the annexation was highly beneficial to the North; and the measure was of course espoused with great zeal by the thousands of influential people of all parties who were owners of what was called Texas script, — a species of property that annexation would render valuable. The candidate of the Freesoilers, Mr. James G. Birney, took votes enough of those who professed opposition to annexation, to have elected Mr. Clay; but those professed Freesoilers were mostly very devout men, and had many objections to Mr. Clay. He had fought one or two duels, and was, moreover, a slaveholder. By voting for Mr. Clay, Mr. Polk and annexation might have been defeated; but the inexorable morals of the Freesoilers would not permit them to do evil that good might come of it. Although the same pious men were afterwards, by some unaccountable subtlety of the enemy, trepanned into the support of Frémont, they were not caught with their eyes shut in 1844. At that day the Freesoilers were not a party; they constituted a faction of voters, and might, had not their consciences been too tender, have defeated what they have ever been loud in proclaiming one of the most unholy acts of the slavery oligarchy. No one doubts but that the Mexican war would have been avoided had Mr. Clay been elected President instead of Mr. Polk; but here, perhaps, God was wiser than man, and subsequent events seem to indicate that the fanaticism of the Free-soilers was providential, and intended as an instrumentality for the development of the mission of America.

Another powerful influence brought to bear against the election of Mr. Clay was British gold. To say nothing of the disbursements in this country for electioneering purposes from the British secret-service fund, the merchants and manufacturers in England openly subscribed money to be employed in effecting the election of Mr. Polk. The tariff of 1842 had checked the excess of importations of British fabrics, and a change of administration was necessary for the prosperity of English trade. The party which had nominated Mr. Polk professed to be in favor of free trade, and the merchants and manufacturers of England knew well enough what the policy of the United States would be under the administration of Mr. Clay. It was well known that British gold was freely made use of during the political campaign of 1844. But so powerful was the impression, on the minds of the mass of the American people, that the principles of the Whigs were indispensable for the prosperity of the country, that a herculean effort was necessary to defeat their candidate. The struggle was fierce, and the efforts of the combined enemies of the Whig party were desperate. Tylerism had stripped the vantage ground attained by the Whigs in 1840 of all its value. Had the administration from 1840 been a sound Whig administration, the defeat of that party in 1844 would not have occurred; and, as it was, if the Whigs had received fair play in that campaign, Mr. Clay would have been elected, and Whig policy become firmly established in the country. This is clearly apparent from the popular vote at the elections of 1840 and 1848, at each of which the Whig candidate received a majority. But the defeat in 1844 was in a great measure to be attributed to the ill-advised nomination of an available candidate in 1840; and the repetition of that foolish policy, in 1848, had a powerful tendency to bring about the annihilation of the Whig party, which soon after ensued.

The administration of Mr. Polk was Democratic. Texas was annexed. The greatest objection that can be made to the admission of that promising sister is as to the manner. It was thought by the Whigs that the movement was premature. The courtship was considered too short. The fact is, some ardent lovers of the fair one proposed the union before her consent had been obtained! The question of annexation, the Whigs thought, was pressed forward too rashly. The Whigs contended that the only constitutional method of acquiring new territory was by treaty. But as every treaty made by the President requires the approval of two-thirds of the Senate, it was found that the annexation scheme could not, through the exercise of the treaty-making power, be consummated. The result was that the admission of Texas was proposed and carried by a joint resolution of the two houses of Congress. The Whigs opposed this method of procedure as unconstitutional. This opposition was not factious or sectional. The Whig party was ever a national party. About every Whig senator from the slave states voted against the act of annexation; but the election of Mr. Polk had put it out of the power of the Whigs to defeat the measure by veto.

The tariff of 1842 was repealed, and its place supplied by the act of 1846, which is a revenue tariff, affording but slight if any protection to the great branches of American industry. The sub-treasury act was also re-enacted, and the country placed under the commercial and revenue system wrought out by Mr. Van Buren, and has thus remained for the past ten or twelve years. Had not Heaven, in its mercy, given us the hundreds of millions of gold from the gulches of California, in what condition should we now, under the operations of that anti-American system, find ourselves? The excess, the monstrous excess of our importations indicates. Figures are reliable things. Bankruptcy may have been avoided; but our commercial system has given Europe the great profits of our mines, and after the lapse of a few years we shall find ourselves, unless our policy be changed, divested of our gold, and in a state of helplessness.

The Mexican war was the great event or measure of Mr. Polk's administration. We will not stop to examine the steps that led to that war. It was the perhaps necessary result of the annexation of Texas, and resulted in the acquisition of California, and the territory of New Mexico. The administration of Mr. Polk will ever be memorable in the annals of the country for having given occasion for the great clamor about Southern aggression. Not that the annexation of Texas, and the consequent acquisition of new territory, were accomplished by the South alone; but as the annexation policy was regarded beneficial to the extension of slavery, the measure was charged to Southern machinations. It was immediately seen, by the Freesoilers of the North, that the defeat of Mr. Clay was a great mistake, and the prodigious events of Mr. Polk's administration gave new life to the anti-slavery sentiment of the free states. While the Mexican war was on our hands, the much talked of Wilmot proviso doctrine took its rise; or rather an old doctrine took a new start under that new name. The annexation of Texas, the stirring events of the Mexican war, and the acquisition of California and New Mexico, all transpired so suddenly that the enemies of these measures had hardly a chance to utter their protestations before they were accomplished. According to Whig principles, the annexation was unconstitutional, and the commencement of the war with Mexico an outrage upon that republic; but the brilliant manner in which that war was conducted by two favorite Whig generals reconciled the party, in a great measure, to those proceedings. The administration was annoyed at the credit accruing to Generals Taylor and Scott, and the Whigs were evidently elated. Outcries and invectives against the war soon ceased to be heard in the Whig ranks, and, at the close of Polk's presidential term, the real issue between the two parties was not so apparent. The old and long-continued discussions in regard to administrative measures had, in a great degree, subsided, and the Whig party, almost with one mind, were disposed to resort to the principle of availability for another party triumph. General Taylor, long prior to the assembling of the National Convention, was announced by Whigs, in all parts of the country, as the next candidate for the presidency. He was no statesman, and had no acquaintance with civil affairs. He was a man of moderate abilities, a skilful and brave general, and an upright and honorable man. But he was no more suitable for the presidency than had been Jackson or Harrison; and, but for one or two splendid victories in Mexico, he would never have been thought of as a candidate for that office.

However, there were many reasons why he might be considered an available candidate. The war was vastly popular with the Democracy, and his good services had endeared him to large numbers of the Democratic party. The expression was often made by Democrats that, if General Taylor should be nominated, they would not vote against him; and many promised, in such an event, to give him their votes. As much support was expected from the ranks of the enemy, it was not prudent for Whigs, in their campaign, to make any unnecessary parade of their political principles. It was calculated that the general's military exploits would advocate his cause, and go further in softening and subduing the hearts of political adversaries than any amount of electioneering about the principles of trade and currency.

The nomination of General Taylor, however, and the campaign that elected him, disclosed in the Whig party elements that bespoke its speedy dissolution. If Texas, New Mexico, and California, had been solid masses of guano, and had been placed upon the root of Freesoilism in the free states, they would not have proved richer and more active fertilizers of that noxious plant than were the proceedings of the administration in acquiring those territories. The outcry of "Southern aggression" rang through the North. Nothing else was, or has since, been talked of. The anti-slavery feeling was greatly excited, and many were forced reluctantly to vote for General Taylor as the least, as they considered it, of three evils. His opponents were General Cass and Martin Van Buren. As for Cass, no Whig of those days could vote for him, as he was regarded quite unsound on the slavery question. Was Van Buren preferable to General Taylor? Strange enough, Mr. Van Buren was the Freesoil candidate, and supported by the Freesoilers of the North! But the imagined change in the sentiments of that gentleman, in regard to slavery, struck the Whigs aghast. His political life, and his administration, his ultra pro-slavery administration, as it had been designated, were fresh in the recollections of all. He had either styled himself, or had by his friends been styled, a Northern man with Southern principles, and, while President, had, with the whole power of his station, done his utmost to crush out Freesoilism; but, nevertheless, in 1848, he was nominated, at the somewhat celebrated Buffalo Convention, as the Freesoil candidate for the presidency. The vote thrown for him shows how profoundly the Northern mind had been stirred on the question of slavery during Mr. Polk's administration. It was hard for old Whigs to support Mr. Van Buren; but thousands did so. General Cass, the nominee of the Democratic party, was well known for his heresy on the subject of slavery, so that between the champion of squatter sovereignty, the conservatism of the slave-owning Whig candidate, and the pretended Freesoil convert, Van Buren, the anti-slavery sentiment of the North was puzzled to choose. It was but late in the campaign, and with much difficulty, that some influential Whig editors could be induced to give in their adhesion to General Taylor; and, although the general was elected, the result of the ballotings was somewhat singular and prophetic. The two strong Whig states, for instance, of Massachusetts and Vermont, elected Taylor electors only by pluralities. In other Northern States Mr. Van Buren had received quite large votes. It will be recollected that there was not perfect harmony in the national convention that nominated General Taylor. The Freesoil sentiment was quite powerful, although conservatism prevailed. So it seems that conservatism triumphed amongst the people ; but that triumph, it should be remarked and recollected, was more owing to the peculiar character of the Freesoil nominee than to the battle of Buena Vista.

The elevation of Zachary Taylor to the presidency was attended with the election of Millard Fillmore, of New York, Vice-President. The events of that administration are too recent to require mention. President Taylor died soon after his inauguration, to wit, on the 9th day of July, by which event Mr. Fillmore became President of the United States. It was necessary for Mr. Fillmore to change his cabinet, and make many changes of office-holders in various parts of the country. These changes at the time were the occasion of much outcry against him by a large section of the Whig party, and were symptoms of a schism which finally involved the party in ruin. In accounting for the course of Mr. Fillmore, we can only revert to the circumstances and impressions of those times.

The history of not a very aged politician, W. H. Seward, is pretty familiar to the generality of Americans. He was born in 1801, and is now less than sixty years of age. His father was a firm Democrat of the Jeffersonian school, and Mr. Seward was himself of the same politics until the revolution in Democratic measures, undertaken by the elevation of General Jackson. At that period, about 1828, Mr. Seward attached himself to the Whig party. Possessing an ambitious spirit, and wielding a somewhat vigorous pen, he soon made himself prominent in his new position. His writings are well known. As to the elegance and perspicuity of his style not many will disagree. He is principally characterized for a speculative turn of thought, and is very pleasing to those who suffer themselves to be floated along in the current of his speculations. But to those who are accustomed to analyze and weigh a writer's positions before giving them acceptance, Mr. Seward's productions are more regarded and admired for their originality and ingenuity, than for their depth and soundness. His organization is not that of a statesman. No man can be a safe counsellor for the state whose mental and moral constitution is such as to render facts, in his deliberations, subordinate to theory. The statesman should avail himself of the aids of the theologian, the philosopher, and the casuist; but he should be neither. If a theologian, his sect will, unquestioned, accept his views, which others might disregard. If a philosopher, one school might admire, while another would denounce, his positions. Perhaps Mr. Seward has shown himself more of a philosopher and sectarian than a statesman, and, as the result, his political opinions are only acceptable to a particular class of a single section of the country. His system of state policy, which he thinks would benefit one part of the country, would involve another in blood and desolation.

For several years Mr. Seward was a consistent conservative Whig, and supported such men as Clay and Harrison for the presidency. His first public life commenced in 1830, when he was elected to the Senate of his native state. In this election he was aided by the anti-masonic spirit, which was at that time quite active.

Later, in 1837, and also in 1839, he was elected Governor of New York; and, in 1849, was, by the New York Legislature, elected to the United States Senate, and to that station was reëlected in 1855. For some years past, Mr. Seward has been noted for his strong anti-slavery principles and feelings. Many of the leading Whigs, especially those who have sympathized with him in his views on the subject of slavery, have been desirous of his nomination for the presidency. That Mr. Seward has partaken of that desire has been quite apparent. There has been to his eyes no reason why he might not aspire to a station which the influence of his native state was mainly instrumental in filling with Mr. Van Buren. The favorite of that mighty state has no occasion to blush for his ambition for presidential honors. Mr. Seward led in the van of the party that overthrew Van Burenism in New York, and why not himself aspire to the fortunes which the influence of that state has been able to open to her sons? But the admirers and followers of that gentleman, although a controlling portion of the late Whig party, never saw a time when they supposed they could present his name for nomination with any prospect of success. His great theme has been anti-slavery for many years. On account of his ultra and impracticable notions about negroes, Mr. Seward has been able to count on no supporters at all in the slave states, and reliably upon none but the abolitionists in the North. For his elevation to the presidency there seems no hope while the states remain united. If all the free states could be brought to act sectionally, and unite on a candidate, perhaps the slavery issue might open the way to the presidency for Mr. Seward; or, if there should be a separation of states, in consequence of the slavery question, Mr. Seward, of course, would be the controlling genius of the Northern republic, and his prominent friends would be placed in all its principal offices. For a few years past the South have looked upon Mr. Seward as Mr. Calhoun was sometimes, in his latter days, regarded by the North. Some of our Northern people thought that in case of a Southern republic, Mr. Calhoun saw the prospect for station and honors which the Union absolutely barred from his reach. He had made himself sectional, it was said, and forever forfeited all confidence of an entire portion of the country. Although many think that Mr. Seward's course has a powerful tendency to produce disunion, perhaps it is not just to charge him with such intentions. He may have hopes of elevation by means short of the creation of a Northern republic. If he can produce the union of the free states, as above suggested; if he can bring the non-slaveholding states to a united action, through the instrumentality of his favorite hobby, anti-slavery, he may yet attain the summit of his glory in the Union. It is true, such an achievement, every sound-minded man must say, would be the ruin of the country; but we need not necessarily conclude that Mr. Seward is of this opinion. He may be innocent in thinking that the presidential elections should turn on the slavery question; that it is the duty of the North to combine (they being the largest portion of the country), and take the United States government into their own hands. He may think that this is not only safe for the country, but likewise just and expedient. We cannot pronounce as to his motives, but, as to his judgment, it is not only our right, but our duty, to speak our opinion.

Although we cannot pronounce Mr. Seward corrupt for his political views, we may be permitted to say that we regard him and his course exceedingly dangerous to the Union. Just such an attempt to unite the free states upon a sectional candidate, as alluded to, was tried by his friends and followers in 1856, and the inauguration speech of that gentleman, made at Albany, upon the occasion of instituting the Republican party, in 1855, is still ringing in the ears of the American people. It is recollected how the duties of the North were pointed out in that speech, and how our Southern fellow-citizens were described. Slaveholders, Mr. Seward labored to instruct us, are a privileged, a dangerous class, whose existence in our government must be dangerous to free institutions ; and the idea was impressed upon us that the people of the North should cherish or cultivate jealous feelings in regard to them. The speech is spoken of from recollection, not having been seen by us since its first appearance in print ; but we can never forget the impression it made at the time, and cannot well mistake its purport.* But the purity

* Since the above was written, Mr. Seward has arrested public attention by his ultra positions in regard to the slavery question. In his speech delivered at Rochester, New York, on the twenty-fifth of October, he deliberately announced that "either the cotton and rice fields of South Carolina, and the sugar plantations of Louisiana, will ultimately be tilled by free labor, and Charleston and New Orleans become the marts for legitimate merchandise alone, or else the rye-fields and wheat-fields of Massachusetts and New York must again be surrendered by their farmers to slave culture and the production of slaves, and Boston and New York become once more markets for trade in the bodies and souls of men."

This position of Mr. Seward, so deliberately taken, and worded with such clearness, care and emphasis, is worthy of the reader's of the conception and birth of that Republican party can be estimated from the fact that its first candidate

most serious reflection, as it but embodies the sentiment of vast numbers of Northern people, who are really of the opinion that the South are endeavoring to extend slavery into the North. There was a time when the Freesoilers of the North professed that they had no desire to meddle with slavery in the states where already established; but the above position of Mr. Seward would indicate that he is the champion of universal emancipation. If he really believes that the only method of preserving Massachusetts and New York from "becoming markets for trade in the bodies and souls of men" is by abolishing slavery in South Carolina and Louisiana, can we doubt that he is, in the strictest sense of the word, an abolitionist? If not an abolitionist, why does he so forcibly inculcate opinions and sentiments which can influence to nothing but the most radical abolitionism? Mr. Seward, it must be recollected, is a senator of one of the most powerful states of the Union, and may fairly be regarded as the leader of the party to which he belongs. There is nothing novel in his language; the orators and editors of his party have continually, for several years past, urged upon the Northern people the same views and sentiments. The more intelligent reader may say that such positions as those alluded to are absurd; that we are not seriously to believe that the continuance of negro-servitude in the South is to result in the establishment of slavery in New England. But how is this with the great mass of the Northern people? There are millions who seriously believe that they must exert themselves, or slavery will be introduced into the North! The activity of the stump, the press and the pulpit, for a few years past, in misrepresenting the objects, efforts and characters, of Southern people, has been marvellous. There is no ridiculous pretence which a political mountebank can attribute to a slaveholder that will not find ready credence in the North. And it is to the stunted, obtuse, bigoted, fanatical, ignorant, jaundiced, self-righteous and self-conceited millions of such in the North that Mr. Seward, and others of his kidney, address such propositions as we have quoted above. It is not expected that they will make any impression on sane and intelligent minds; but the empire of such men is in the hearts of the victims of fraud and fanaticism. When such language, in one of the first cities in the for the presidency was selected solely on the ground of availability. The party itself was sufficiently animated by the opinions and spirit of Seward, and was justly regarded as an organization to promote the anti-slavery feelings and doctrines of the North; but the most eloquent, talented and long-tried champions of Freesoilism were, at the very first presidential campaign, ignored, and a talented and sprightly young Southern Democrat, famous for anything but zeal in the cause of anti-slavery, was put upon the track:

The acquiescence of the leading organs and mouthpieces of Mr. Seward, in General Taylor's nomination, had not been cheerful and with alacrity, although their support was finally accorded to him. As Mr. Seward's friends represented the Freesoil wing of the Whig party, their support of Taylor looked like a sacrifice; and, on the general's ascendency to the presidential chair, he was made aware of the vast importance of recognizing the power that had so graciously or ungraciously made him President; and the result was that in the appointments Mr. Fillmore had but little voice or influence. If this was so, removals, on the death of President Taylor, would become quite natural.

But, during the administration of Taylor and Fillmore, Freesoilism increased rapidly throughout the

North, is deliberately put forth by a senator of the United States, and is hailed as a grateful and worthy speech, by millions of Northern people, who heartily respond to every word, we think that it is time for the patriot — the true lover of his country — to open his eyes. No one, with the dimmest vision, can fail to see to what such political agitations are tending. The issue, as presented by the above extract from Mr. Seward's speech, is emphatically and essentially a disunion issue.

North. It was the duty of their administrations to frame laws for the new territories acquired by the Mexican war, and to receive into the Union California. The subjects connected with the new territories, although the fruits of the administration of Mr. Polk, were left for the management and disposal of the Whigs, and were the cause of great commotion and strife. The Whig party, so called, had triumphed under Taylor; but it stood over an abyss. The old party issues were fading from the minds of the people, and a new one of fearful omen making its appearance. A glance at the steps of the spirit of disorganization, then gnawing upon the vitals of the Whig party, is all that is requisite; the history is pretty minutely familiar to all.

CHAPTER XXVIII.

CAMPAIGN OF 1852 THE LAST WHIG CAMPAIGN. — CAUSES OF THE RUIN OF THE WHIG PARTY. — SLAVERY ISSUE. — PROPAGATION OF ANTI-SLAVERY FEELINGS IN THE NORTH. — HATRED OF SLAVERY APPLIED TO NEGRO SERVITUDE BY THE IGNORANT. — ALIENATION OF THE NORTH FROM THE SOUTH. — FUGITIVE LAWS OF 1793 AND 1850, ETC.

THE campaign of 1852 was the last presidential one that saw the Whigs in the field as a national party. After an existence of about twenty-five years, that party was broken up and dissolved into thin air by the disorganizing touch of fanaticism. The causes that promoted the growth of this fanaticism have been alluded to. To secure place, to enjoy the spoils of office, to attain honors and power, political parties at length seized hold of the jealousy which the dissimilarity of the institutions of two great sections of the country have given rise to, and made it the basis of party action. It was foreseen, at the formation of our government, that slavery was to be the rock on which our institutions were to wreck. To bring our national vessel upon this rock has ever been the aim of internal and external enemies, and already she has, on several occasions, experienced very narrow escapes from their efforts. The future looks discouraging. Human nature has been the same in all ages of the world. From our knowledge of what man has ever been, we can form a tolerably accurate estimate of what may be expected of him hereafter. The motives and passions that swayed him two thousand years ago will influence him now; and we may rest perfectly assured that no god has yet bestowed on him that wisdom, and prudence, and self-constraint, the lack of which ever has been the cause of his ruin and degradation. Fanaticism, of course, is a species of madness. It has been the ruin of every free people that has ever existed. When people are seized with a peculiar idea that takes command of their minds, they lose their reason, and can no longer act with prudence. There is no compromise with a fanatic; he is a monomaniac; he will have his insane idea gratified, or encounter the consequences. Ordinarily the result has been the ruin of the madman. Centuries ago it was uttered as a proverb, *Quem deus vult perdere, prius dementat:* that those whom God would destroy, he first renders fanatical.

The last presidential election saw the people of the United States divided at the polls upon no question but that of slavery! The patriotic statesman expressed himself alarmed at such a spectacle, to be laughed at as a fool by those who constantly pray for the destruction of the Union! The men of the North have become too pure to worship and vote with the men of the South. Is it strange they should be impatient to be cut entirely adrift from such monsters as they are now disposed to think slaveholders to be? The last President was elected nearly by the votes of a section of the country, although belonging to a different section from the one mainly instrumental in his election. The day may come when our elections will be purely sectional. But we have no disposition to speak much of the present or future. Our chief lessons are in the past.

At the formation of our Union, the whole subject of slavery, as our worthy Revolutionary statesmen and patriots thought, was fully and finally settled by the compromises in the Constitution. It was then hoped that that fiend of discord was allayed forever. It was early declared by all parts of the country that what was yielded to slaveholders by the Constitution they should enjoy. Quite a minority in the North are willing now that the compromises of the Constitution should be faithfully observed. As this was the general feeling of our Northern people in the early and purer days of our republic, there was no possible chance for making a party question out of slavery. The Constitution covered the whole ground. There was no point at which slavery could be attacked save through the Constitution, and the people of those days had a sacred regard for that instrument. The voice of the British agitator was heard in America, and an anti-slavery sentiment was awakened in the hearts of thousands; but that sentiment never found vent in the politics of the country until 1820, when Missouri was admitted as a state into the Union.

At the achievement of our independence, at the close of the Revolutionary war, which resulted in the peace of 1783, all of the unoccupied territories in the confederation were in the possession of the Southern States. The great North-western Territory then belonged to Virginia; and soon after the formation of the Union, the purchase of Louisiana gave us all of Texas; so that, under the administrations of our early Presidents, it is apparent that there could have been but little made by agitating the subject of slavery in the territories. Virginia, prior to the adoption of the Constitution, ceded all of the North-west Territory to the general government, under a restriction that it was to be forever exempt from slavery. Texas, a territory purchased with Louisiana in 1803, and devoted to slavery by local laws, was by Mr. Monroe ceded away in 1819, thus divesting the South of wide domains well adapted to their institutions. Thus far the South had made no aggressions on the North! In fact, the imperial states of the Great West were formed from territories originally belonging to the Southern States; and it was not until Missouri asked for admission that the religious and humane feeling of the North burst forth in a clamor against receiving into the Union any more slave states. No leakage, no crevasse, however slight, is safe in the dike that forms a barrier to long pent up and agitated floods.

But, notwithstanding the barrenness of the slave controversy while limited to constitutional grounds, the subject of slavery has never ceased, from the origin of our government to the present time, to be a constant theme of sermon, prayer, lecture, alms, or anathema, amongst the masses of the Northern people. The old emancipation and colonization movements were common to Northern and Southern people, the former doing most by way of prayer, the latter by contributions and sacrifices. While all sections were harmonious and worked together upon the subject, much good was accomplished. Thousands of slaves were emancipated and conveyed to Liberia; and the interchange of sympathies, views, and labors, led to valuable improvements in the South of the condition of those remaining in bondage. But these good services were destined soon to end.

That there were in New England bitter haters of the South at an early period of our government, has already been shown; but the change of feeling amongst the masses of Northern men, in regard to Southern institutions, by which enmity to the South has become more general in the North, has been the work of time. Unfortunately for the prevalence of sound views on the subject of slavery, the great body of the people of the Northern States are unacquainted with the institution, and know comparatively nothing of slaves, or of what they gain or lose by their servitude. They draw their sentiment of anti-slavery directly from God, and acquire it at their birth. We know this from our own Northern birth. We do not allow ourselves to discuss the question as to the rightfulness of slavery; we know it is wrong. We will not insult our understandings by doubting the great enormity of so foul a thing as human bondage. Abhorrence of slavery comes into our hearts as naturally as breath into our nostrils, and we have nothing to do throughout our whole lives but denounce the monster. In this we are not singular. Reverse our circumstances with the people of the South, and they would do the same. In 1776 no fiercer words in condemnation of slavery were coined by anybody than by the patriots of the South. The Declaration of Independence was drawn by a slaveholder. In regard to detestation of slavery, there is no difference between the people of the North and South; they are both from the same stock, and in the veins of both runs the same blood. But these two people differ widely in their feelings in regard to negro servitude. The people of the North have long cultivated their anti-slavery sentiment unmodified by any knowledge, or scarcely inquiry, as to what negro slavery really is; and while the people of the South have abated no jot of their love of liberty, their daily and intimate knowledge of the native incapacity of negroes for the enjoyment of civil liberty, reconciles them to the continuance of a species of servitude which contains not a single element of the slavery so odious to the Northern heart. It is only the illiterate, illiberal, and bigoted ultra of the North that consigns all the slaveholders of the South to infamy, pronouncing them all to be wicked and vile for holding negroes in bondage. Still, too few in the free states are disposed to concede that religion, morality, and virtue, can flourish in what are called the slave states. There is in the North a woful misapprehension upon the subject of negro servitude and Southern society. The fact that the Southern people are humane, virtuous, high-minded, liberal, and upright, is not appreciated; and that the millions of helpless negroes of the South have no hope for elevation and happiness saving through subordination to their Southern masters, is not considered or known; and the fact that negro bondage in the Southern States has already accomplished more for the welfare and happiness of the negro race than has ever before been wrought out for him upon earth since his creation, is with fanatical hysterics denied or not admitted. The fact is, the people of the North have condemned their Southern brethren as slaveholders, and attach to them all the odium their hearts have ever felt for slavery.

The propagation of an ultra anti-slavery feeling amongst the people of the North has been going forward for many years, from various motives, and in various methods, many of which have already been alluded to. It is not strange that much delusion upon the subject should exist, especially in the extreme North, where but little is known of negro slavery or of the negro race. The people of the North are progressive. They are a reading, inquiring, and reforming people. There are a few subjects that have, it is true, received more than ordinary attention at their hands; but it must not be inferred from this that the Northern people are indifferent to things in general. The subject of slavery has been one of their specialities; to this they have given uncommon attention in their way. There are a few other subjects also that have been extensively agitated in New England, and among them temperance and capital punishment may be named. Scarcely does a Northern child leave his cradle, before he is embarked upon the limitless ocean of discussion upon such topics as before named, and slavery is the first and last that is found engaging his heart and understanding. Not only is the subject discussed over the newspaper at the fireside, but the boy's first effort at composition is upon the most thrilling of all subjects, to wit, slavery; as the current and household ideas of the day upon this topic will flow when the poor lad would be mute upon most others. Declamations in the schools, also, are generally upon that subject; and slavery has been the standing and never-ending subject for debating societies for time out of mind. The youthful mental faculties of Northern people for over half a century have been disciplined on that subject. If there is any theme on which the New England mind is active, and the tongue glib and eloquent, it is upon this. The same stereotyped ideas have passed through generations, and by the cultivation of constant exercise are kept lively and inspiring. This must necessarily be so. It is impossible to chain down the faculties of an active mind. The poverty and laborious lot of millions of our countrymen preclude their research and investigation into subjects requiring a preliminary education, and the knowledge which reading and science can alone supply; and consequently the native activity and vivacity of their mental energies must be brought into play upon topics upon which reason can act with but little aid save a resort to its own resources. Not only to such, but likewise to many a poverty-stricken intellect in the schools, the question of slavery is a god-send, affording a theme for composition or declamation when no other subject can "start a spirit." Many a schoolboy debater has shown his nascent oratorical powers in depicting the stripes and chains and other standing accompaniments of slavery; and, from the renown won in such exercises, been promoted to the pulpit, or to the station of a travelling lecturer for some anti-slavery society. No clergyman reaches the sacred desk without more or less use of this subject for the exercise of his faculties. And there is but one manner in which slavery is uniformly treated by such young and old orators. It is made the subject of declamation. All such efforts are highly drawn pictures of the horrors of slavery, produced for effect. Not only this, but no sooner does the schoolboy find that he can put ideas together upon paper, than some village print groans under a lucid exposition upon this fruitful topic from his pen. Thus, by orators, editors, and poets, all the outrages by slave owners ever committed are collected together, and with passion-breathing accents pressed upon Northern auditors and readers; and it would not be at all strange if upon this subject the minds of the Northern people were tolerably united. But the slightest glance shows that the Northern mind, in arriving at its present position on the question of negro slavery, has been educated wholly by its feelings. It has never been informed upon the real merits of the subject. We all know this very well, as we can reflect back upon the earlier period of our lives, and recollect the accounts uniformly given us by our teachers of Southern slavery. Was our childhood ever notified of a single bright spot in it? Were we ever told that such a thing as a good slaveholder could exist? Did we ever imagine that a slave could utter anything but groans, or that the poor negro's life could be anything but an unintermitted torture? Let us revert in recollection to the accounts of slavery in the South that the books and papers our teachers used to place before us presented to us. We even see now, in memory, the pictures in our Sabbath-school books of the poor blacks, with manacled hands outstretched to heaven, with woe and agony depicted upon their countenances. No glimpse of the exact truth in regard to the matter ever entered the mind of the Northern youth; but the whole subject, from some cause or other, has been shrouded with an impenetrable cloud of error and falsehood. We demand to know by what Northern writer, teacher, or lecturer, for the past fifty years, the youth of New England have been instructed that of the millions of negroes in servitude in the South, the great mass are contented, happy, well cared for, and enjoying every blessing their natures are susceptible of? Who has taught that the highest happiness the negro has ever known upon earth, has, beyond all controversy, been realized in Southern servitude? Where is now the Northern lecturer, editor, teacher, or divine, that will admit that the overthrow of Southern slavery would be the ruin of the comfort, civilization, and happiness of those millions of negroes now in bondage? When and by whom were we ever told that the Southern people are a civilized, polished, humane, and Christian people? And, in speaking evil of them, when were we ever rebuked for bearing false evidence against our neighbor?

The history of the progress of the sentiment of anti-slavery in the North is familiar to all. Many events in that history have been alluded to. A revolution in the feelings of the Northern people has been gradually, but surely, going on,—a revolution that will bring with it important consequences to mankind. It is a revolution that will change the face of affairs in the moral and political world. The dismemberment of the American Republic will restore legitimacy throughout the whole earth, and this dismemberment can only be achieved through the agency of Northern feeling upon the subject of slavery. The process by which foreign enemies of Republicanism are accomplishing this has been pointed out, and any one can see the fruits of their labors. The revolution is progressing. The Northern churches first withdraw their fellowship and connection with those of the South. To hold slaves is pronounced sinful; a gulf is to be interposed between the Northern and Southern Christian. The Northern Christian smites his breast, and thanks God that he is better than his Southern brother, with whom he deems it a sin to commune. Other religious societies are crumbling beneath the breath of the fiend of civil discord, and every day the fierce purity of the North is pouring its destructive and wrathful bolts into the South; and so outrageous is the hatred of the South in the hearts of Northern Christians, that that unhappy part of the world is hardly considered worthy of a missionary's care, hardly considered worth saving.

But, passing over the invidious designs and means by which the enemies of our institutions are working their destruction, we will note some of the evidences of the progress of the fatal revolution which is going on amongst us. For years after the formation of our Union the compromises of the Constitution were regarded as sacred, and no one thought of refusing obedience. The right of holding slaves was recognized, as well as the right of all the states and territories to import slaves, at least until the year 1808. The Constitution preserved to the people of the states and territories the right of carrying on the slave-trade for twenty years after its adoption, which would indicate that by that instrument slavery was not viewed as a local institution. The Constitution also provided that if one held to labor in one state should escape into another, he should not be discharged from such service by any laws of the state into which he should flee; but, on demand, be surrendered up. The provision was plainly penned, and was inserted in the Constitution for the protection of the owners of slaves. During the administration of President Washington, a fugitive law, as it has been called, was enacted by Congress, by which negroes escaping into free states were arrested and carried back to their masters. To this law there was no objection for years. In fact, the escape, or attempt at escape, of a slave — a full-blooded negro slave — is a rare occurrence, save when enticed by the deceptive wiles of abolitionists. For many years the fugitive law was rarely called for. The escape of slaves, never very large in proportion to the number in the South, was always very small until systematic efforts for running them off were instituted by a set of men who have made themselves rich out of the pockets of deluded Northern people. Coëval with the outburst of radical abolition, with the construction of those under-ground railroads for decoying away slaves from their owners, the Northern States began to pass laws in contravention of the fugitive law of 1793. This law prescribed the manner of procedure in apprehending the fugitive, looking to the use of the officers of the law, sheriffs, jailers, and so forth, of the several states. The legislatures of the free states did not, in terms, nullify the letter of the law of 1793, but they passed laws forbidding the use of their jails for the purposes specified in that law, and forbidding the state officers, under heavy penalties, from aiding in the arrest of a fugitive. Probably every free state passed such laws, and many states made repeated enactments upon the subject. The result was that the law of 1793 became a dead letter. The enactment stood, but the agencies, by which the Congress of '93 supposed they had provided for its execution, were paralyzed. In effect, the law for restoring fugitives was nullified. All this occurred, in the extreme Northern States, many years ago, and before the South had begun to feel alarmed for their safety, and make the horrid aggressions on the North of which we have recently heard so much. What was the occasion of this attack on the constitutional right of the South? The Constitution says, plainly and explicitly, that such fugitive escaping into a neighboring state shall, on demand, be given up. Now, is it complying with that Constitution for a state not only to refuse to surrender such fugitive, but to pass penal laws for the prevention of its officers in aiding in such surrender? Is it honest for sensible Northern men to pretend that such legislative acts are not in open defiance of the constitutional rights of the slave states? It is true that there are shallow, sophistical knaves, who sometimes pretend that the word used in the Constitution for fugitives does not mean slaves; but for every honest man it is sufficient to know that the Supreme Court of the United States, as well as the highest courts in such states as Massachusetts and New York, have pronounced that provision in the Constitution to relate to slaves; and every man of common sense and common honesty must see and, at once, admit this. But what Northern lecturer or editor, while enlarging upon the subject of Southern encroachments, ever mentions this palpable and flagrant outrage upon the clear rights of the South? The man that, for a moment, moved by conscience, should presume to suggest that the people of the North had been in error upon the subject, would be quite universally stigmatized as a dough-face and a pro-slaveryite. But one side ever has or ever will be heard in the North. The Northern mind is fixed upon the subject, and fixed by fraud and falsehood. But the despots of Europe know the force of fixed ideas. The human heart loves a falsehood, when adopted, as ardently as it does a truth. If any one doubts this, let him attempt to reason with a follower of Mahomet, Joe Smith, or Lloyd Garrison.

When the intrigues of Europe commenced the anti-slavery enterprise in the North, there was but a narrow field for political action. The District of Columbia was the only territory we had in which slaves could be held, and the fierce crusade against the institutions of that district is well remembered. In those days the South was the party attacked, vilified, and outraged. On slight pretexts, the enemies of the country took occasion in the South to blacken the North, and in the North to traduce the South. All remember how, by degrees, the sensitiveness of the Northern mind upon the subject of slavery was increased, and how politicians, lecturers, authors, and editors, began to avail themselves of that sensitiveness to advance their selfish purposes. Northern legislatures, year after year, for a long series of years, have constantly put forth strong resolutions denouncing slavery and slaveholders. These resolutions, many of them, have been of the most insulting kind, and forwarded to the executives of Southern states, seemingly for no purpose but insult. The country for years has been overrun with anti-slavery lecturers, whose sole mission it has been to abuse the Southern people. Miserable negroes and negro-wenches have repeated to Northern audiences the committed slang compiled from abolition writings; and dishonest, swindling white lecturers, male and female, have, year after year, poured into Northern ears their slandering falsehoods about the South; and all this has been done not to show the propriety of political action as to slavery, but to embitter the feelings of the men, women, and children of one section of the country against another. The object of the work has been to produce an alienation of feeling between the North and the South. Those careless and unreflecting or unsuspecting men and women of the North, who have professed that they had no desire to interfere with slavery in the states where it exists, have listened complacently to the foul fiends whose mission it has been to sow the seeds of dissension and anarchy in their hearts. False accounts have been uniformly given of Southern institutions. The lectures repeated to Northern auditors have uniformly been tissues of exaggeration or lies; and the feelings produced by them in the hearts of Northern people have been, in the highest degree, unjust to their Southern friends. And editors are now almost universally committed against the South. Unless the newspaper ministers to the diseased feeling of the Northern mind, upon the subject of slavery, it will find but slim support. Journals, that twenty years ago were national and conservative, now freely devote themselves to the abuse of the Southern people. Such could be mentioned, but every reader knows the fact. We see in such journals the fiercest invectives against slaveholders as such; and purely for the purpose of arraying the North against the South, of carrying forward the great work of embittering one section against another, of making the North hate the South, Southern advertisements for runaway slaves, and for the auction of slaves, are freely copied into their columns, and sent abroad amongst the Northern people. There can be but one object in such a course, and that has been to increase the ill-feeling between the two sections of the country. And authors and writers of fiction have gathered a rich harvest from the matured enmity existing in the North against the the South, and are doing their part to forward the work of alienation.

CHAPTER XXIX.

THE ACQUISITION OF NEW TERRITORY OCCASIONED THE INCREASE OF FREESOILISM. — ACTION OF THE SOUTH. — SECESSION MEDITATED. — J. C. CALHOUN'S SPEECH AND POSITION. — CONTROVERSIES IN REGARD TO CALIFORNIA, NEW MEXICO AND UTAH. — THE WILMOT PROVISO. — DISUNION IMMINENT. — COMPROMISE MEASURES OF MR. CLAY. — WEBSTER'S SEVENTH OF MARCH SPEECH. — CALIFORNIA PREFERS FREE-LABOR. — SLAVERY FOUND TO BE A QUESTION OF CLIMATE. — COMPROMISE MEASURES PASS. — THE FUGITIVE SLAVE LAW. — NEW ENGLAND OFFENDED AT WEBSTER FOR FAVORING THAT LAW. — CHANGE OF THE POPULAR MIND, AND THE ANCIENT FEELING ON THE SUBJECT, ETC.

The election of General Taylor, in 1848, was, for the Whigs, the fortunate result of a singular combination of circumstances. The events of Mr. Polk's administration had deeply stirred the anti-slavery feeling of the North; but that feeling, owing to the peculiar nominations of the different parties, was wasted like useless steam. Mr. Van Buren was the best abolitionist offered to the anti-slavery men of the free states! But the long-cherished anti-slavery sentiment of the North was soon aroused into unwonted activity. It was at once decided, by old and by young, by men and by women, that the new territories must be free. The question of the freedom of the territories was, in the free states, of course, magnified into vast importance; and, as the free-state party was the largest, the South at once imagined herself divested of her rights in property acquired by the blood of her sons.

The newly-aroused crusade in the North against slavery in the territories, or the admission of more slave states, provoked the indignation of the South. The idea that the people of New England should dictate to the people of a territory or state, as to their domestic institutions, was to Southern people repulsive and exciting. The course taken by the South, in consequence of that pursued by the North, is well recollected. The Southern manifesto, signed by forty-two members of Congress; the Southern Convention at Nashville; the establishment of the Southern Press at Washington to advocate secession; and the open organization of a plan of secession and disunion by some of the Southern people, are recollected as features of the history of those times. The excitement in the South was intense, and the country was regarded as in uncommon peril. The factions in both the North and the South were aroused into energetic action, and seemed inspired with a common purpose — to wit, the overthrow of the Union. And this long-meditated purpose of the enemies of the American Union seemed in a fair way of accomplishment. The North was, it appeared, on the point of excluding slavery from the territories by legislation; and the South, it was well known, would never submit to what she regarded as an act of usurpation. It appeared inevitable that a collision between the North and the South must ensue, and that the strength of the government was on the eve of a trial. Mr. Calhoun's celebrated speech cannot be forgotten. He virtually pronounced the Union at an end. But in this he no more than repeated his prophecy of an earlier date. Mr. Calhoun has been much derided, in years past, for pronouncing a dissolution of the Union inevitable; and, as the Union has continued as yet unbroken, his speeches and prognostications are treated as unworthy of notice. But perhaps he who fifty years, or twenty years, or ten years hence, shall read the works of the American statesmen of the age just past, will find in those of Mr. Calhoun the clearest insight into the spirit of the institutions of the country, and by far the greatest foresight as to the tendency of the events and measures of his day. There was nothing dim, obscure, or shadowy, in his mental vision. The future to him was the present. He saw as in sun-light that the agitation of the slavery question would infallibly rupture the ligaments that connect the American states. As he saw that this result must inevitably and certainly occur, it was his opinion that the South should take advantage of the period when she was nearly on equality with the North, and meet the coming issue at once; and, if to be settled disastrously to the Union, have it settled when the South might meet the storm with less peril to herself. The nature of fanaticism, the objects of Northern fanatics, the tendency of Northern preaching and lecturing, and the results to be apprehended from the constant outpouring from the Northern press of anti-slavery sentiments, were clearly, strongly and vividly portrayed, time and time again, in the speeches of that clear-minded man. The agitations of the last three or four years, and the present universal anti-slavery excitement of the North, are but the realizations of his early prophecies, for which he was, when he uttered them, unheeded, or regarded as wild and visionary. Nothing but the ruin of this Union, through the agency of the slavery agitation, is requisite to show that Mr. Calhoun was the clearest-minded man of his times, and to establish the wisdom of his counsel for that section of the country which he saw must some day become the victim of a fanatical crusade. Upon the occasion of which we are speaking, Mr. Calhoun, deciding what the South should do by the light of what he thought she ought to do, pronounced disunion inevitable. He saw that the North had ceased to recognize the constitutional rights of the South; that the restoration of fugitives was refused; and that the territories were to be closed to Southern occupation. Mr. Clay and Mr. Webster were at that time in the United States Senate, and both solemnly and earnestly admonished the country that the Union was in danger; and this was the unanimous opinion of every right-minded and sound-minded statesman in the land.

But how idle, how futile, how uncalled-for and unnecessary the whole uproar of the North as to the question of slavery in the territories! How strange, how wonderful have been the developments of Providence! And how short-sighted and contemptible have appeared the aims and labors of our Northern people in regard to these territorial questions! To such men as Clay and Webster the unexpected and marvellous course of events in California opened the first gleam of sunshine through the dense clouds that overhung the horizon. California! — the land of gold — the fruits of the war, and undoubtedly the gift of Providence! Her gold discoveries immediately filled her with American citizens; and, before the quarrel about the territories was well under way, she was knocking for admission into the Union as a sovereign state! She had taken a large emigration from the South, as well as other parts of the land; but, to the astonishment of the world, when her convention assembled to form a Constitution, her delegates were unanimous for the exclusion of slavery! And for the proposed state a Constitution excluding slavery was adopted. Nearly one-half of the delegates in that constitutional convention were persons who had emigrated from the South! The marvel of California in this respect has recently been repeated in the territory of Kansas. A goodly portion of the settlers of Kansas are from the South, and three-fifths of those derived from slave states are in favor of excluding slaves from the territory! Such facts at once divest Northern preaching upon the subject of slavery of all its importance! The course of California threw the first ray of light upon the subject, and taught all reasonable men what reason had before suggested — that is, slavery is a question of climate and soil. It cannot exist where the Saxon race can cultivate the land, as it cannot compete with white labor. The negro slave has been moving southwards ever since the establishment of our independence; and white labor will, at no very distant future day, crowd him still further south.

But, in 1850, the Northern mind was busy and big with the destiny of the territories. The action of California had providentially opened a door for compromise. Mr. Clay, in the United States Senate, proposed a series of compromise measures which, it was thought and hoped, would at once and forever put the agitation of the slavery question in the United States at an end. Among other things, he proposed the admission of California with her free Constitution; the adoption of territorial governments for New Mexico and Utah on the principle of popular sovereignty; the passage of a fugitive slave law to carry out a provision of the Constitution; and the abolishment of the slave-trade in the District of Columbia. The result of these propositions of Mr. Clay needs no particular description. They were supported by that statesman by a most powerful and patriotic speech; and in favor of them Mr. Webster made his celebrated seventh of March effort. The three great American statesmen were again brought together in the United States Senate, and signalized themselves by masterly efforts upon an occasion full of uncertainty, fear, and danger, to their country. Mr. Calhoun was very feeble; his great speech was read to the Senate by a friend. He died the last day of March, but had heard the efforts of his powerful opponents. Mr. Webster was transferred from the Senate to the state department by Mr. Fillmore, and Mr. Clay's voice soon died away from the Senate, to be heard there no more. Neither Mr. Clay nor Mr. Webster lived to witness another presidential election. The death of Mr. Clay occurred in June, 1852, and that of Mr. Webster in October.

The pacification measures of Mr. Clay were finally carried through both houses of Congress, and received the approbation of the President; but the fiend of sectional discord was far from allayed. No one not a witness by personal presence can have any adequate conception of the true state of Northern feeling upon all the topics of the slavery question. Against the law for the restoration of fugitives the prejudices of the Northern people were and are very strong. This prejudice was felt by Mr. Webster, and was remarked upon in the Senate, in July, 1850. "It was created," he truly said, "by the incessant action on the public mind of abolition societies, abolition presses, and abolition lecturers. No drum head, in the longest day's march, was ever more incessantly beaten and smitten, than public sentiment in the North has been, every month, and day, and hour, by the din, and roll, and rub-a-dub of abolition writers and abolition lecturers." It is true the voice of Clay and Webster was somewhat heeded in the United States Senate, but much less than upon former occasions; and amongst the people of the North their influence was at an end. Of the Whig delegation in Congress from Massachusetts, Mr. Webster stood alone upon those compromise measures, and it was soon apparent that the old leaven of conservatism had departed from the Whig ranks. No candid man will pretend that either of these venerable statesmen had at all changed his opinions upon the subject of slavery, or did or said anything in 1850 inconsistent with the principles advocated by him in former years; yet their course upon the compromise measures of 1850 gave offence to the great mass of the Whigs of the free states. The usage of Mr. Webster by the people of the North, — of his own state, — for the positions taken by him in his seventh of March speech, is fresh in the recollection of every one. He incurred the condemnation of Massachusetts, and the censure of the whole North, for the most patriotic service he ever rendered his country. No man can point out an opinion or statement in that celebrated speech that is not founded in reason, justice and truth. His positions were all eminently correct, and his sentiments the very soul of patriotism. The unfortunate events of Mr. Polk's administration had involved the country in a fierce sectional controversy, that was threatening civil war and disunion, and Mr. Webster, in coming forward to support measures of pacification, was not guilty of making improper concessions to the South; he did not offer to yield any right of the North, or grant the South anything not theirs by every legal and moral principle. No; his fault was in making that hated section any concessions, however justly their due. Those who have read and reflected upon Mr. Webster's course in that crisis know this very well. It was seen by intelligent men that if such territories as Kansas and California are not adapted to negro labor, it is mockery to talk of carrying slaves into the sterile plains and barren heights of Utah and New Mexico! Mr. Webster saw that the established freedom of California was the end of all legitimate controversy about slavery in the territories, and deemed it unnecessary to cover the arid mountains of New Mexico with Wilmot provisos. For this perhaps he was not particularly censured; but for consenting to the enactment of a fugitive slave law he brought down upon himself the vengeance of the whole Freesoil and abolition posse of the free states. He had been guilty of remaining stationary in his political and moral principles. In the great progress around him, Mr. Webster had made no advance. He saw clearly that the conservatism which had ever rendered the Whigs a national party was disappearing; and foresaw, in fact saw, the dissolution and ruin of that party. He saw and felt the tendency of the times during the presidential campaign of 1848, and was deeply sensible of the great change the anti-slavery sentiment had wrought in the hearts of Northern Whigs, when he made his seventh of March speech. The embarrassments of his situation were trying; but he proved true to his mission, to the honor of his state, and to his country. He found it necessary to encounter the prejudices of those whom he loved, and he did it because he loved them. "*Vera pro gratis;*" that is, instead of pandering agreeably to their peculiar sentiments, he found himself obliged to tell them truths. He was not so ignorant and short-sighted as to be unaware that his course would bring upon him the displeasure of the great mass of the Northern people; but it was not in his power to hesitate when duty to his country called upon him to take his stand.

The odium piled upon Mr. Webster for his support of the fugitive slave act has not yet wholly abated. All that he did in regard to the measure was to make that seventh of March speech. Every one can read his words, and judge of his guilt or innocence as to that enactment. He was clear that such a law is plainly demanded by the Constitution. No one denies this. He further gave it as his opinion that the provisions of the Constitution are obligatory, and ought to be honestly, fairly, and with good faith, carried out and executed. As the Constitution secures the rights of Southern masters to the restoration of their fugitive slaves, he argued that it is no more than just and right that those rights should be observed. This was the head and front of his offending; so his offence consisted in his following the example of Washington, rather than espousing as a guide the modern preachers of a higher law, who ignore all constitutional provisions that contravene the law of God!

The history of the fugitive-slave law of 1793, enacted at the recommendation of George Washington, we are all pretty well acquainted with. The North had laboriously and most cautiously nullified its effect. Enactment after enactment had been passed by state legislatures to defeat its operation ; and, long prior to 1850, it had become, in the free states, completely a dead letter. The return of fugitives had been lectured against, written against, preached against, and legislated against, by thousands and thousands of persons who probably never had read the Constitution of the United States during their whole lives. Perhaps it is not fair to say that the Northern people deliberately set themselves at work to rob the South of their constitutional rights, for we know that such has not been the case. There has been no *deliberation* in the matter. The whole movement has been emotional. The understanding and conscience have had no part in the work. Never was anything intended but a blow in the cause of freedom ; the rights of others are things never considered by the great mass of those who have followed the hue-and-cry of British emissaries and American fanatics and traitors. Were prejudiced men capable of reason and justice, the people of the North would at once see and acknowledge their inconsistency and error. Fugitives from slavery are quite rare. The right of their capture is a small thing compared with the question of holding some three millions of negroes in bondage. Nevertheless, nearly one-half (perhaps more) of the Northern people will say at once that they are not for disturbing slavery in the states where located, because in these states slavery has the sanction of the Constitution. It is only in the territories, say many, that the Constitution does not protect the institution ; but in the slave states they have no desire to meddle with it. Then, if content that such states enjoy their negroes, why is the master opposed in pursuing one who escapes; especially as the Constitution particularly guards and preserves the owner's right to recapture such fugitive? But so it is. The great mass of the Northern people have been educated into the feeling that slaveholders must not be allowed to carry back their fugitives. This feeling has become a holy sentiment, — an item of religious faith amongst Northern people, — a principle for which they are willing to peril life and everything valuable. Constitutions, unions, laws, the highest hopes of a country or of mankind, form no barrier to the onward course of a religious idea, or a fanatical ism. The arrest of fugitives in Massachusetts has been tried. The people in a mass arise against the laws of the United States! The Supreme Court of that state is appealed to (by *habeas corpus*), and its decision that the law of 1850 is constitutional, does not stay the resistance to the owner of the fugitive. Those having custody of the runaway under process of the general government are beset by a mob, and life is sacrificed! The sentiment of the people arises against the slave owner; and the population, *en masse*, go forth to obstruct a citizen of the South in the pursuit of his constitutional right.

But few of the Northern people stop to consider their position in regard to the slave question, or to note the changes wrought in their feelings by the insidious influences which have been at work upon them for years. And a smaller number still condescend to inquire into the practical utility of the measures they are induced to advocate, or even attempt to give any reason for their course but the pretended commands of God, which they cannot resist; not knowing whether their labors will bring good or ill to the objects of their concern. Never on earth was a moral movement urged forward by the sons of men with less regard for consequences than the anti-slavery crusade of the present day. What benefit to the negroes can possibly accrue from the measures agitated by anti-slavery philanthropists, no one can imagine. The emancipation of the slaves of the South would be disastrous to them. There is no disputing this. There is no sane philanthropist in New England that would to-day enfranchise all the slaves in the United States, were the power so to do committed to his hands. But Northern men, with a blindness and prejudice befitting idiots, say no slaveholder shall come upon Northern soil with his negro, and retain him in servitude! Indeed! How wise and pure! New England, whose money and enterprise transported Sambo from Africa to the South, will probably escape accountability by this extreme and most holy horror of the bare sight of slavery! No; no slave must be brought to the North! Slavery is well enough in its place! It would be impossible to abolish it in Carolina or Georgia; this is forbidden both by the welfare of the slave and the constitutional rights of the master; but the poor negro must draw out his servile life on those Southern plantations! The luxurious master, who annually spends months at Niagara, Saratoga, the White Mountains, and other Northern places of resort, must not bring the poor slave to catch a gleam of Northern happiness! And why? The puritans of the North cannot endure so sad a sight as a human being in bondage! Some good to the slave might result from spending a part of his time in the free states; he might come in contact with genuine piety, which is thought to be a stranger in the South; he might gain from intercourse with Northern philanthropists much useful knowledge, and become inspired with ideas that, on his return to the South, would be valuable to his brethren in bondage; and that portion of his life spent in the North might be passed more happily than if confined on the plantation at home; but what holy Northern man, for the sake of such advantages to miserable negroes, could think of permitting the foul sin of slavery for a moment to offend his eyes? And if one of these slaves escape to the North, his freedom must be upheld against the Constitution and the laws of the land! It is seen by a glance that in this the benefit of the negro is not consulted, but sacrificed.

How long has it been since the North has shown herself so extremely cautious of her pure and unstained skirts? How long have we been thus over-righteous? Under Washington and our first presidents, masters could bring their slaves at pleasure, reside with them as long as they pleased, and in case of an escape, even while residing in the North, the fugitive would be restored by the laws of the land. Under this fraternal feeling existing between the citizens of different states, Southern gentlemen used to come into the North with their slaves; and, finding life pass pleasantly, continued their residence here for large portions of the year. To guard against the abuse of this comity, — to prevent legalizing slavery by the master's making the Northern state his permanent residence under such circumstances, — some of the free states, to wit, Pennsylvania and New York, passed laws limiting the right of Southern gentlemen coming North with slaves, to a residence of six and nine months, with the privilege of retaining their servants. Should a Southern gentleman continue his residence over nine months, it was to be considered that his Southern residence was abandoned, and his home made permanent in the North, and, consequently, he no longer entitled to retain his slaves. Can there be a doubt that such an arrangement was, in a high degree, beneficial to both the slave and his master? Then whence opposition to it? The objection, we are told, is on account of the repugnance felt by the humane and freedom-loving people of the North to the mere sight of slavery. The whole movement upon this subject had its origin in the feelings. There is no judgment, no conscience, no humanity in the matter. The sentiment of the North has been aroused by the wiles of an enemy.

It was the fortune or misfortune of Mr. Webster, the most upright and patriotic statesman of his age, to encounter the fierce prejudice of the Northern people upon this subject. In 1852, but for his stand upon the rights of the South to her fugitives, he would have been nominated for the presidency. The friends and followers of Mr. Seward defeated his claims in the national convention; and the most that could be urged against Mr. Webster was that he had not changed his position on the slavery question, while all around him had embraced new views and feelings. As an evidence of the remarkable change that had come over the feelings of even Mr. Seward, we will quote his reply to Gerrit Smith in 1838, when a candidate for governor of New York. Mr. Smith demanded to know what Governor Seward thought of the law then existing, allowing slaveholders to retain their slaves in that state during a temporary sojourn; and Mr. Seward answered that he was opposed to its repeal. His answer was such as any candid man would make, and contains the following sensible remarks:

"But, gentlemen, being desirous to be entirely candid in this communication, it is proper I should add that *I am not convinced it would be either wise, expedient or humane, to declare to our fellow-citizens of the Southern or South-western States that if they travel to or from, or pass through the State of New York, they shall not bring with them the attendants whom custom, or education, or habit, may have rendered necessary to them.* I have not been able to discover any good object to be attained by such an act of inhospitality. It certainly can work no injury to us, nor can it be injurious to the unfortunate beings held in bondage, to permit them, once perhaps in their lives, and at most on occasions few and far between, to visit a country where slavery is unknown. I can even conceive of benefits to the great cause of human liberty from the cultivation of this intercourse with the South. I can imagine but one ground of objection, which is, that it may be regarded as an implication that this state sanctions slavery. If this objection were well grounded, I should at once condemn the law. But, in truth, the law does not imply any such sanction. The same statute which, in necessary obedience to the Constitution of the United States as expounded, declares the exception, condemns, in the most clear and definite terms, all human bondage. I will not press the considerations flowing from the nature of our Union, and the mutual concessions on which it was founded, against the propriety of such an exclusion as your question contemplates, apparently for the purpose only of avoiding an application not founded in fact, and which the history of our state so nobly contradicts. It is sufficient to say that such an exclusion could have no good effect practically, and would accomplish nothing in the great cause of human liberty."

CHAPTER XXX.

CAMPAIGN OF 1852. — THE PLATFORMS OF THE TWO PARTIES. — ADMINISTRATION OF PIERCE. — DOUGLAS, AND THE NEBRASKA MEASURE. — EFFORTS IN THE NORTH. — REPUBLICAN PARTY. — NOMINATIONS AND ELECTION OF '56. — CINCINNATI CONVENTION. — FRÉMONT. — ELECTION OF BUCHANAN. — HIS ADMINISTRATION, ETC.

The result of the campaign of 1852 is instructive. That General Scott was a genuine Whig no one doubted; but his nomination through the influence of the Freesoil wing of the party, his tacit recognition of the right of that wing to control his political action, and the emphatic and contemptuous rejection, by those who had been mainly instrumental in his nomination, of the national platform on which he had been placed at the Baltimore Convention, shocked and disgusted thousands of national Whigs, and drove them into the ranks of the opposition. Both the Whig and Democratic National Conventions had approbated the compromise of 1850 by their platforms. The champions of Scott accepted his nomination, but said, "We spit upon the platform." It was a declaration that a large portion of the Whig party were resolved to repudiate the national principles of the Baltimore Convention; and it was not considered safe to throw into the hands of those sectionalists so powerful an instrument as the presidency. The national Whigs were not prepared to exalt to that powerful station a person who might, by possibility, become the organ or chief of a sectional faction. And the support of General Pierce, by those disappointed Whigs, involved but a slight sacrifice of principle. General Pierce and the party that nominated him were unanimous in the support of a platform with scarcely any perceptible difference from that put forth by the Whig National Convention. It is a significant fact that the Democratic party have, for the last twenty years, been drifting back into the wholèsome principles inaugurated by Madison and Monroe, from which the storm of Jacksonism had, as has been shown, driven them so far. The acquisitions from the Whigs in 1852 and 1856 have had a tendency to hasten the return to those conservative and valuable measures so necessary to our country, and so much desired by the patriot. But, unfortunately, the Democrats in 1852, as well as the Whigs, adopted, in making their nomination, the principle of availability, and bitter experiences have been the result.

Of the administration of President Pierce, which is of so recent date, it is not necessary to say much. But few readers will care to have their opinions of that administration revised at present. The friends of the general look upon it as a model one; his enemies regard it as fatally unfortunate. Without impeaching the motives of that President, which may have been upright and patriotic, we may say, with safety, that the election, in his place, of Buchanan or Marcy, would have saved the Democratic party from severe misfortunes, if not degradation, and the country from the most imminent perils. That President Pierce was actuated by high-toned national sentiments, most of his opponents concede; that, with some exceptions, his administration was conservative and judicious, is not denied. If there were errors, they were those of the head rather than of the heart. His Secretary of State, Mr. Marcy, was a statesman of first-rate abilities, who, in his administration of the foreign policy of our country, met the hearty approbation of every Whig. A man of unwavering integrity, Mr. Guthrie, was placed at the head of the Treasury department, quite to the satisfaction of every well-wisher of the country; and a gentleman of known conservative principles, James Buchanan, was sent minister to the British court. His other secretaries were all able men.

But, as the Nebraska-Kansas bubble is not entirely exploded yet, and, like other bubbles, reflects from its magnificent sides so many dazzling hues, and still commands the gaze of millions with trance-like power, anything like a calm and reasonable consideration of its substance and importance could scarcely be expected. A few remarks touching that subject, however, will readily occur to every mind. The apparent object of the Nebraska bill has failed. The origin of the project was attributed to the Hon. S. A. Douglas, who had, in 1852, been a candidate for nomination to the presidency. He had made, so it was said, almost superhuman efforts upon that occasion to secure his nomination. Such things were charged against him as the purchase of the influence of the Democratic Review, and the enlistment of office-seekers in his interest by liberal promises in way of promotion. When, therefore, the Nebraska bill, so called, repealing the Missouri compromise restriction, was brought forward in Congress, and powerfully championed by Mr. Douglas, the North were pretty unanimous in the opinion that the move was political. It was generally supposed that Mr. Douglas was looking for support in the next National Convention of his party. Kansas was a rich territory, just opening for settlement, and it was thought that, by a removal of the Missouri restriction, a benefit would be conferred on the South. Unless that act was regarded as beneficial to the South, the action of Southern Congressmen cannot well be explained. All of the Democratic and many of the Whig members of the South supported the Nebraska bill, while it was opposed by all of the Whigs and a fair minority of the Democratic members of the North. It was said, it is true, that the object of the repeal of the Missouri restriction was to obliterate that badge of Southern inequality and oppression; to wipe out a stain that had long rested upon Southern honor; but, when it is recollected that that restriction, whether a stain or otherwise, was, by the South, though, as an escape from worse consequences, self-imposed, and that by the most brilliant statesmen she has ever produced, we can hardly credit that by the repeal nothing was expected but a victory of empty honors. The proposition added to the already excited feelings of the North, and was the watchword for renewed frenzy. And it was frenzy, and nothing else. This is proved by the fact that those who then denounced the idea of repeal, and of popular sovereignty, now bless the former, and glory in the latter. The outcry of the abolitionists of the North against the proposed repeal of the Missouri compromise was a thoughtless spasm of those who were afflicted with a frightful disease of the nervous system. It was involuntary. The judgment had no part in the action.

Every sane and sensible man in the country sees that the Missouri compromise restriction was originally the peace-offering extorted from the South by the blind fanaticism of the North, and should, in justice, never have been exacted; but still, the conservative men of the North, as they knew the deranged and diseased condition of Northern minds, and well understood with what excitement the reöpening of that old controversy would be attended, were grieved at the step of Mr. Douglas, and highly incensed against him for his course.

This movement of Mr. Douglas, it was seen, was embarrassing to President Pierce. It appeared that Pierce had an ambition for a reëlection, and no doubt this influenced him materially in his course. The measure was the subject of consultations in a cabinet that was not harmonious. It was the *on dit* that Mr. Marcy stoutly opposed the scheme; but, however that was, President Pierce gave the Nebraska bill his support, and it was passed. The result is known to every one. If the South approbate Mr. Douglas' heart in regard to the measure, they must, by this time, distrust his head, as that section has been a severe sufferer by the result. If intended as an offering to the South, the measure has turned out an acquisition to the North. However, the greatest calamity of the transaction falls upon the country. A new impulse was given to the long maturing anti-slavery feeling of the North, and the two great sections of the country were brought into collision with each other. The hatred between these sections is becoming extremely bitter. The excitement was fierce beyond precedent. Those who had been for years regarded as ultraists, who had been recognized as the special enemies of the South, were, by the commotion occasioned by the Nebraska bill, at once thrown into the lead in the great popular movements that ensued in the free states. The American party which, in ordinary times, would have become firm and imposing, was, almost as soon as formed, shattered by the spirit of abolition; and a new — the Republican — party was formed under the lead and auspices of the old and long-recognized ultraists of the North. As significant of what this party was, we may say that Garrisonians gave it their sympathies; and many, such as Wendell Phillips and Miss Lucy Stone, gave it their support. Before the breath of the popular tornado the last vestiges of the Whig party disappeared, and the great and powerful Democratic party was razed almost to its foundations. A party with fearful vitality had sprung up in the North; it was a party based on fanaticism, — such a party as made Cromwell the ruler of England. Cromwell, it has been said, affected Puritanism for purposes of power; and we cannot say but many of the Republican leaders embarked in that sectional organization more out of love for office and honors than from any real sympathy with the fanatical feelings of their followers. As to how this is we shall soon know. The presidential campaign of 1860 will probably reveal much that now can only be conjectured, and we must desist.

In 1856, the Republican party put in nomination John C. Frémont, a Southern-born Democrat. He had much celebrity as an explorer; and his nomination, it was said, was a suggestion, "in a fit of prophetic fury," of the Hon. N. P. Banks, a brother Democrat of the free-trade school. The claims of Freesoil veterans were ignored, and availability tried in the nomination of Mr. Frémont. Mr. Frémont's antecedents were well known.

He had been a Democrat of the Young America stamp from his youth, and much of his celebrity arose from his *coup de Fillibuster* in California. But he was young and ambitious; and, as it was of vast importance fcr the Republican leaders to secure to their party the presidency, he was put upon the track with no other capital than a letter, in which he had announced himself in favor of Kansas becoming a free state. What sort of President Mr. Frémont would have made it is unimportant to consider. It was no doubt expected that he would be the President of those who should elect him. What his course would have been, or what the results of his election, each one may judge for himself.

The Democrats in 1856 made their nomination at a convention held at Cincinnati. Never did such responsibilities rest upon a party convention in America as rested upon the Democratic Convention of 1856. The conservative feeling in America looked to it as the hope of the country. The ambition and efforts of Mr. Pierce and of Mr. Douglas for nomination were well known, and regarded with unfeigned apprehensions. It was viewed as almost certain that neither of these gentlemen could save the country from the impending calamity of the election of a sectional President; and when the news of Mr. Buchanan's nomination was conveyed by the telegraph wires throughout the land, a sensation of relief and high gratification thrilled the heart of every conservative patriot.

The presidential campaign of 1856 was one that should never be forgotten, although another such should never be desired. The Kansas bubble was blown to still grander proportions, and was the only capital on which the election of Frémont was sought to be effected. A description of that bubble must not be expected here.

It is enough to say that, from an early period of the Kansas troubles, it was perfectly apparent that she was destined to be free. At the time of the election of delegates to the Lecompton Constitutional Convention, there were about nine thousand registered voters in the territory, of which but about two thousand were in favor of slavery. In electing those delegates, scarcely any but those pro-slavery men voted, the free-state voters remaining away from the polls. But with such a vast preponderance of voters in favor of freedom, there cannot be any doubts about the final condition of that territory in regard to slavery. Whatever may have prompted the Freesoil electors in submitting to the triumph of pro-slavery delegates in the Constitutional Convention, there can be no doubt but, sooner or later, slavery will be excluded from Kansas.

The waves of fanaticism found a barrier in the mountains of Pennsylvania. The triumph of abolition was prevented by those states that border upon the slave states. The silly delusions of Northern fanatics have made but little impression upon those people who live upon the borders of slavery, and who really know what opinion to entertain in regard to negroes and their masters. The furor of the Northern mind in respect to negro servitude is in consequence of its gross ignorance in regard to the objects of its gratuitous sympathy. The southern part of Ohio, where the institution is understood and appreciated, repudiated with indignation the cant of British philanthropy; and the common sense and patriotism of Indiana and Illinois gave a sturdy check to fanaticism. The patriot of Wheatland occupies the presidential chair, and old and new aspirants are busy at work in laying their respective tracks for the race of 1860. The active scenes occasioned by the labors of these gentlemen but little disturb, it seems, the placid temper of the President. They did annoy him much, for a while, in regard to the admission of Kansas. His best endeavors to secure the people of that territory equal rights were thwarted by factionists, and that people are made to suffer by the intrigues of politicians; but, as her overwhelming preponderance of free-state voters over those in favor of slavery clearly negatives the idea that she can ever be made a slave state, the prospect of making her longer the football of politicians is discouraging. All that is needed to restore the measures which once made the country prosperous and happy, is peace from the sectional anti-slavery spirit which has, for a long time, been distracting the country, and occupying the minds of our legislators to the exclusion of higher and nobler objects. The efforts of our present President to allay this fiend of discord are appreciated by the considerate and patriotic. No one denies Mr. Buchanan eminent patriotism and statesmanship; and every lover of his country must rejoice that a man of so much worth and ability is at the head of our government. In his administration we see the efficacy of intelligence and self-reliance, and the importance of elevating to the highest office in our gift men of superior ability. When Mr. Douglas attempted, under Mr. Buchanan, to repeat the Nebraska experiment in his Lecompton move, we see that the unconcern of the President contrasted strangely with the anxieties, jealousies, and fears of his predecessor under similar circumstances. The President relied upon his own judgment, and encountered the opposition of the little giant with little loss of sleep or of political influence with the better class of our people.

CHAPTER XXXI.

THE REPUBLICAN, AMERICAN AND DEMOCRATIC PARTIES. — THEIR FEATURES AND CHARACTERISTICS. — DEMOCRATIC THE ONLY NATIONAL PARTY. — NECESSITY OF A NATIONAL CONSERVATIVE OPPOSITION, WITHOUT WHICH THAT PARTY MUST SOON BECOME SECTIONAL. — WHIG PRINCIPLES, AND THE SPIRIT OF THE OLD WHIG PARTY CONSIDERED. — THE NECESSITY OF THE REVIVAL OF THE WHIG PARTY, ETC., ETC.

On the dissolution of the Whig party, the Whigs who remained true to their principles found that there was no party in existence with which they could cordially connect themselves. The Democratic party remained substantially unchanged. Its principles and tendencies were known. In many of its measures it differed from Whig policy; and its tactics were not in accordance with Whig sentiments. Although, at that time, on the question that was shaking the country to its centre, — the question which was paramount for the moment to all others, — the Whig sympathized with the Democrat, and saw that the safety of the Union depended on coöperation, it was upon that great national question only that fellowship with the Democracy was hearty and cordial. The Democratic party is composed of discordant elements, and is held together by a principle that could never be available in the Whig party. There are in the Democracy conservative and progressive elements, which are so blended and united as to give conservatism more life, and to divest agrarianism of its aggressive and revolutionary power. In that party the highest patriotism and most accomplished statesmanship come in contact, under the momentum characteristic of great forces, with the fiercest demagogism ; but, not meeting, as in the Whig party, in a direct line of opposition, but obliquely, the force of each, though increased, is modified. If either act for a while in excess, if occasionally the demagogue power get the ascendency, the patriotic element does not expire ; but, providentially favored by outside influences, such, for instance, as the antagonism of the Whig party, is fortunate in regaining an equilibrium. The existence of a conservative, enlightened and patriotic opposition party is the necessary condition of the existence of the Democracy as a national party. The extinction of the Federal organization, during the administration of Monroe, led to the dismemberment of the Democratic party in 1824, and the complete overthrow, under the demagogic Jackson-Van-Buren dynasty, of the political measures established under the administrations of Madison and Monroe. Although, as now constituted, the Democratic party is national, its nationality is by no means likely to be of long continuance in the absence of a national opposition.

There are at present arrayed against the Democracy but two parties, — the Republican and the American, — neither of which is a national party, supported in all parts of the Union by persons entertaining a similarity of opinions and sentiments on national questions. The Republican party, formed in 1855, after the passage of the celebrated Kansas or Nebraska Act, was not, at its creation, intended as a national organization. The old Whig party had become much degenerated from its original purity and tone; and, at the first clang of the bugle of the pretentious disorganizer, the mass of its adherents broke the ranks for new banners. At the very instant that the preservation of Democratic conservatism required, more than usual, the stability and the confronting and resisting power of their old national adversaries, and at the moment when Democracy, from the triumph of its demagogue element, had shocked its conservatism, and had thus, on account of the disturbance of its elements, endangered its safety, and offered the opposition an advantageous opportunity for victory, the ancient Whig party itself was rent asunder by the spirit of fanaticism, as described in a former chapter. In 1852 the Democracy was an overwhelming party, carrying all the states of the Union but four. The administration of President Pierce had not expired before the free states were all substantially under the control of the opposition. By the Nebraska measure, which resulted in the repeal of the Missouri Compromise, the administration justly forfeited the confidence of the country; and, in 1856, but for the frightful aspect of that "lower deep" opened by the fanaticism of Republicanism, the Democratic party would have been swallowed up in ruin. Destruction was averted only by the folly and madness of the opposition. But, although ruin was thus stayed, the doom due that awful iniquity yet awaits the party, and will overtake it, unless it make living sacrifices upon the altar of violated justice. The reäppearance of the Whig party would find the Democracy with that Cain-mark upon its brow. The author, or at least the chief engineer, of the Nebraska measure through the two houses of Congress, having failed in 1856, through the insanity of Republicanism, to destroy his party, has since, with a peculiar tact for destructive conceptions, so adjusted his course as to render the overthrow of the Democracy certain in 1860. His Southern extremes, which, in 1856, failed to consummate his purposes, will be surrendered in 1860 for the trial of an appeal to Northern prejudices. The Democratic party, it appears, is threatened with a division. If its conservative and patriotic elements, in case of such disruption, can be made available to the country by the reörganization of the Whig party, the ascendency of sectionalism may be prevented.

The Republican party was formed by the union of men of all parties; it only professed to unite those agreeing in sentiment on the slavery question. Its ranks, consequently, embrace people of all varieties of political faith. Mr. Frémont, like many other Democrats, North and South, announced himself of the opinion that Kansas should be left free to settle her own domestic institutions, and exclude slavery, if she should think proper; and, in consequence of his somewhat liberal position on that topic, was deemed by the Republicans a suitable candidate for the presidency. His Southern birth and thorough-bred Democracy did not seem to disqualify him for the support of Northern Whigs. Many of the most influential leaders in the Republican organization, as well as their candidate for the presidency, were of the Democratic school in politics. The rallying cry was, "Those opposed to the extension of slavery." Many Whigs recoiled with horror from all connection with such a party. Not that any Whig was more in favor of the extension of slavery into the territories, by the general government, than Mr. Frémont, or the best Republican at his back; but the idea of the formation of a party based on the slavery question could not be entertained for a moment by one imbued with genuine Whig sentiments. In the nature of things, such a party must be sectional, and calculated to engender the most bitter and violent sectional animosities. But, notwithstanding this, and notwithstanding the Republican party was headed by the most violent anti-slavery men, and was warmly supported by many open and leading disunionists, — that its conventions, its platforms, its resolves, its orators and editors, continually abounded in fierce denunciations of the South, of Southern institutions, of the fugitive slave law, and of slaveholders, thus breathing a dangerous sectional spirit, many honest-hearted Whigs, for the moment outraged by the wanton repeal of the Missouri compromise, and indignant at what they regarded a breach of faith by the South, suffered themselves to be led into that combination, which can hardly be dignified with the title of party. The step was rather the effect of passion than of the reason ; and many, in acting with the Republicans, feeling the impropriety of such an organization, premised the act with the declaration, "We will go with them this time." We are sorry to record this, — to be obliged to show that a Whig was ever moved by his feelings to act in defiance of his judgment ; but, in taking that rash step, we feel grateful to him for first surrendering the Whig name. It is not for a moment to be credited that Whigs can continue to be members of a sectional party ; and it is easily perceived that Republicanism offers them no congenial home.

The American can never be a substitute for the Whig party. Many of its leaders are exalted statesmen and patriots; but it lacks nationality and consistency. Many of its teachers and high officers in the North, while they claim equality for the negro, — the most ignorant and degraded of all the races of the earth, — exhibit great jealousy and suspicion of their intelligent, economical and virtuous German brother, who brings from the father-land that love of home and that patriotism peculiar to the Teutonic heart. In the North, the American is the advocate of personal liberty bills, and an opponent of fugitive slave laws; while in the South he may be a conservative, or even an ultra-slavery propagandist. North and South, East and West, the members of the American party may be concurrent in their views upon the subject of naturalization laws, as applied to all races but that of Africa, called the negro; but there is not much agreement between them on the most of political topics. The question of the reformation of our naturalization laws is hardly a fit basis for a party organization.

Thus we see that neither the Democratic, the Republican, nor the American party will answer, to the Whig, as a substitute for the genuine Whig party. The feelings of each Whig will instinctively teach him this. And what could be more proper and advisable than the reörganization of that estimable and highly respected party? When this is asked, only the interests of the country, and the satisfaction and pleasure of the Whigs, are considered. The name is excellent, suggestive of intelligence, virtue and patriotism. When spoken of here, the Whig party, as it existed in this country during the last years of its existence, is not referred to. Success, the prospects of success even, proved too much for its poor human nature, as constituted in its latter days. When, therefore, we speak of Whig principles, we have in mind the party as it appeared in its period of purity.

The Whig party of old caught its inspiration from the spirit of the founders of our institutions, and derived its principles from those statesmen and patriots over whose counsels the great and good Washington presided; and, when viewed in its purity, discloses none of the appearances of art and policy, contrived for the captivation of the masses, by pandering to their passions and prejudices.

Although we have a Democratic party, and our government is becoming in effect democratic, it is clear that a democracy was not intended by the framers of our institutions. The reader needs not be told that a democracy is a government where measures are adopted by the direct vote of the people. Of course such a government cannot exist saving in small states that will admit of the assemblage, for the purpose of legislation, of all the people into one forum. Such for a while was the government of ancient Athens. The people were rulers, and ruled in their assembled omnipotence, without the aid of senates, legislatures or monarchs. The popular will, expressed by the vote of a popular assembly, was the supreme law of the land. The workings of that Athenian Democracy are familiar to every school-boy. If wisdom, and virtue, and justice, are now the possessions of the people, and the characteristics of the masses, they were not the attributes of the people of Athens. The men most noted for virtue, talents and patriotism, were banished, by popular vote, from the state; and her purest citizens fell victims to the fanaticism of the ignorant multitude. The story of the ancient democracies is a sad one.

Although not flattering to the too much flattered "dear people," it must be owned that the absurdity of the democratic system is glaring. In all communities are intelligence and ignorance, virtue and vice; and there never yet was a very large country in which political wisdom resided in the majority of its people, and probably such a spectacle will never be witnessed. Thorough discipline of the moral and intellectual faculties is the rare achievement of the few; and of the highly cultivated, the number of those that fathom the principles of the Constitution of their country is still less. The authors necessary for a comprehension of the principles of our government are never seen by one out of a thousand of the American people. The writings of Adams and Jefferson are found in large libraries, and are perused by but few. The able and interesting essays by Hamilton, Madison and Jay, — essays that afford a masterly exposition of republican institutions and their tendencies, — although published under the title of "The Federalist," and purchased by the wealthy, are far from being a popular or common work. The profound and lucid treatise on the Constitution, by Judge Story, one of our most illustrious American jurists, a son and ornament of Massachusetts, and the glory of his age, has probably never been heard of by the great mass of the voters in the United States. The "Madison Papers," as they are called, being his minutes of the debates in the convention that framed the Constitution, — a work that, as by a window, throws light into the very framework of that structure; an authentic document that gives an accurate key to the meaning of its founders on all the exciting questions so flippantly settled at the present day by the million; a sure guide to its spirit and force,—is found in the libraries of congressmen and some scholars; but as a guide to political action is never heard of by the tens of thousands whose education in such matters is from Uncle Tom's Cabin and kindred works. To govern the country; to adopt appropriate measures for developing its resources, for regulating our foreign trade, establishing and maintaining diplomatic intercourse with other nations, adjusting a system of duties to afford revenue and protection, carrying forward suitable works of internal improvement, protecting and managing the public property, governing and preserving the navy, etc, etc., require such intelligence as only long-continued and attentive application can furnish; and, to be plain and honest in the matter, will the reader please state the proportion of the people of the United States that have ever given themselves any trouble upon any of these subjects? The masses of our people are not so well posted on public measures as were the ancient Athenians, for the reason that those Athenians, before voting upon any question, heard full discussions by their orators. It was quaintly remarked by Anacharsis, a Scythian traveller, who happened to be at Athens when some measure was debated by her orators, and decided by the assembled masses: "This is a queer country, where the wise men discuss important measures of government, and the ignorant decide them!" And the remark made at Athens some two thousand years ago, by the shrewd Scythian, in regard to the system of the Athenian, is equally applicable now to the American Democracy, which, for the voice of an independent congress of our choicest and wisest men, would substitute the voice or incongruous voices of the ignorant masses, as gathered from all sections, and borne into the national legislature by representatives who consider the discharge of such duties a calling sufficiently high and honorable, provided the salary be remunerative!

The founders of our institutions sought to place them on a different basis, and secure, in the governing power, the highest intelligence, ripest wisdom, and most exalted virtue of the country. Even the executive, those founders intended, should, through the instrumentality of the college of electors, be chosen by a select number of the soundest men the states could produce; and, to shape our policy, frame our laws, and guard our rights at home and abroad, it was intended that the legislature should be composed of our wisest, best, and most experienced men; and that their wisdom, and not the prejudices of party, should at all times prevail in the national councils.

To realize and carry out these objects, contemplated by the founders of our institutions, is the chief aim of Whig principles; and all resorts to sectional interests and local jealousies, and all appeals that are calculated to render the people the judges of what our institutions intend shall be left to the unbiassed judgment of their representatives, are in direct hostility to the fundamental doctrines of the Whig party.

The slightest reflection, after even a superficial observation of the condition of our country, will satisfy any candid person of ordinary ability that the reconstruction of the Whig party is indispensable to the perpetuity of the Union. The Democratic party, though now national, if left to the sole opposition of the Republican, which is a sectional party, must inevitably, sooner or later, itself degenerate into sectionalism. This must be the necessary result of such antagonism. And there are thousands now in the Democratic, Republican, and American parties, who are longing, with the impatience of the repentant prodigal, for the appearance of a new organization, in whose congenial bosom they may find repose from their wanderings.

But, as will at once be seen by all, a party based on intelligence and moral worth will be liable to encounter the jealousies of the ignorant and vicious, and must most of the time be in the minority of the country, and much of the time exceedingly small. This the Whigs see, and readily accept the conditions of their existence. It is not their study, their purpose, to shape their politics for their own interests. The acquisition of office, for the honors and emoluments thereof, forms no part of the inducements that should constitute one a Whig. The party was conceived in the loftiest patriotism. The good of the country, and that alone, was contemplated. In the pursuit of so noble an object, self-sacrifice, rather than self-interest, was the inspiration of each heart. An office-seeker in the ranks of the true Whig party would be an anomaly. As the elevation of the incompetent and unworthy to high offices of trust is never imagined by the Whig, a proper stimulant is offered to ambition for improvement, and the attainment of superior excellence. Those who embrace that party must do so prompted by purely patriotic emotions; must enter its ranks without hopes of personal advancement. In the hearts of true Whigs reigns an ardent, abiding, and intelligent patriotism; as all political association and action are prompted solely by the love of country.

By intelligent patriotism, is meant that noble love of country which, as developed through the culture of the moral and intellectual nature, becomes an absorbing passion. There have been sublime examples of such patriotism in both ancient and modern times. Brutus, whose inflexible devotion to his country impelled him to yield his paternal to his patriotic feelings, and execute his own son for treason against the state, is a notable case of Roman virtue. But nothing in ancient history so well illustrates our idea of a true Whig, as the life and character of that noble Athenian, Aristides. The life of that great man is full of instances evincing a love of justice and of country superior to all considerations of self. It will be recollected that, amongst the Democrats of Athens, the competition for office was as fierce as ever manifested in the United States, and that office-holders were, by their competitors, subjected to criticism, detraction, and every species of abuse. From the accounts given us by history, it appears that the more exalted the virtue of the statesman, the surer were his rivals to bring upon him the jealousy and hatred of the people. This, though occasioned by an attribute having the effect of a law of nature, is, in fact, owing to a weakness of human nature which is almost universal,— a weakness that has ever subjected the innocent blind to the wiles of the subtle and crafty. Intelligence has always rendered its possessor an object of suspicion and fear to the ignorant; and we see that, in all ages and countries, superior wisdom and worth have been obliged, so far as popular influences have been felt, to give place to persons more on a level with the multitude. But Aristides, by a life of marked self-sacrificing probity, became so distinguished for equity as to acquire from the people of Athens the title of *The Just.* As an instance illustrative of the estimation in which he was held by the people, the reader will recollect that his fellow-citizens had become so accustomed to refer to him their disputes, that it was finally made a grave charge against him, by those envious of his position, that he was usurping the occupation of the courts, which, in consequence of him, were left deserted! And, notwithstanding his uprightness and justice were eminent, while he had the care of the government treasury, he was charged with frauds, peculations, and all kinds of corruptions. Such things are common in all countries. In this country we have rarely had an administration that has not been accused of such corruptions; and the reader will readily recollect the solemn and specific charges brought against our American Aristides, Webster, by a Mr. Ingersoll. But the officers of our government have better facilities for vindicating their honesty, in the care of government funds, than had the chief treasury-officer of the Athenian Democracy. Aristides, who was charged with the custody and disbursement of the revenues of his state, necessarily had under him many subordinate officers, such as collectors, sub-treasurers, and pay-masters. As in all the Eastern nations, these revenue officers had, time out of mind, been oppressors, peculators, and plunderers. The ancient systems of raising and collecting revenues, put it in the power of the farmers thereof, or collecting officers, to despoil the people, and to defraud the state, there having been no check but in the superior of the department. As might have been expected, the vigilance which Aristides, when at the head of the treasury, exercised over his officers, raised against him their united hostility. Though his integrity was the only real cause of complaint by his enemies, they commenced and kept up against him a constant clamor for peculation! So large was their number, so numerous and respectable their connections and associations, and so extensive their relations and influence with society, that their united and continued accusations were injurious even to Aristides. He was publicly accused and tried in presence of the democracy of Athens, and convicted! The witnesses against him were those under-officers whose falsehoods there were no means of exposing. But the sense of justice of the better part of the Athenian public was shocked at the outrageous decision. The sentence was not only stayed, but he was, by the active interposition of the best of the Athenians, continued in his office. After this trial, it is said that Aristides seemed less vigilant in regard to the frauds of his sub-officers, and appeared not to notice their corruptions; and, as a consequence of his easy administration, his character for integrity was restored. His accusers became his eulogists and warm supporters, and solicited from the people his continuance in his responsible trust. As the people of Athens were about to confer that trust again upon him, he indignantly rebuked them, saying: "While I managed your finances with all the fidelity of an honest man, I was loaded with calumnies; and now, when I suffer them to become a prey to public robbers, I am become a mighty good citizen; but, I assure you, I am more ashamed of the present honor than I was of the former disgrace; and it is with indignation and alarm that I see you esteem it more meritorious to oblige a set of corrupt office-holders, than to take proper care of the public revenue."

That our country abounds in patriotism no one doubts; but in how much intelligent patriotism? And, if not intelligent, is that virtue of much value, especially in a republic? Like paternal love, the love of country, unless enlightened, may be the ruin of its object. Unless judicious, the son but little profits by his parent's affection. And of what avail to the state is the blind passion called love of country, unless its sphere be illuminated by the light of a cultivated understanding, and all the duties incident to its nature be brought into exercise, and be enforced? The duties of patriotism are many and severe; but who, from the commencement to the close of his life, concerns himself in regard to them? As a general rule, we think, with the masses of our citizens private affairs chiefly occupy the mind and engage the attention, to the almost total disregard of public duties. Who are to take care of the republic? Who are to watch over its necessities, its interests, and its perils? Who can tell? Who feel concern for the general welfare,—the public weal,—and take pains to obtain the information necessary for its protection? This one is disturbed about the rights of a fugitive negro from a Virginia plantation; that one is exercised with grief in view of the habits of his fellow-citizens in matters of drink; and on their specialities—temperance and slavery, two subjects profoundly mastered by large numbers—each is ripe for public action. Many people have heard much of protection, and will vote for none but tariff men; while others, struck with the sound *free*, in the term free trade, will only support such as are in its favor. One party will not support a candidate not in favor of the extension of our national boundaries; another is equally intent on adhering to our country as now bounded, without any enlargement of its area. On several subjects the ideas of certain people are fixed, and their support is a matter of passion. These ideas, whatever they may be, have become a bias; their advocacy a matter of feeling; and the candidate is expected to be as much their slave as is the deluded elector himself. The elector, or voter, may be native or foreign born, wise or ignorant, competent to judge intelligently on political subjects or not; it is all the same; he will trust no officer not pledged, by a liberal amount of professions, to sustain his views. The impropriety of bringing down to such mental vassalage superior intellects seems to be felt and tacitly acknowledged by the multitude, in the general distrust entertained of great men as the champions of popular ideas. The candidate, the representative, must be one not capable, by possession of great abilities, of transcending in action the intellectual sphere of his constituents, and of being actuated by motives and reasons beyond their comprehension or appreciation. He must be their representative in every respect. He may drag out long sessions in Congress; may listen to able arguments by his colleagues; may, by resort to congressional libraries, and by researches into the statistics of his country, and by mastering works of political economy, get better and more satisfactory light on many subjects than he ever before enjoyed; but such must prove vain acquisitions. The prejudices of his constituents, and not the light evoked in halls of legislation, must be his guide!

The consequence of our democratic tendencies is, that our national legislature reflects the local prejudices of every section of the land; is a mirror, that reflects not only the education of our statesmen, but the schools, also, in which they are tutored. Each member, instead of being a representative in contemplation of the Constitution, is rather a *specimen* of his constituents. Instead of a long and patient investigation of the varied interests of the country, — of endeavoring to master the principles of the Constitution, and ascertain their application to legislative measures, — of making himself acquainted with the numerous questions of political economy, — the representative only finds it necessary to learn to echo the predominant and perhaps temporary feeling or whim of his constituents ; and the acquisition of a knowledge of their prejudices is all the political education he finds necessary to enable him to fill his post with entire satisfaction to his electors.

The Whig idea was the original one observed in the construction of our institutions ; and this would place the representative in the national legislature free to act in accordance with the conclusions of his unbiassed judgment. Legislation is the exercise of a trust power, whose scope is not any single congressional district, but the whole Union. The practice of holding members obedient to local views and prejudices, in effect changes our government from a representative republic to a democracy. Instead of vesting the executive and legislative power in the hands of persons selected on account of their being most noted for wisdom and virtue, the ignorant and prejudiced virtually take the whole subject of legislation into their own hands, and all that is required of their member is to see their purposes carried out. Any other than the Whig system must lead to fatal consequences. In times of great political excitement, especially when sectional controversies run high, it is very clear that people of such diversified and opposing interests, as those associated in our Union, could not long remain united under institutions which are democratic in spirit. The people of Boston, Mass., or Charlestown, S. C., may think themselves safe in holding their representatives to a strict compliance with local views and feelings; but it must be evident to the shallowest perceptions that without the freedom of a higher stand-point in legislation; without, where interests are really conflicting, some latitude for compromise, or the privilege to the legislator of basing his decisions on principles of justice in view of the interests of all sections, when duly examined and weighed, a conflict of sections must inevitably take place. It is in view of such considerations as these that the Whig remains what is called an "old fogy." In times of "remarkable political activity," as elegantly expressed by the leading Republican journal of the country, not to make any advance with the popular tide is cause of grave reproach by those who are dancing in the foam upon the very crest of the billow. The more ignorance the more zeal; as in proportion as the reason is dormant the passions predominate. Under the play of skilful agitators, the masses will warm themselves into a sectional warfare much faster than the more experienced and thoughtful, and will naturally enough be disposed to repose more confidence in the young and ardent champion of reform, whose sympathies are with them, than in those who, although of more experience, knowledge and natural ability, are less progressive, and too little inspired by the astonishing "political activity" of their time.

Hence, as our government can only exist on the

basis on which it was founded, and by carrying out the principles of its organization; as its creation is perceived to have been a compromise, all sections yielding individual rights, and surrendering advantages for the security and good of the whole; as the adoption of democratic principles — that is, leaving to the people of each section to legislate or decide on national measures — was seen by its founders to be impracticable, and the general government made to absorb, to a certain extent, all local jurisdictions; as the national legislature was, under the qualifications expressed in the Constitution, created with power absolute and unquestionable; and as in the exercise of its functions the members should be considered as the officers, not of any locality, but of the whole nation, charged with the duty of legislating for the best good of the whole, it is the duty and peculiar mission of the Whig to stand up as a barrier against the popular tide which the breath of demagogues has put in motion; to use his best efforts to resist the tendency of the country to sectionalism; to endeavor to allay the strife of sectional feelings, which is already so fierce in the country and in Congress, and to make the utmost exertions to restore to the administration of the general government those national principles on which it was founded. There is in his mission something noble — something grateful to the heart of the intelligent patriot and philanthropist. He has not the gratification of a present passion in view; but crushes out and sacrifices private feelings and interests, and compromises with antagonistic views, to secure the stability of the country, develop its resources, and place its future on a safe and enduring basis. His ideas are not formed on partial views, nor inspired by local interests; but are liberal, enlarged, comprehensive, and are the growth of long-continued and mature reflection, drawn not only from a close examination of his own country, but also from the contemplation of it as one of the great family of nations; from an observation of the feelings, interests, aims and machinations of surrounding monarchies and despotisms, the natural enemies of republics; and a study of the dangers, the perils, within and without, that beset the path and cloud the future of his beloved republic.

The Whig is not a professional alarmist, but still deems it wholesome to keep the dangers that surround his country constantly before his eyes. The epithet, "Union-saver," bestowed upon him by the sectionalists as a slur, he accepts as a compliment. Not that he would arrogantly assume patriotic achievements, but the attempted slur virtually accords to him patriotic motives. It imports that he has paid attention to the solemn warnings of the FAREWELL ADDRESS, and that the manifestation of fear — unnecessary fear, if the reader pleases — for the safety of our Union, indicates love for it. He is not so shallow as to believe that his beloved country is entirely safe and free from perils, when he sees abroad every power on earth arrayed against it, and at home beholds its integrity and unity assailed and warred upon by hordes of enemies, open and disguised. He loves his country; he praises God continually for its bestowal upon him; he looks upon it as the richest gift ever before bestowed upon man; and that his heart should bound in the very excitement of alarm, when the lightest blow is aimed at its safety, should not, by the honest and worthy, be made the subject of jesting remark. And when this is with impunity done, we think the cause of free institutions is not very auspicious.

The Whig cannot force his mind into the view that the administration of government is a fit subject for political huckstering; that the whole matter is but a mere game of party politics, with no nobler objects than the acquisition of place. He looks on government as something more than the mere arrangement or adjustment of temporary interests; as something more than present protection, even; he views it as the exercise of a trust conferred upon him from above; he regards government itself as something bestowed on him as the reward for moral and intellectual excellence, and which can only be preserved by the cultivation and continuance of the virtues for the reward of which it was bestowed. And regarding his institutions so rare and precious, the Whig is astonished and shocked that any citizen should for a moment be so thoughtless and reckless as to suffer the "first dawnings" of a spirit that may imperil their stability to go unrebuked. He catches his inspiration from the Farewell Address, and shares the solicitudes and anxieties, in regard to the future, of the great and good Washington, and recoils with horror from those partisans who with treasonous hands minister at the altar of sectional discord.

Many may think the Whig not sufficiently hopeful; but what has he to encourage him? He is not lulled into apathetic confidence by the cheering expression, "Freedom is universal; slavery is local." For the Whig does not look solely at the present time, nor does he limit his view to one section of the globe, for lessons of instruction and grounds of hope; he searches the records of human history for the boasted universality of liberty, and finds, throughout the great track of time, scarcely a trace of its footsteps; but, in its stead, crushing, bloody, and continued despotism. In Asia, Europe and America, the record of human history is a bloody and a sad one; and the Whig sees nothing in its countless pages to excite his hopes in regard to his own country. In glancing his eye over the world, it first rests on the Celestial Empire, so called, which has for untold centuries groaned under a despotism that has extinguished from the heart and minds of a nation, embracing almost a third of the human family, the last hope or even thought of liberty. There he sees, swayed by one man, three hundred millions of human beings, who seek no law but his imperial will, and who, regarding him as not less than a deity, repose in peace under his rule. Then fall under his vision the Indies, with their different castes and races; their successive dynasties; a peculiar people, from the earliest dawn of history steeped in the most abasing superstitions; a theocratic despotism, the features of which are reflected in the bloody rites of Juggernaut; a system of rule based on the bigotry of the people, and fashioned by the all-moulding craft of kings, lords, and priests, who, from ages unknown, have revelled on the sweat and blood of the masses; — the Persian and Assyrian dynasties, under which billions of people have been the instruments and supports of luxurious and lustful despots; people who, under the divine teachings of their priests, became the easy and yielding victims of oppression, with no pretensions, no aspirations for freedom, and no efforts to acquire it; — the Hebrew dynasties, — the Hebrew commonwealth, — institutions delivered from on high, a precious gift to a precious, a peculiar people, for their own benefit; institutions, by the terms and spirit of which all other races were but fit subjects of Hebrew servitude; institutions under which that people were vouchsafed more than usual freedom, until overthrown by the factions engendered by uncompromising Jewish bigotry, and thus the first glimmerings of liberty on earth extinguished by the hot breath of fanaticism;—Egypt, whose pyramids are monuments of immemorial generations of slavery and priestly domination; a land that for more than five thousand years has never even had a dream of freedom;—Europe, ancient and modern, whose countless billions of civilized and barbarous peoples have presented an almost unbroken scene of riotous passion, brutal lust, fierce fanaticism, blind bigotry, and bloody oppression; whose best states, in their most palmy days, have only, as in a disturbed dream, shaken off a single for the substitution of a horde of tyrants; chasing away a rapacious king for a democracy still more rapacious; and whose numerous races and peoples at the present day, from the huge Russian despotism on the East, to the luxurious lords of the British isles on the West, are but the beasts of burden that bear upon their backs a banded brotherhood of kings, flanked by a consuming priesthood, and the most crushing aristocracy the world has ever beheld; millions of the children of idleness and pleasure entrenched with irresistible power upon the shoulders of the downtrodden and toiling masses, and whose great and principal concern in life is, by aid of holy alliances and quintruple treaties, to perpetuate security to themselves and their descendants;—the numberless hordes that inhabit the African continent, fifty millions in number, that have for ages lived in degradation and crime;—the cannibals of the Eastern isles ; — the savage tribes of North and South America ; — the scarcely animated lump of mortality of the extreme North, the stupid Esquimaux, and the scarcely human form of the uncouth Patagonian, of the extreme South ; — yes, turn his view where he may, and, not only at the present day, but during all past ages of the world, in all parts and sections of the earth, he sees that men have been divided into hostile, barbarous and warlike families, and that, as compared with the whole, the civilization of the past has been confined to but a small speck of the human family. He sees, he feels, he cannot help feeling, that the republic of the United States is the marvel of time, — the miracle of earth, — a shrub that, like the century plant, may bloom at stated periods, but the intervals are of such countless ages as to leave its nature unknown. Where in history have we the description of anything like this republic? And it is yet but in its infancy. It has been styled an experiment; and, guided by the history of the world in the formation of their apprehensions, our fathers may well have trembled for its success. At first small and feeble, and now but a speck upon the globe, — but twenty-five millions of freemen out of the ten hundred millions of human beings that inhabit the earth! And still the Whig is sneered at for regarding free institutions as a fit matter for solicitude! No! the Whig, with his most enthusiastic political opponent, has confidence in the mission of his beloved country, and joins in the universal faith of his countrymen ; but without works, faithful, intelligent, and unremitting works, he has no right to expect that faith to be a living and saving power.

www.ingramcontent.com/pod-product-compliance
Lightning Source LLC
LaVergne TN
LVHW022039110826
845151LV00007B/288
* 9 7 8 1 4 2 5 5 4 0 6 0 9 *